DISCOURSE ANALYSIS

Routledge English Language Introductions cover core areas of language study and are one-stop resources for students.

Assuming no prior knowledge, books in the series offer an accessible overview of the subject, with activities, study questions, sample analyses, commentaries and key readings – all in the same volume. The innovative and flexible 'two-dimensional' structure is built around four sections – introduction, development, exploration and extension – which offer self-contained stages for study. Each topic can also be read across these sections, enabling the reader to build gradually on the knowledge gained. Each book in the series has a companion website with extra resources for teachers, lecturers and students.

Discourse Analysis:

❑ provides a comprehensive overview of the major approaches to and methodological tools used in discourse analysis;
❑ introduces both traditional perspectives on the analysis of texts and talk as well as more recent approaches that address technologically mediated and multimodal discourse;
❑ incorporates practical examples using real data;
❑ includes articles from key authors in the field, including Jan Blommaert, William Labov, Paul Baker, Penelope Brown and Stephen Levinson;
❑ is supported by a companion website featuring extra activities, additional guidance, useful links and multimedia examples including sound files and YouTube videos.

Features of the new edition include: new readings featuring cutting-edge research; updated references; revised and refreshed examples; and a wider range of material from social media that includes Twitter, Instagram and Snapchat.

Written by an experienced teacher and author, this accessible textbook is essential reading for all students of English language and linguistics.

Rodney H. Jones is Head of the Department of English Language and Applied Linguistics at the University of Reading, UK.

ROUTLEDGE ENGLISH LANGUAGE INTRODUCTIONS

SERIES CONSULTANT: PETER STOCKWELL

Peter Stockwell is Professor of Literary Linguistics in the School of English at the University of Nottingham, UK, where his interests include sociolinguistics, stylistics and cognitive poetics. His recent publications include *The Cambridge Handbook of Stylistics* (2014), *Cognitive Grammar in Literature* (2014) and *The Language and Literature Reader* (2008).

SERIES CONSULTANT: RONALD CARTER

Ronald Carter is Research Professor of Modern English Language in the School of English at the University of Nottingham, UK. He is the co-series editor of the Routledge Applied Linguistics, Routledge Introductions to Applied Linguistics and Routledge Applied Corpus Linguistics series.

TITLES IN THE SERIES:

Sociolinguistics
Peter Stockwell

History of English
Dan McIntyre

Language and Media
Alan Durant and Marina Lambrou

Researching English Language
Alison Sealey

Practical Phonetics and Phonology, Third Edition
Beverley Collins and Inger M. Mees

Stylistics, Second Edition
Paul Simpson

Global Englishes, Third Edition
(previously published as *World Englishes*)
Jennifer Jenkins

Pragmatics, Third Edition
(previously published as *Pragmatics and Discourse*)
Joan Cutting

Introducing English Language, Second Edition
Louise Mullany and Peter Stockwell

Language and Law
Alan Durant and Janny HC Leung

English Grammar, Second Edition
Roger Berry

Language and Power, Second Edition
Paul Simpson, Andrea Mayr and Simon Statham

Discourse Analysis, Second Edition
Rodney Jones

For more information on any of these titles, or to order, please go to
www.routledge.com/series/RELI

DISCOURSE ANALYSIS

A Resource Book for Students

Second Edition

RODNEY H. JONES

Routledge
Taylor & Francis Group

LONDON AND NEW YORK

Second edition published 2019
by Routledge
2 Park Square, Milton Park, Abingdon, Oxon, OX14 4RN

and by Routledge
711 Third Avenue, New York, NY 10017

Routledge is an imprint of the Taylor & Francis Group, an informa business

First edition published by Routledge 2012

British Library Cataloguing-in-Publication Data
A catalogue record for this book is available from the British Library

Library of Congress Cataloging-in-Publication Data
Names: Jones, Rodney H., author.
Title: Discourse analysis: a resource book for students / Rodney Jones.
Description: Second edition. | Abingdon, Oxon; New York, NY: Routledge, 2019. |
Series: Routledge English language introductions | Includes bibliographical references and indexes.
Identifiers: LCCN 2018023902 | ISBN 9781138669666 (hardback) |
ISBN 9781138669673 (paperback)
Subjects: LCSH: Discourse analysis.
Classification: LCC P302 .J66 2019 | DDC 401/.41–dc23
LC record available at https://lccn.loc.gov/2018023902

ISBN: 978-1-138-66966-6 (hbk)
ISBN: 978-1-138-66967-3 (pbk)

Typeset in Minion Pro
by Deanta Global Publishing Services, Chennai, India

Visit the companion website: www.routledge.com/cw/jones

HOW TO USE THIS BOOK

The Routledge English Language Introductions (RELI) are 'flexi-texts' that you can use to suit your own style of study. The books are divided into four sections:

A: Introduction – sets out the key concepts for the area of study. The units of this section take you through the foundational concepts, providing you with an initial toolkit for your own study. By the end of the section, you will have a good overview of the whole field.

B: Development – adds to your knowledge and builds on the key ideas already introduced. Units in this section also introduce key analytical tools and techniques. By the end of this section, you will already have a good and fairly detailed grasp of the field and will be ready to undertake your own exploration and thinking.

C: Exploration – provides examples of language data and guides you through your own investigation of the topic or area. The units in this section will be more open-ended and exploratory and you will be encouraged to try out your ideas and think for yourself, using your newly acquired knowledge.

D: Extension – offers you the chance to compare your expertise with key readings in the area. These are taken from the work of important writers and are provided with guidance and questions for your further thought.

You can read this book like a traditional textbook, 'vertically' straight through from beginning to end. So you would establish a broad sense of the key ideas by reading through section A, and deepen your knowledge by reading section B. Section C would then present you with one or more activities to test out different aspects of your broad knowledge. Finally, having gained a good level of competence, you can read the section D articles and follow up the further reading.

However, the Routledge English Language Introductions have been designed so that you can read them in another dimension, 'horizontally' across the numbered units. For example, units A1, B1, C1 and D1 constitute a strand first introducing a topic, then developing your knowledge, then testing out and exploring some key ideas, and finally offering you a key case study to read. The strand across A2, B2, C2, D2 and the other strands 3, 4, 5, and so on all work in the same way. Reading across the strands will take you rapidly from the key concepts of a specific topic to a level of expertise in that precise topic, all with a very close focus. You can match your way of reading with the best way that you work. The glossarial index at the end together with the suggestions for further reading for each strand will help to keep you orientated. Each textbook has a supporting website with extra commentary, suggestions, additional material and support for teachers and students.

Discourse analysis

This book covers the vast field of discourse analysis. Strand 1 gives a general introduction to the field, and the following strands are broadly arranged across three areas. Strands 1 to 4 cover the study of written discourse, examining cohesion and coherence, the social functions of texts and the ways ideology is expressed in written texts. Strands 5 to 7 focus more on spoken discourse and more interactive written discourse such as that which occurs in computer-mediated communication, examining how conversations are structured and how conversational participants strategically construct identities and activities in their talk, as well as how social contexts affect the way utterances are produced and interpreted. The last three strands focus on three relatively new approaches to discourse: mediated discourse analysis, an approach that examines, among other things, the way media affect the kinds of discourse we can produce and what we can do with it; multimodal discourse analysis, an approach that considers modes of communication beyond spoken and written language such as images and gestures; and corpus-assisted discourse analysis, an approach that uses computers to aid in the analysis of large collections of texts or transcripts.

Discourse analysis is a diverse and rapidly developing field; nearly every observation we have made about discourse in this book is open to debate and nearly every analytical technique we have introduced is open to criticism or further refinement. The real aim of this book is to provide you with the basic background to be able to engage in these debates and to assemble a toolkit of analytical techniques that best fit your needs. If you wish to know more about the ways discourse analysis fits into or relates to other approaches to the study of English, there are other books in the RELI series such as *Introducing English Language: A Resource Book for Students* by Louise Mullany and Peter Stockwell, *Pragmatics and Discourse: A Resource Book for Students* by Joan Cutting and *Language and Power: A Resource Book for Students* by Paul Simpson and Andrea Mayr.

The RELI books do not aim to replace your teacher or lecturer, but instead, they offer both student and expert a resource for you to adapt as you think most appropriate. You will want to critically examine what is presented here, test out the assumptions and – we hope – feel motivated to read and explore further. There is always space for tutors to mediate the material and for students to explore beyond the book.

CONTENTS

Contents cross-referenced   x
List of figures and tables   xiii
Acknowledgements   xv

**A Introduction: key topics in the
study of discourse analysis**   **1**
1   What is discourse analysis?   2
2   Texts and texture   5
3   Texts and their social functions   7
4   Discourse and ideology   11
5   Spoken discourse   17
6   Strategic interaction   21
7   Context, culture and communication   25
8   Mediated discourse analysis   28
9   Multimodal discourse analysis   31
10   Corpus-assisted discourse analysis   34

**B Development: approaches to
discourse analysis**   **37**
1   Three ways of looking at discourse   38
2   Cohesion, coherence and intertextuality   41
3   All the right moves   49
4   Constructing reality   55
5   The texture of talk   62
6   Negotiating relationships and activities   68
7   The speaking model   73
8   Mediation   76
9   Modes, meaning and action   80
10   Procedures for corpus-assisted discourse analysis   87

C Exploration: analysing discourse   **93**
1   Doing discourse analysis: first steps   94
2   Analysing texture   97
3   Analysing genres   104
4   Competing ideologies   107
5   Analysing speech acts and implicature   110
6   Analysing conversational strategies   114

7 Analysing contexts   118
8 Doing mediated discourse analysis   123
9 Analysing multimodality   125
10 Analysing corpora   132

**D Extension: readings in
    discourse analysis**   **139**
1 Three perspectives on discourse   140
2 Three perspectives on texture   146
3 Genres, discourse communities and creativity   156
4 Ideologies in discourse   162
5 Two perspectives on conversation   171
6 Politeness and framing in interaction   178
7 The ethnography of communication   186
8 Discourse and action   191
9 Two perspectives on multimodality   200
10 Corpus-assisted discourse analysis   207

Further reading   **215**

References   **218**

Author index   **228**

Glossarial index   **229**

A **INTRODUCTION**
Key topics in the study of discourse analysis

B **DEVELOPMENT**
Approaches to discourse analysis

1	

What is discourse analysis?	Three ways of looking at discourse
2	38

2	Texts and texture	Cohesion, coherence and intertextuality
	5	41

3	Texts and their social functions	All the right moves
	7	49

4	Discourse and ideology	Constructing reality
	11	55

5	Spoken discourse	The texture of talk
	17	62

6	Strategic interaction	Negotiating relationships and activities
	21	68

7	Context, culture and communication	The speaking model
	25	73

8	Mediated discourse analysis	Mediation
	28	76

9	Multimodal discourse analysis	Modes, meaning and action
	31	80

10	Corpus-assisted discourse analysis	Procedures for corpus-assisted discourse analysis
	34	87

Further reading

References

Author index

Glossarial index

C EXPLORATION *Analysing discourse*	**D** EXTENSION *Readings in discourse analysis*	

Doing discourse analysis: first steps 94	Three perspectives on discourse 140	**1**
Analysing texture 97	Three perspectives on texture 146	**2**
Analysing genres 104	Genres, discourse communities and creativity 156	**3**
Competing ideologies 107	Ideologies in discourse 162	**4**
Analysing speech acts and implicature 110	Two perspectives on conversation 171	**5**
Analysing conversational strategies 114	Politeness and framing in interaction 178	**6**
Analysing contexts 118	The ethnography of communication 186	**7**
Doing mediated discourse analysis 123	Discourse and action 191	**8**
Analysing multimodality 125	Two perspectives on multimodality 200	**9**
Analysing corpora 132	Corpus-assisted discourse analysis 207	**10**

Further reading

References

Author index

Glossarial index

FIGURES AND TABLES

Figures

A5.1   Calvin and Hobbes (© 1985 Watterson.
Reprinted with permission. All rights reserved)   19

B2.1   Advertisement for Body Coach.Net
(Duval Guillaume, Brussels, Belgium)   46

B4.1   Sign at US-Mexico border (photo credit: AT2663-commonswiki)   58

B4.2   Currency exchange booth (photo credit: author)   59

B4.3   Sign in luxury hotel (photo credit: author)   60

B8.1   Crossing the street   79

B9.1   Warriors (photo credit Claudio Gennari)   82

B9.2   Selfie (credit Robert Couse-Baker)   82

B9.3   Child (photo credit Denis Mihailov)   83

B9.4   Selfie II (photo credit hannesdesmet)   84

B9.5   Rape infographic (photo credit Snipegirl)   85

C1.1   Sign from men's lavatory, University of Reading   94

C1.2   Sign from men's lavatory, Paddington Station   97

C2.1   One of the photos shows a child appearing to accidentally
cover the dolphin's blowhole (from Equinac's Facebook page)   98

C2.2   From Equinac's Facebook page   102

C3.1   Review from Trip Advisor I   105

C3.2   Review from Trip Advisor II   106

C6.1   Excerpt from the author's Facebook newsfeed   116

C6.2   WhatsApp conversation   117

C6.3   Emojis (from Twitter)   118

C9.1   Life is hard in translation class, from Albwardi   127

C9.2   Eyeliner on fleek, from Albwardi, 2018   128

C9.3   An interaction in a writing centre   130

C10.1   Partial concordance list for 'I'm' in pre-2012 corpus   135

C10.2   Partial concordance list for 'I'm' in post-2012 corpus   135

D9.1   Bath I   202

D9.2   Bath II   202

D10.1   Overall frequencies of extreme belief words occurring
before or after Muslim(s), Islamic and Islam for each newspaper   209

D10.2   Proportion of times (per cent) that extreme belief words occur
before or after Muslim(s), Islamic and Islam for each newspaper   210

Tables

A4.1	Different forms of discourse representation	16
A6.1	Face strategies	23
C3.1	Analysing YouTube genres	106
C7.1	Analysing a speech event	121
C8.1	Cultural tools for breaking up	124
C10.1	Size of corpora and type token ratio	133
C10.2	Top five words	133
C10.3	Right collocates of 'I'	134
C10.4	'Keywords' in the pre- and post-2012 corpora	136
D10.1	Word sketch of extreme belief words	208

ACKNOWLEDGEMENTS

I wish to thank my colleagues and students at City University of Hong Kong and the University of Reading, the United Kingdom, for their valuable suggestions and support while I was writing this book.

The articles listed below have been reproduced with kind permission. Whilst every effort has been made to trace copyright holders, this has not been possible in all cases. Any omissions brought to our attention will be remedied in further editions.

Calvin and Hobbes © 1985 Watterson. Reprinted with permission of Andrews McMeel Syndication. All rights reserved.

Advertisement for BodyCoach.Net (Retrieved from http://adsoftheworld.com/media/print/bodycoach_net_before_after): Duval Guillaume, Brussels, Belgium. All rights reserved.

Claudio Gennari, Warriors (Retrieved from http://www.flickr.com/photos/claudio-gennari/3557886648/) licenced under the Creative Commons for reuse with attribution.

Denis Mihailov, Child (photo retrieved from http://www.flickr.com/photos/svintus2010/4549150256/) licensed under the Creative Commons for reuse with attribution.

Harris, Zellig (1952). Discourse analysis. *Language 28*(1), 1–30. Language by Linguistic Society of America. © 2012. Reproduced with permission of Linguistic Society of America in the format Textbook via Copyright Clearance Center.

Widdowson, Henry (1973). An applied linguistic approach to discourse analysis. Ph.D. thesis, Department of Linguistics, University of Edinburgh. Reproduced with kind permission of the author.

Gee, James Paul (2010). *Introduction to discourse analysis* 3rd Edition. London: Routledge (pp. 28–29). Reproduced with permission.

Halliday, Michael and Hasan, R. (1976). *Cohesion in English*. London: Pearson Education Ltd (pp. 1–6). Reproduced with permission.

Swales, John (1990). *Genre Analysis.* Cambridge: Cambridge University Press. © Cambridge University Press. Reproduced with permission.

Austin, J.L. (1962). *How to do things with words*. Oxford: Oxford University Press. By permission of Oxford University Press.

Tannen, Deborah and Wallat, Cynthia (1987). Interactive frames and knowledge schemas in interaction: examples from a medical examination/interview. *Social Psychology Quarterly 50*(2), 205–216. Reproduced with kind permission of Deborah Tannen and the American Sociological Association.

Saville-Troike, Muriel (2003). *The ethnography of communication*. Oxford: Blackwell. Copyright © 2011 Blackwell Publishing Ltd. Reproduced with permission of Blackwell Publishing Ltd.

Scollon, R. (2001). *Mediated discourse: the nexus of practice*. London: Routledge. (pp. 1–8). Reproduced with permission.

Kress, Gunther and van Leeuwen, Theo (2006). *Reading images: the grammar of visual design*, 2nd edition. London and New York: Routledge. Reproduced with permission.

Norris, S. (2004). *Analyzing multimodal interaction: a methodological framework*. London: Routledge. Reproduced with permission.

Re, Daniel E., Wang, Sylvia A., He, Joyce C. and Rule, Nicholas O. (2016). *Social Psychological and Personality Science*, Sage Publications 7(6), copyright © 2016 by Sage Publications. Reprinted by permission of Sage Publications, Inc.

Twitter Emoji is a coloured font for Emoji, developed by Twitter and released on Github under CC-BY 4.0 license (Retrieved from https://en.blog.wordpress.com/2014/11/06/emoji-everywhere/).

O'Neill, M. (2011). Infographic: Mobile daters more likely to 'hook up' than online daters, *Adweek*, 7 Nov. (Retrieved from http://www.adweek.com/digital/infographic-mobile-daters-more-likely-to-hook-up-than-online-daters/). © Snap-interactive.com. Reproduced with permission.

Labov, W. (1973). *Language in the inner city: studies in the Black English vernacular*, pp. 359–370. Reprinted with permission of the University of Pennsylvania Press.

Blommaert, J. (2007). Sociolinguistics and discourse analysis: orders of indexicality and polycentricity, *Journal of Multicultural Discourses* 2, 1115–1130, Taylor and Francis Ltd, http://www.tandfonline.com. Reprinted by permission of the publisher.

Brown, P. and Levinson, S.C. (1987). *Politeness: some universals in language usage*, (pp. 61–71). © Cambridge University Press 1978, 1987, reproduced with permission.

Jones, R. (2014). Mediated discourse analysis. In S. Norris and C.D. Maier (eds.) *Interactions, images and texts: a reader in multimodality*. New York: Mouton de Gruyter, pp. 40, 42–49. Reproduced with permission of the publisher.

Gee, James Paul (1996). *Social linguistics and literacies*, pp. 69–73 and 77–79. London: Taylor and Francis. Reproduced with permission.

Schegloff, E.A. and Sacks, H. (1973). Opening up closings. *Semiotica* 7, 289–327. Reproduced by permission of De Gruyter.

Baynes, C. (2017). Baby dolphin dies after being passed around for selfies with tourists. *The Independent*, 16 Aug. (Retrieved from https://www.independent.co.uk/news/world/europe/baby-dolphin-dies-passed-tourists-photographed-almeira-spain-moj-car-a7896376.html). © 2017 Independent Digital News and Media Ltd. (Independent.co.uk).

King, Lorraine, *et al.* (2013). Big Debate: CCTV cameras—Tackling crime or invading our privacy?, *Newham Recorder*, 27 Mar. (Retrieved from http://www.newham-recorder.co.uk/news/politics/big-debate-cctv-cameras-tackling-crime-or-invading-our-privacy-1-1993243). Reproduced with permission of Newham Recorder/Archant.

Scollon, R., Tsang, W.K., Li, D., Yung, V. and Jones, R. (1998). Voice appropriation and discourse representation in a student writing task. *Linguistics and Education* 9(3), 227–250. With permission from Elsevier.

Bhatia, Vijay K. (2017). *Critical genre analysis: investigating interdiscursive performance in professional practice*, pp. 39–44. London: Routledge. Reproduced with permission.

Varis, P. (2016). Digital ethnography. In A. Georgakopoulou and T. Spilioti (eds.) *The Routledge handbook of language and digital communication*, pp. 55–68. London: Routledge. Reproduced with permission.

Baker, P. (2012) Acceptable bias? Using corpus linguistics methods with critical discourse analysis. In *Critical Discourse Studies* 9(3), pp. 247–256. London: Taylor and Francis. Reproduced with permission.

Section A

INTRODUCTION
KEY TOPICS IN THE STUDY OF DISCOURSE ANALYSIS

A

A1   WHAT IS DISCOURSE ANALYSIS?

Our first step in the study of discourse analysis has to be figuring out exactly what we mean by **discourse** and why it is so important to learn how to analyse it.

In one sense, we can say that discourse analysis is the study of language. Many people would define discourse analysis as a sub-field of linguistics, which is the scientific study of language. Linguistics has many sub-fields, each of which looks at a different aspect of language. **Phonology** is the study of the sounds of languages and how people put them together to form words. **Grammar** is the study of how words are put together to form sentences and spoken utterances. And **discourse analysis** is the study of the ways sentences and utterances are put together to make texts and interactions and how those texts and interactions fit into the social world.

But discourse analysis is not *just* the study of language. It is a way of looking at language that focuses on how people use it in real life to do things such as joke and argue and persuade and flirt, and to show that they are certain kinds of people or belong to certain groups. This way of looking at language is based on four main assumptions:

1   *Language is ambiguous.* What things mean is never absolutely clear. All communication involves interpreting what other people mean and what they are trying to do.
2   *Language is always 'in the world'.* That is, what language means is always a matter of where and when it is used and what it is used to do.
3   *The way we use language is inseparable from who we are and the different social groups to which we belong.* We use language to display different kinds of social identities and to show that we belong to different groups.
4   *Language is never used all by itself.* It is always combined with other things, such as our tone of voice, our facial expressions and gestures when we speak, and the fonts, layout and graphics we use in written texts. What language means and what we can do with it is often a matter of how it is combined with these other things.

The ambiguity of language

Everyone has had the experience of puzzling over what someone – a lover, a parent, a friend, or a politician – 'really meant' by what he or she said. In fact, nearly all communication contains some elements of meaning that are not expressed directly by the words that are spoken or written. Even when we think we are expressing ourselves clearly and directly, we may not be. For example, you may want to borrow a pen from someone and express this desire with the question, 'Do you have a pen?' Strictly speaking, though, this question does not *directly* communicate that you need a pen. It only asks if the other person is in possession of one. In order to understand this question as a request, the other person needs to undertake a process of 'figuring out' what you meant, a process that in this case may be largely unconscious and automatic but is, all the same, a process of interpretation.

So, we can take as a starting point for our study of discourse analysis the fact that *people don't always say what they mean, and people don't always mean what they say*. This is not because people are trying to trick or deceive each other (though sometimes they are), but because language is, by its very nature, ambiguous. To say exactly what we mean all the time would be impossible: first, because as poets, lovers and even lawyers know, language is an imperfect tool for the precise expression of many things we think and feel; and second, because whenever we communicate, we always mean to communicate more than just one thing. When you ask your friend if he or she has a pen, for example, you mean to communicate not just that you need a pen but also that you do not wish to impose on your friend or that you feel a bit shy about borrowing a pen, which is one of the reasons why you approach the whole business of requesting indirectly by asking if they have a pen, even though you may know very well that they have one.

At the same time, there are instances in which people *are* trying to deceive you, and discourse analysis can also help you to detect these moments and to call out those people. Politicians, advertisers and others who are trying to win your loyalty, patronage or compliance also depend on the ambiguity of language to persuade you to vote for them, buy their products, or otherwise go along with their program. For example, the manufacturer of a product that does not meet the government's criteria to claim that it is 'low in sugar' may write 'less sweet' on the label instead to give customers the impression that it is healthy. Politicians frequently speak in ambiguous language in order to avoid taking clear positions or to send different messages to different audiences. A politician who touts 'law and order' might be signalling that he or she wishes to crack down on political dissent, and one who calls refugees 'migrants' may be subtly calling into question their right to seek refuge.

Language in the world

One of the most important ways we understand what people mean when they communicate is by making reference to the social context within which they are speaking or writing. The meaning of an utterance can change dramatically depending on who is saying it, when and where it is said and to whom it is said. If a teacher asks a student who is about to take an examination the same question we discussed above, 'Do you have a pen?' it is rather unlikely that this is a request or that the teacher is a bit shy about communicating with the student. Rather, this utterance is probably designed to make sure that the student has the proper tool to take the examination, or to inform the student that a pen (rather than a pencil) must be used.

In other words, when we speak of discourse, we are always speaking of language that is in some way **situated**. Language is always situated in at least four ways. First, language is situated within the material world, and where we encounter it, whether it be on a shop sign or in a textbook or on a particular website, will contribute to the way we interpret it. Second, language is situated within relationships; one of the main ways we understand what people mean when they speak or write is by referring to who they are, how well we know them and whether or not they have some kind of power over us. Third, language is situated in history, that is, in relation to what happened before and what we expect to happen afterwards. Finally, language is situated in relation to other language – utterances and texts always respond to or refer to other utterances and texts; that is, everything that we say or write is situated in a kind of web of discourse.

Language and social identity

Not only is discourse situated partly by who says (or writes) what to whom, but people – the 'whos' and the 'whoms' who say or write these things – are also situated by discourse. What I mean by this is that whenever people speak or write, they are, through their discourse, somehow demonstrating who they are and what their relationship is to other people. They are enacting their identities through discourse, or, to put it another way, the discourse they are using is helping to create 'who they are'.

The important thing about identities is that they are multiple and fluid rather than singular and fixed. The identity I enact at the dance club on Friday night is not the same identity I enact at the office on Monday morning. The reason for this is not that I change my personality in any fundamental way, but rather that I change the way I use language.

Language and other modes

Changing the way I use language when I enact the identity of a dance-club diva or a yoga teacher or a university professor, of course, is not enough to fully enact these identities. I also have to dress in certain ways, act in certain ways and hang out in certain places with certain people. In other words, language alone cannot achieve all the things I need to do to be a certain kind of person. I always have to combine that language with other things such as fashion, gestures and the handling of various kinds of objects.

In the same way, most of the written texts that we encounter consist of more than just words. They convey their messages through a combination of words, images, layout and sometimes even sound files or video clips.

Partially because of its roots in linguistics, discourse analysts used to focus almost exclusively on written or spoken language. Now, people are increasingly realising not just that we communicate in a lot of ways that do not involve language, but also that in order to understand what people mean when they use language, we need to pay attention to the way it is combined with other communicative **modes** such as pictures, gestures, music and the layout of physical environments.

So what good is discourse analysis?

Given these four principles, we can begin to understand some of the reasons why learning how to analyse discourse might be useful. The chief reason is that we *already* engage in discourse analysis all the time, when we try to figure out what people mean by what they say and when we try to express our multiple and complicated meanings to them. Much of what you will learn in this book will be about making processes that already take place beneath the surface of your consciousness more explicit. But what is the point of that, you might ask, if all of this communication and interpretation is going on so smoothly without us having to attend to it? But the fact is, it's not. None of us are immune to misunderstandings, to offending people by saying the wrong thing, to struggling to get our message across, or to being taken in by someone who is trying somehow to deceive us. Hopefully, by understanding how discourse works, we will be able to understand people better and communicate more effectively.

Studying discourse analysis, however, can teach you more than that. Since the way we use discourse is tied up with our social identities and our social relationships, discourse analysis can also help us to understand how the societies in which we live are put together and how they are maintained through our day-to-day activities of speaking, writing and making use of other modes of communication. It can help us to understand why people interact with one another the way they do and how they exert power and influence over one another. It can help us to understand how people view reality differently and why, and how the texts that we are exposed to come to create our view of reality. The study of discourse analysis, then, is not just the study of how we use language. It is also indirectly the study of politics, power, psychology, romance and a whole lot of other things.

👁 **Look deeper into why people don't say what they mean or mean what they say on the companion website.**

TEXTS AND TEXTURE   A2

Discourse analysts analyse 'texts' and 'conversations'. But what is a 'text' and what is a 'conversation'? What distinguishes texts and conversations from random collections of sentences and utterances? These are the questions taken up in this section. For now, we will mostly be considering written texts. Conversations will be dealt with in later units.

Consider the following list of words:

- ☐ milk
- ☐ spaghetti
- ☐ tomatoes
- ☐ rocket
- ☐ light bulbs

You might look at this list and conclude that this is not a text for the simple reason that it 'makes no sense' to you – that it has no **meaning**. According to the linguist M.A.K. Halliday, meaning is the most important thing that makes a text a text; it has to *make sense*. A text, in his view, is everything that is meaningful in a particular situation. And the basis for *meaning* is *choice* (Halliday 1978: 137). Whenever I choose one thing rather than another from a set of alternatives (yes or no, up or down, red or green), I am making meaning. This focus on meaning, in fact, is one of the main things that distinguishes Halliday's brand of linguistics from that of other linguists who are concerned chiefly with linguistic *forms*. Historically, the study of linguistics, he points out (1994: xiv), first involved studying the way the language was put together (syntax and morphology), *followed by* the study of meaning. In his view, however, the reverse approach is more useful.

As he puts it, 'A language is ... *a system of meanings*, accompanied by forms through which the meanings can be expressed' [emphasis mine].

So one way you can begin to make sense of the list of words above is to consider them as a series of choices. In other words, I wrote 'milk' instead of 'juice' and 'spaghetti' instead of 'linguini'. There must be some reason for this. You will still probably not be able to recognise this as a text because you do not have any understanding of what motivated these choices (why I wrote down these particular words) and the relationship between one set of choices (e.g. 'milk' vs. 'juice') and another.

It is these two pieces of missing information – the *context* of these choices and the *relationships* between them – that form the basis for what is known as **texture** – that quality that makes a particular set of words or sentences a *text* rather than a random collection of linguistic items. A language speaker's 'ability to discriminate between a random string of sentences and one forming a discourse', Halliday explains, 'is due to the inherent texture in the language and to his awareness of it' (Halliday 1968: 210). According to this formulation, there are two important things that make a text a text. One has to do with features inherent in the language itself (things, for example, such as grammatical 'rules'), which help us to understand the relationship among the different words and sentences and other elements in the text. It is these features that help you to figure out the relationship between the various sets of choices (either lexical or grammatical) that you encounter. The problem with the text above is that there is not much in the language itself that helps you to do this. There are, however, two very basic things that help you to establish a connection among these words. The first is the fact that they appear in a list – they come one after another. This very fact helps to connect them together, because you automatically think that they would not have been put together in the same list if they did not have something to do with one another.

Another 'internal' thing that holds these words together as a potential text is that they are similar; with the exception of 'light bulbs', they all belong to the same **semantic field** (i.e. words having to do with food). In fact, it is because of words such as 'milk' and 'tomatoes' that you are able to infer that what is meant by the word 'rocket' is 'rocket lettuce' (or *arugula*) rather than the kind of rocket that shoots satellites into space. This semantic relationship among the words, however, is probably still not enough for you to make sense of this list as a text as long as you are relying only on features that are intrinsic to the language. The reason for this is that there are no grammatical elements that join these words together. It would be much easier for you to understand the relationship among these words if they appeared in a conversation like this:

> *Franny:*   What do we need to get at the shop?
> *Zoe:*   Well, we need some milk. And I want to make a salad, so let's get some tomatoes and rocket. And, oh yeah, the light bulb in the living room is burnt out. We'd better get some new ones.

In this conversation, the relationship between the different words is much clearer because new words have been added. One important word that joins these words together is 'and', which creates an *additive* relationship among them, indicating that they are all part of a cumulative list. Other important words are 'we' and 'need'. The verb 'need' connects the things in the list to some kind of *action* that is associated with them, and the word 'we' connects them to some people who are also involved in this action.

This second part of Halliday's formulation has to do with something that cannot be found in the language itself but rather exists inside the minds of the people who are perceiving the text – what Halliday calls an *awareness* of the conventions of the language (and, by extension, broader conventions of communication in a given society) that helps us to work out the relationships among words, sentences, paragraphs, pictures and other textual elements, as well as the relationships between these combinations of textual elements and certain social situations or communicative purposes. These conventions give us a kind of 'framework' within which we can fit the language. The framework for the text above, for example, is 'a shopping list'. As soon as you have that framework, this list of words makes perfect sense as a text. In fact, you do not even need to refer back to the conversation above to understand what the text means and how it will be used. All of the information about what people do with shopping lists is already part of your **common knowledge** (the knowledge you share with other people in society).

There is still one more thing that helps you to make sense of this as a text, and that has to do with the connections that exist between this particular collection of words and other texts that exist outside of it. For example, this text might be related to the conversation above. In fact, it might be the result of that conversation: Franny might have written down this list as Zoe dictated it to her. It might also be related to other texts, like a recipe for rocket salad Zoe found in a cookbook. Finally, when Franny and Zoe go to the supermarket, they will connect this text to other texts, like signs advertising the price of tomatoes or the label on the milk carton telling them the expiry date. In other words, all texts are somehow related to other texts, and sometimes, in order to make sense of them or use them to perform social actions, you need to make reference to these other texts.

To sum up, the main thing that makes a text a text is *relationships* or *connections*. Sometimes these relationships are between words, sentences or other elements *inside* the text. These kinds of relationships create what we refer to as **cohesion**. Another kind of relationship exists between the text and the person who is reading it or using it in some way. Here, meaning comes chiefly from the background knowledge the person has about certain social conventions regarding texts as well as the social situation in which the text is found and what the person wants to do with the text. This kind of relationship creates what we call **coherence**. Finally, there is the relationship between one text and other texts in the world that one might, at some point, need to refer to in the process of making sense of this text. This kind of relationship creates what we call **intertextuality**.

👁 **Look deeper into what makes a text a text on the companion website.**

TEXTS AND THEIR SOCIAL FUNCTIONS A3

In the previous section, we explored how the internal structure of a text and the expectations we have about it contribute to the text's *texture*. We also saw how different patterns of texture are often associated with particular kinds of texts and, by extension, particular kinds of text producers. Newspaper articles, for example, tend to favour particular kinds of cohesive devices and are structured in a conventional way, with a summary of the main points in the beginning and the details coming later, a convention that all journalists must learn if they want to get a job (see C2). To understand *why* such textual conventions are associated with certain kinds of texts, however, we need to understand something about what the people who produce these texts are trying to *do* with them, and how this *doing* is mixed up with their social or professional identities. In this section, we will examine how the structures and expectations associated with different kinds of texts contribute to how they function in the social world, and how they help to define social activities and the groups of people who take part in them. The study of the social functions of different kinds of texts is called **genre analysis**.

The notion of **genre** is probably familiar to you from your experience as a movie-goer. Different films belong to different genres: there are love stories, horror movies, thrillers, 'chick flicks', and many other film genres. Before we go to the movies, we always have some idea about the film we are about to see based on the genre that it belongs to. These expectations include ideas about the kind of story the film will tell and the kinds of characters it will include. At the same time, of course, not all films fit neatly into genres. We might go to a film called *Scary Movie*, for example, and find that it is actually a comedy, and sometimes what makes a film successful is that it creatively confounds our expectations by mixing different genres together. We are also familiar with genres in other media as well. On *YouTube*, for instance, we can watch product reviews, gaming videos, 'vlogs' (video web logs), 'unboxing' videos (which portray people unpacking an item they have just bought) and 'how to' videos (which teach viewers how to perform some kind of task) (see C3).

The notion of *genre* in discourse analysis goes beyond examining the features of different kinds of texts to ask what the structures of these texts can tell us about the people who use them and what they are using them to do. Bhatia (1993: 13) defines genre as follows:

> (A genre is) a recognisable communicative *event* characterised by a set of *communicative purposes* identified and mutually understood by members of the community in which it occurs. Most often it is highly structured and *conventionalised* with *constraints* on allowable contributions in terms of their intent, positioning, form and functional value. These constraints, however, are often *exploited by expert members* of the discourse community to achieve private intentions within the framework of the socially recognised purpose(s) [emphases mine].

There are three important aspects to this definition that need to be further explained: first, that genres are not defined as types of text but rather as types of **communicative events**; second, that these events are characterised by **constraints** on what can and cannot be done within them; and third, that *expert* users often *exploit* these constraints in creative and unexpected ways.

Genres are communicative events

While it might not seem unusual to refer to spoken genres such as conversations and debates and political speeches as 'events', thinking of written texts such as newspaper articles, recipes and job application letters as 'events' might at first seem rather strange. We are in many ways accustomed to thinking of texts as 'objects'. Seeing them as 'events', however, highlights the fact that all texts are basically instances of people *doing* things with or to other people: a newspaper article is an instance of someone *informing* someone else about some recent event; a recipe is an instance of someone *instructing* another person how to prepare a particular kind of food; and a job application letter is an instance of someone *requesting* that another person give him or her a job. As Martin (1985: 250) points out, 'genres are how things get done, when language is used to accomplish them'.

Of course, most texts are not just trying to get only one thing done. The **communicative purposes** of texts are often multiple and complex. A recipe, for example, may be *persuading* you to make a certain dish (or to buy a certain product with which to make it) as much as it is *instructing* you how to do it, and a newspaper article might be attempting not just to *inform* you about a particular event but also to somehow affect your opinion about it. The different people using the text might also have different purposes in mind: while a job applicant sees his or her application letter as a way to convince a prospective employer to hire him or her, the employer might see the very same application letter as a means of 'weeding out' unsuitable candidates.

Conventions and constraints

Because genres are about 'getting things done', the way they are structured and the kinds of features they contain are largely determined by what people want to do with them. The kinds of information I might include in a job application, for example, would be designed to convince a prospective employer that I am the right person for the job. This information would probably not include my fondness for taking selfies with injured animals or my opinion about some event I read about in a newspaper. Genres, therefore, come with 'built-in' *constraints* as to what kinds of things they can include and what kinds of things they cannot, based on the activity they are trying to accomplish.

These constraints govern not just *what* can be included but also *how* it should be included. In my job application letter, for example, I would probably want to present the information in a certain order, beginning by indicating the post I am applying for, then going on to describe my qualifications and experience, and ending by requesting an appointment for an interview. Putting this information in a different order – for example, waiting until the end of the letter to indicate the post for which I am applying – would be considered odd. The order in which I do things in a genre, what in genre analysis is called the **move structure** of a particular genre, often determines how successfully I am able to fulfil the communicative purpose of the genre.

But what is important about these conventions and constraints is not only that they make communicative events more efficient but also that they demonstrate that the person who produced the text knows 'how we do things'. Prospective employers read application letters not just to find out what post an applicant is applying for and what qualifications or experience that person has, but also to find out if that person *knows how to write a job application letter*. In other words, the ability to successfully produce this type of genre following particular conventions is taken as an indication that the writer is a 'certain kind of person' who 'knows how to communicate like us'.

In fact, for some employers, the qualifications that applicants demonstrate through successfully producing this genre are far more important than those they describe in the letter itself.

Creativity

That is not to say that all job application letters or other genres such as newspaper articles and recipes, are always exactly the same. Often, the most successful texts are those that defy conventions and push the boundaries of constraints. Expert producers of texts, for example, sometimes mix different kinds of text together, or embed one genre into another, or alter the moves that are included or the order in which they are presented. Of course, there are limitations to how much a genre can be altered and still be successful at accomplishing what its producers want to accomplish. There are always risks associated with being creative.

There are several important points to be made here. The first is that such creativity would not be possible without the existence of conventions and constraints, and the reason innovations can be effective is that they exploit previously formed expectations. The second is that such creativity must itself have some relationship to the communicative purpose of the genre and the context in which it is used. Writing a job application letter in the form of a sonnet, for example, may be more effective if I want to get a job as an editor at a literary magazine than if I want to get a job as a software engineer. Finally, being able to successfully defy conventions is very much a matter of and a marker of expertise: in order to break the rules effectively, you must also be able to show that you have mastered the rules.

Discourse communities

It should be clear by now that at the centre of the concept of genre is the idea of *belonging*. We produce and use genres not just in order to get things done but also to show ourselves to be members of particular groups and to demonstrate that we are qualified to participate in particular activities. Genres are always associated with certain groups of people that have certain common goals and common ways of reaching these goals.

John Swales calls these groups **discourse communities**. In the excerpt from his book *Genre Analysis* (1990), which is included in D3, he describes a number of features that define discourse communities, among which are that they consist of 'expert' members whose job it is to socialise new members into 'how things are done', that members have ways of regularly communicating with and providing feedback to one another, and that members tend to share a certain vocabulary or 'jargon'. The two most important characteristics of discourse communities are that members have common goals and common means of reaching those goals (genres). These goals and the means of reaching them work to reinforce each other. Every time a member makes use of a particular genre, he or she not only moves the group closer to the shared goals but also validates these goals as worthy and legitimate and shows him or herself to be a worthy and legitimate member of the group.

Thus, genres not only link people together; they also link people with certain activities, identities, roles and responsibilities. In a very real way, then, genres help to regulate and control what people can do and who people can 'be' in various contexts.

This regulation is exercised in a number of ways. First of all, since the goals of the community and the ways those goals are to be accomplished are 'built in' to the texts that members of a discourse community use on a daily basis, it becomes much more difficult to question those goals. Since mastery of the genre is a requirement for membership, members must also 'buy into' the goals of the community. Finally, since texts always create certain kinds of relationships between those who have produced them and those who are using them, when the conventions and constraints associated with texts become fixed and difficult to change, these roles and relationships also become fixed and difficult to change. When looked at in this way, genres are not just 'text types' that are structured in certain ways; they are important tools through which people, groups and institutions define, organise, and structure social life.

👁 **Look deeper into the idea of discourse communities on the companion website.**

DISCOURSE AND IDEOLOGY   **A4**

In the last two units, we looked at the ways texts are structured and the social functions they fulfil for different groups of people. In this section, we will examine how texts promote certain points of view or **ideologies**. We will focus on four things:

1   the ways authors create *'versions of reality'* based on their choice of words and how they combine words together;
2   the ways authors construct certain *relationships* between themselves and their readers;
3   the ways authors represent *the words of other people* and position themselves in relation to those words (and those people);
4   the ways authors of texts **index** or 'invoke' larger concepts, systems of social organisation or relationships of power and, by doing so, reinforce these concepts, systems and relationships.

I will talk about the first three things in this section and focus on the fourth thing in section B4.

Whether we are aware of it or not, our words are never neutral. They always represent the world in a certain way and create certain relationships with the people with whom we are communicating. For this reason, texts always, to some degree, promote a particular **ideology**. An ideology is a specific set of beliefs and assumptions people have about things such as what is good and bad, what is right and wrong and what is normal and abnormal. Ideologies provide us with models of how the world is 'supposed to be'. In some respects, ideologies help to create a shared worldview and sense of purpose among people in a particular group. Ideologies also limit the way we look at reality and tend to marginalise or exclude altogether people, things and ideas that do not fit into these models.

All texts, even those that seem rather innocuous or banal, somehow involve these systems of inclusion and exclusion. Often, when you fill out a form, such as a university application form or an application for a driver's licence, you are asked to indicate whether you are married or single. One thing that this question does is reinforce the idea that your marital status is an important aspect of your identity (although it may have very little bearing on whether or not you are qualified to either study in university or drive a car). Another thing it does is limit this aspect of your identity to one of only two choices. Other choices such as divorced, widowed or in a civil partnership are often not offered, nor are choices having to do with other important relationships in your life, such as your relationship with your parents or your siblings. In China, such forms often ask this question slightly differently, offering the categories of 結婚 ('married') or 未婚 ('single', or literally 'not yet married'). These two choices not only exclude people in the kinds of relationships mentioned above but also people such as Buddhist monks and 'confirmed bachelors' who have no intention of getting married. They also promote the idea that being married is somehow the 'natural' or 'normal' state of affairs.

In such cases, it is fair to ask how much you are answering questions about yourself and how much the forms themselves are *constructing* you as a certain kind of person by enabling some choices and constraining others. In other words, are you filling out the form, or is the form filling out you?

'Whos doing whats'

The linguist Michael Halliday (1985, 1994) pointed out that whenever we use language we are always doing three things at once: we are in some way representing the world, which he called the **ideational** function of language; we are creating, ratifying or negotiating our relationships with the people with whom we are communicating, which he called the **interpersonal** function of language; and we are joining sentences and ideas together in particular ways to form cohesive and coherent texts, which he called the **textual** function of language. All of these functions play a role in the way a text promotes a particular ideology or worldview. In A2, we looked at the *textual* function, discussing how different ways of connecting ideas together and of structuring them based on larger sets of expectations not only help us to make sense of texts but can also reinforce certain assumptions about people, things and ideas and how they are linked together. In this section, the *ideational* and the *interpersonal* functions of language will be the focus.

According to Halliday, we represent the world through language by choosing words that represent people, things or concepts (**participants**), and words about what these participants are *doing* to, with, or for one another (**processes**). All texts contain these two elements: *participants* and *processes*. James Paul Gee (2010) calls them '**whos doing whats**'.

Rather than talking about texts representing reality, however, it might be better to talk about texts 'constructing' reality, since, depending on the words they choose to represent the 'whos doing whats' in a particular situation, people can create very different impressions of what is going on. First of all, we might choose different words to represent the same kinds of participant. In traditional church wedding ceremonies in many places, for example, the convener of the ceremony (often a priest or a minister), after the couple have taken their vows, will pronounce them 'man and wife'. By using different kinds of words to describe the groom and the bride, this utterance portrays them as two different kinds of people, and as fundamentally unequal. This choice of words gives to the 'man' an independent identity but makes the woman's (the 'wife's') identity contingent on her relationship to the man. Nowadays, many churches have changed their liturgies to make this 'I now pronounce you husband and wife' in order to present the two individuals as more equal.

The words we use for processes and how we use them to link participants together can also create different impressions of what is going on. One of the key things about *processes* is that they always construct a certain kind of *relationship* between participants. Halliday calls this relationship **transitivity**. An important aspect of transitivity when it comes to ideology has to do with which participants are portrayed as performing actions and which are portrayed as having actions performed to or for them. In the same kinds of traditional church weddings described above, after pronouncing the couple 'man and wife', the convener might turn to the man and say, 'you may now kiss the bride'. Making the male participant the *actor* in the process (kissing) constructs him as the person 'in charge' of the situation and the woman as a passive recipient of his kiss. We call the actor in processes the **agent** and refer to his or her ability to 'take charge' of the process **agency**. In this sentence, the agency that is given to the male participant reinforces many assumptions about the roles of men and women, especially in romantic and sexual relationships, that are still deeply held in some societies. As with the statement, 'I now pronounce you man and wife', in many places this has changed in recent years, with the couple either simply kissing after the declaration of marriage or the convener saying something like 'you may now kiss each other'.

Different kinds of processes link participants in different ways. Processes involving some kind of physical action like kissing link participants in ways in which one participant is portrayed as doing something to or for the other (**action processes**). Processes involving saying or writing, on the other hand, often link participants so that one participant takes the position of the speaker or writer and the other takes the position of the listener or reader (**verbal processes**). Processes involving thinking and feeling link participants to ideas or emotions in various ways (**mental processes**).

Participants can also be linked in ways that show their relationship with each other (**relational processes**): they might be portrayed as equal or equivalent with linking verbs such as 'to be' or 'to seem' (as in 'this ice cream is my dinner'); one participant might be portrayed as possessing another with words such as 'to have' or 'to contain' (as in 'this ice cream contains nuts'); and participants might be linked to each other in other kinds of relationship such as cause and effect with words such as 'to cause', 'to lead to', or 'to result in' (as in 'ice cream leads to obesity').

Finally, processes themselves can sometimes be transformed into participants and linked to other participants or other processes (as in 'kissing is a custom at many wedding ceremonies'). In this last example, the action of kissing is turned into a 'thing' and then linked to another thing (a custom) with a **relational process**. Turning a process into a participant is known as **nominalisation** and is often a characteristic of technical or academic texts.

A good example of how 'whose doing whats' can change the way we perceive something can be seen in the warnings that come on the side of packets of cigarettes. Different countries require cigarette manufacturers to put different warnings on cigarette packets, and lawmakers change these requirements from time to time. Here are two examples from the United States, one (a) that was required in the 1970s, and the other (b) that is required today.

a   Warning: The Surgeon General Has Determined that Cigarette Smoking is Dangerous to Your Health (US circ. 1970s).
b   SURGEON GENERAL'S WARNING: Smoking Causes Lung Cancer, Heart Disease, Emphysema and May Complicate Pregnancy (US circ. 1980s).

In the first warning, the main participant is a person (the Surgeon General), and he or she is portrayed carrying out a mental process (determining something). The fact that 'cigarette smoking is dangerous to your health' is **backgrounded** as the thing that has been determined rather than the main 'whose doing what' of the sentence. Even in this clause, however, 'cigarette smoking' (a *nominalisation* of the *action* of smoking cigarettes) is not portrayed as doing anything; rather it is linked with a relational process to an attribute: 'Dangerous'. In the second warning, however, the nominalisation of 'smoking' is portrayed as the main participant, and one that actually *does* something: '*causing* lung cancer, heart disease …'. This formulation portrays a version of reality in which cigarette smoking is construed as much more 'dangerous' than in the first warning. Other examples of such warnings can be even more menacing, depending on the kinds of participants and processes that are chosen. A common warning on cigarette packets in the EU, for example, is 'Smoking Kills!' with the action process 'kills' making 'smoking' seem even more like a something with *agency* and that intentionally wants to harm you.

We have to assume that these differences in wordings on cigarette packets are in some way deliberate choices. Lawmakers spend a great deal of time writing and debating legislation to require these warnings, and cigarette companies spend a great deal of time and money trying to get lawmakers to make them seem less menacing. Looking at such warnings, then, can tell us not just about the 'ideology' around smoking and health in a particular country but also about who is more powerful: lawmakers or corporations.

Relationships

Another important way texts promote ideology is in the *relationships* they create between the people who are communicating, what Halliday calls the *interpersonal* function of language. We construct relationships through words we choose to express – things such as certainty and obligation (known as the system of **modality** in a language). The traditional priest or minister described above, for example, typically says 'you may now kiss the bride' rather than 'kiss the bride!' constructing the action as a matter of permission rather than obligation and constructing himself or herself as someone who is there to assist them in doing what they want to do rather than to force them to do things they do not want to do.

Another way we use language to construct relationships is through the style of speaking or writing that we choose. To take the example of the convener of the wedding ceremony again, he or she says, 'you many now kiss the bride' rather than something such as 'why don't you give her a kiss!' This use of more formal language helps create a relationship of respectful distance between the couple and the convener and maintains an air of seriousness in the occasion.

Halliday sees the degree of 'formality' of language as a matter of what he calls **register**, the different ways we use language in different situations depending on the topic we are communicating about, the people with whom we are communicating and the channel through which we are communicating (e.g. formal writing, instant messaging, face-to-face conversation) (see section A7).

Like genres, registers tend to communicate that we are 'certain kinds of people' and show something about the relationships we have with the people with whom we are communicating. Most people, for instance, use a different register when they are talking or writing to their boss than when they are talking or writing to their peers. The American discourse analyst James Paul Gee refers to these different ways of speaking and writing as **social languages** (see D4).

The use of different registers to create a different kind of relationship between authors and readers can also be seen in cigarette warnings. Consider the two examples below:

1   Smoking when pregnant harms your baby (EU).
2   SURGEON GENERAL'S WARNING: Smoking By Pregnant Women May Result in Fetal Injury, Premature Birth And Low Birth Weight (US).

Both of these examples are about the same thing: smoking by pregnant women. The first text, however, positions the reader as someone who is herself a pregnant woman, whereas the second positions the reader as someone who, while he or she may be interested in 'pregnant women', may not be one. Furthermore, the first example uses common, everyday language and few nominalisations, constructing the author as a person not so different from the reader, someone akin to a friend or a relative. The second example, on the other hand, uses very dense scientific language and nominalisations such as 'fetal injury' in which the process of 'harming' from the first example is transformed into a noun, and the participant 'your baby' is transformed into an adjective modifying that noun ('fetal'). This sort of language constructs the author as some kind of expert, perhaps a doctor or a research scientist and creates a considerable distance between him or her and the reader.

Discourse representation

As I mentioned in section A2, texts often refer to or somehow depend on other texts for their meaning. We called the relationship texts create with other texts *intertextuality*, and intertextuality is another important way ideologies are promoted in discourse.

When we appropriate the words and ideas of others in our texts and utterances, we almost always end up communicating how we think about those words and ideas (and the people who have said or written them) in the way we represent them. We might, for example, quote them verbatim, **paraphrase** them or refer to them in an indirect way, and we might characterise them in certain ways using different **reporting** words such as 'said', or 'insisted', or 'claimed'. Sometimes the effect of direct **quotation** can be to validate the words of the other person by implying that what they said or wrote is so important and profound that it is worth repeating word for word. Ironically, however, this technique can also have the opposite effect, creating a distance between the author and the words he or she is quoting and sometimes implying a certain scepticism towards those words – a way of saying, 'please note that these are not *my* words'. Often in cases of direct quotation, the reporting word that is used is important in indicating the author's attitude towards the words being quoted; it is quite a different thing to 'note' something, to 'claim' something, or to 'admit' something.

Another way authors represent the words of other people is to paraphrase (or 'summarise') them. An example of this is the following sentence: 'The Surgeon General has determined that cigarette smoking is dangerous to your health'. Here, rather than directly quoting what the Surgeon General said (or wrote in his or her report), the warning gives the 'gist' of what the Surgeon General said.

Sometimes authors will employ a mixture of quotation and paraphrase, using quotation marks only for selected words or phrases. This is most often done when authors want to highlight particular parts of what has been said, either to validate those words or to express scepticism about them. Quotes that are put around single words or phrases are sometimes called 'scare quotes' and are usually a way of saying things such as 'so called …' or 'as s/he put it …'.

By far the most common way to appropriate the words of others is by *not* attributing them to another person at all but by simply asserting them as facts. For example, the sentence 'Smoking kills' is just as much a matter of borrowing the words of others as is the sentence above that is attributed to the Surgeon General. The difference is that in this sentence, the author does not tell us who said this. Obviously, this makes for a stronger warning, since the danger of cigarettes is presented as 'a fact' rather than as the opinion of one person (the Surgeon General).

Finally, often the words and ideas of other people are not directly asserted but rather indirectly *presumed* in texts. Presuppositions are implicit assumptions about background beliefs that are presented as taken-for-granted facts. They are among the main devices authors use to promote their ideological positions. They are particularly effective in influencing people because they portray ideas as established truths and pre-empt opportunities to question or debate them.

Table A4.1 gives examples of these different forms of discourse representation.

Table A4.1 Different forms of discourse representation

Direct quotation	According to the Surgeon General, 'Smoking is the leading cause of preventable death in the United States'.
Paraphrase	The Surgeon General has determined that cigarette smoking is dangerous to your health.
Selective quotation	The Surgeon General has long warned that smoking is 'dangerous'.
Assertion	Smoking kills.
Presupposition	The purpose of the legislation is to reduce the harms caused by tobacco.

Intertextuality does not just involve mixing other people's words with ours. It can also involve mixing genres and mixing social languages, a practice that we call **inter-discursivity**. In the discussion of genres (A3), for example, I talked about how some people creatively mix together different genres, and the excerpt from James Paul Gee reprinted in section D4 examines how the authors of the label on an aspirin bottle mix together different social languages.

Discourses

It should be quite clear by now that even a seemingly innocent phrase such as 'you may now kiss the bride' can be seen as *ideological*. That is to say, it promotes what James Paul Gee calls **cultural models** (see B2) – 'frozen theories' or generalisations about the world and how people should behave, in this case generalisations about brides and grooms and men and women and how they are supposed to act in the context of marriage. Cultural models serve an important role in helping us make sense of the texts and the situations that we encounter in our lives. At the same time, however, they also function to exclude certain people or certain ways of behaving from our consideration.

Cultural models are not random and free floating. They are parts of larger systems of knowledge, values and social relationships that grow up within societies and cultures, which Gee calls 'Discourses' (with a capital 'D'). Other people have used different terms. The French philosopher Michel Foucault calls these systems '**orders of discourse**' and gives as examples things such as 'clinical discourse, economic discourse, the discourse of natural history, psychiatric discourse' (1972: 121).

The phrase 'you may now kiss the bride', then, does not just reinforce a theory about how brides and grooms are supposed to act *during* a marriage ceremony, but also invokes broader theories about marriage, gender relations, love, sex, morality and economics. All of these theories are part of a system of discourse that we might call the 'Discourse of marriage'.

👁 **Look deeper into ideology, cultural models and discourses on the companion website.**

SPOKEN DISCOURSE

So far, we have been focusing mostly on the analysis of written texts. In this section, we will begin to consider some of the special aspects of spoken discourse. In many ways, speech is not so different from writing. When people speak, they also produce different kinds of *genres* (such as casual conversations, debates, lectures and speeches of various kinds) and use different kinds of *registers* or *social languages*. They also promote particular versions of reality or *ideologies*. But there are some ways in which speech is very different from writing.

First of all, speech is more interactive. While we do often expect and receive feedback for our writing, especially when it comes to new media genres such as blogs and social media posts, this feedback is not always immediate the way it is in face-to-face communication. When we speak we usually do so in 'real time' with other people, and we receive their responses to what we have said right away. As we carry on conversations, we decide what to say based on what the previous speaker has said as well as what we expect the subsequent speaker to say after we have finished speaking. We can even alter what we are saying as we go along based on how other people seem to be reacting to it. Similarly, listeners can let us know immediately whether they object to, or do not understand, what we are saying. In other words, conversations are always *co-constructed* between or among the different parties having them.

Second, speech tends to be more transient and spontaneous than writing. When we write, we often plan what we are going to write carefully, and we often read over, revise and edit what we have written before showing it to other people. Because writing has a certain 'permanence', people can also read what we have written more carefully. They can read it quickly or slowly, and they can re-read it as many times as they like. They can also show it to other people and get their opinions about it. Speech, on the other hand, is usually not as well planned as writing. While some genres such as formal speeches and lectures are planned, most casual conversation is just made up as we go along. It is also transient; that is to say, our words usually disappear the moment we utter them. This makes listening in some ways more challenging than reading. Unless our words are recorded, people cannot return to them, save them, or transport them into other contexts. While they might be able to remember what we have said and repeat it to other people, it is never exactly the same as what we have actually said.

Finally, speech tends to be less *explicit* than writing. The reason for this is that when we are speaking, we often also depend on other methods of getting our message across. We communicate with our gaze, our gestures, our facial expressions and the tone of our voice. When we are writing we do not have these tools at our disposal, and so we often need to depend more on the words themselves to express our meaning. Speech also usually takes place in some kind of physical and social *context* that participants share, and often the meaning of what we say is dependent on this context. We can use **deictic expressions** (see section B3) such as 'this' and 'that' and 'here' and 'there' and expect that the people we are speaking to can understand what we are talking about based on the physical environment in which the conversation takes place, and we can usually assume more about our relationship with the people that are communicating with us in the case of spoken discourse than we can when it comes to written communication.

Of course, there are many kinds of speech that do not share all of the features we have discussed above. People engaged in telephone conversations, for example, like readers and writers, are situated in different places and cannot rely on physical cues such as gestures and facial expressions to convey meaning, although their conversations are still interactive. When people speak to us through television or YouTube, on the other hand, while we can see their gestures and facial expressions, we cannot usually respond to what they are saying in real time, although, in the case of YouTube, we can leave a comment. There are also certain kinds of conversations that share features of *both* speech and writing. Messaging and 'texting' using applications like WhatsApp and Facebook Messenger, for example, are, like speech, interactive and usually fairly unplanned, while at the same time, like writing, they involve a certain amount of permanence (the words we write remain in chat windows for some time after we have written them and may be stored on our and our **interlocutor's** phone or computer). They also lack the non-verbal cues that are part of physical co-presence (though users might resort to other non-verbal cues like 'emojis'). Other more 'hybrid' kinds of interaction are those involving apps like Snapchat, in which users exchange messages that might combine written text, drawings and pictures of themselves or their environments; or Skype and FaceTime, which in many ways enable conversations that resemble face-to-face conversations but also might involve users typing into chat windows, exchanging files, sharing their computer screens, or pointing their cameras towards other people or things in their environments. This kind of **mediated communication** will be considered later. In this unit, the focus is mainly on real-time, face-to-face interaction.

Making sense of conversations

As I mentioned in section A1, one of the main problems that people have when communicating is that quite often *people do not mean what they say, and people do not say what they mean.* This is true of both written and spoken discourse, but it can be more dramatic in spoken discourse since speech is usually less explicit and more context dependent. In the first unit, we encountered the example of someone asking to borrow a pen with the words 'Do you have a pen?' and I pointed out that, strictly speaking, this utterance is *literally* a question about whether or not someone possesses a pen rather than a *request* to borrow one, even though most people would not take it literally but instead 'hear' it as a request. Similarly, in the comic strip in Figure A5.1, when Calvin's mother says 'What are you doing to the coffee table?!' she is not so much asking a question as she is expressing shock and disapproval – offering a *rebuke*. The humour in Calvin's response lies in the fact that he has taken her utterance *literally*, responding to it as if it were meant as a question rather than a rebuke. Interestingly, we regard Calvin, who operates on the principle that people *should* mean what they say, as the uncooperative party in this conversation rather than his mother, who, strictly speaking, does not say what she means.

It is, of course, not at all unusual for people to say things like 'Do you have a pen?' and 'What are you doing to the coffee table?' and not mean these questions literally. And so, the question is, if people do not say what they mean or mean what they say, how are we able to successfully engage in conversations with one another, especially in the context

Figure A5.1 Calvin and Hobbes (© 1985 Watterson. Reprinted with permission. All rights reserved).

of face-to-face conversation, in which we have to make decisions about what we *think* people mean rather quickly in order for the conversation to proceed smoothly.

Furthermore, sometimes the way we interpret what people say can lead to misunderstandings or even be the source of broader political or ideological disagreements or prejudices, as when someone replies to the slogan 'Black lives matter!' with the words: '*All* lives matter!' In a way, this person is not unlike Calvin in the cartoon above, who uncooperatively takes his mother's words literally rather than interpreting them in relation to the *context* in which they are spoken. The phrase 'Black lives matter' is not meant to imply that *all* lives (including white lives) don't matter, but to highlight a social situation in which black lives do not seem to matter to police officers or to the government, and least not in the same way white lives do, and to reply to this utterance with '*All* lives matter!' actually serves to discount or ignore this reality.

In order to understand how conversational participants deal with situations in which interpreting what people mean requires that they go beyond the literal meanings of the words, we can turn to two different analytical traditions in discourse analysis, one with its roots in philosophy and the other with its roots in sociology. These two traditions are called **pragmatics** and **conversation analysis**.

Pragmatics is the study of how people use words to accomplish actions in their conversations – actions such as requesting, threatening and apologising. It aims to help us understand how people figure out what actions other people are trying to take with their words and respond appropriately. It has its roots primarily in the work of three philosophers of language: Herbert Paul Grice, John Austin and John Searle.

Conversation analysis, on the other hand, comes out of a tradition in sociology called **ethnomethodology**, which focuses on the 'methods' ordinary members of a society use to interact with one another and interpret their experiences. It was developed by three sociologists – Harvey Sacks, Emanuel Schegloff and Gail Jefferson – and studies the 'procedural rules' that people use to cooperatively manage conversations and figure out what other people mean.

Because these two analytical frameworks come out of such different intellectual traditions, they approach the problem discussed above in two very different ways. With its roots in philosophy, pragmatics tends to approach the problem as a matter of *logic*, asking what conditions need to be present for a participant in a conversation to logically conclude that a given utterance has a certain meaning (or pragmatic 'force'). With its roots in sociology, conversation analysis approaches the problem not as one of abstract logic, but as one of *locally contingent action*. According to this perspective, people make sense of what other people say not by 'figuring it out' logically, but by paying attention to the local conditions of the conversation itself, especially the sequence of utterances.

Rather than being mutually exclusive, these two approaches represent two different windows on the phenomenon of conversation, with each illuminating a different aspect of it. In the sections that follow, even more perspectives will be introduced that focus on different aspects of spoken interaction. Taking these various perspectives together will lead to a rich and comprehensive understanding of what people are doing when they engage in conversation and how they cope with the unique challenges of spoken discourse as well as more interactive forms of written and multimodal discourse which people engage in using digital media.

👁 **Look deeper into the differences between pragmatics and conversation analysis on the companion website.**

STRATEGIC INTERACTION   A6

When we have conversations with others, we are always engaged in some kind of activity – we are arguing, or flirting, or commiserating, or gossiping, or doing other things with our conversations, and a big part of understanding what somebody means is understanding what he or she is 'doing' and what is 'going on' in the social situation that the conversation is part of. At the same time, we also use conversations to show that we are certain kinds of people and to establish and maintain certain kinds of relationships with the people with whom we are talking. Understanding who somebody is 'trying to be' in a conversation is also an important part of understanding what they mean by what they say.

We do not, however, engage in these activities and construct these identities all by ourselves. We must always negotiate 'what we are doing' and 'who we are being' with the people with whom we are interacting. The methods we use to engage in these negotiations are called **conversational strategies**.

In this unit, we will focus on two basic kinds of conversational strategies: **face strategies** and **framing strategies**. Face strategies have to do primarily with showing who we are and what kind of relationship we have with the people with whom we are talking. Framing strategies have more to do with showing what we are doing in the conversation, whether we are, for example, arguing, teasing, flirting or gossiping.

These two concepts for analysing how we manage conversations come from an approach to discourse known as **interactional sociolinguistics**, which is concerned with the sometimes very subtle ways people signal and interpret what they think they are doing and who they think they are being in social interaction. It is grounded in the work of the anthropologist John Gumperz (1982), who drew on insights from anthropology and linguistics as well as the fields of pragmatics and conversation analysis, which were introduced in the previous unit. One of the most important insights Gumperz had was that people belonging to different groups have different ways of signalling and interpreting cues about 'what they are doing' and 'who they are being', and this can sometimes result in misunderstandings and even conflict. Not surprisingly, interactional sociolinguistics has been used widely in studies of intercultural communication, including some of the early studies by Gumperz himself on communication between Anglo-British and South Asian immigrants to the United Kingdom.

Another important influence on interactional sociolinguistics comes from the American sociologist Erving Goffman, who, in his classic book *The Presentation of Self in Everyday Life* (1959), compared social interaction to a dramatic performance. Social actors in everyday life, he argued, like stage actors, use certain 'expressive equipment' such as costumes, props and settings to perform certain 'roles' and 'routines'. Our goal in these performances is to promote our particular 'line' or version of who we are and what is going on. Most of the time, other people help us to maintain our line, especially if we are willing to help them to maintain theirs. Sometimes, however, people's 'lines' are not entirely compatible, which means they need to negotiate an acceptable common 'definition of the situation' or else risk spoiling the performance for one or more of the participants.

It was Goffman who contributed to discourse analysis the concepts of **face** and **frames**. By 'face' he meant 'the positive social value a person effectively claims for himself by the line others assume he has taken' (1967: 41). In other words, for Goffman, a person's 'face' is tied up with how successful he or she is at 'pulling off' his or her performance and getting others to accept his or her 'line'. What he meant by 'frames' was 'definitions of a situation (that) are built up in accordance with principles of organisation which govern events' (1974: 10). The concept of 'framing' relates to how we negotiate these 'definitions of situations' with other people and use them as a basis for communicating and interpreting meaning.

Showing who we are: face strategies

Social identity is a complex topic and one that will be further explored in the coming units. For now, the focus will be on one fundamental aspect of identity: the fact that our identities are always constructed *in relation to* the people with whom we are interacting. Some people are our friends, and others are complete strangers. Some people are our superiors, and others are our subordinates. When we talk, along with conveying information about the topic about which we are talking, we always convey information about how close to or distant from the people with whom we are talking we think we are, along with information about whether we are social equals or whether one has more power than the other. The strategies we use to do this are called face strategies.

The concept of face in its more everyday sense will be familiar to many readers. The term is often used to denote a person's honour or reputation. Many cultures have the notions of 'giving' people face (helping them to maintain a sense of dignity or honour) and of 'losing face' (when people, for some reason or another, suffer a loss of dignity or honour). Interactional sociolinguists, however, have a rather more specific definition of face. They define it as 'the negotiated public image mutually granted to each other by participants in a communicative event' (Scollon *et al.* 2012).

There are three important aspects to this definition: the first is that one's face is one's public image rather than one's 'true self'. This means that the social image that constitutes face is not the same in every interaction in which we engage. We 'wear' different faces for different people. The second important aspect of this definition is that this image is 'negotiated'. That is to say, it is always the result of a kind of 'give and take' with the person or people with whom we are interacting, and throughout a given interaction, the image that we present and the images others project onto us may undergo multiple adjustments. Finally, this image is 'mutually granted'. In other words, successfully presenting a certain face in interaction depends on the people with whom we are interacting cooperating with us. This is because face is the aspect of our identity that defines us *in relation* to others. If one person's idea of the relationship is different from the other person's idea, chances are one or the other will end up 'losing face'. And so, in this regard, the everyday ideas of 'giving face' and 'losing face' are also quite important in this more specialised definition of face.

There are basically two broad kinds of strategies we use to negotiate our identities and relationships in interaction. The first we will call **involvement strategies**. They are strategies we use to establish or maintain closeness with the people with whom we are interacting – to show them that we consider them our friends. These include things such as calling people by their first names or using nicknames; using informal language; showing interest in someone by, for example, asking personal questions; and emphasising our common experiences or points of view. While such strategies can be used to show friendliness – as we will see in the next section – they can also be used to assert power over people. Teachers, for example, often use such strategies when interacting with young students, and bosses sometimes use them when interacting with their employees.

The second class of face strategies is known as **independence strategies**. These are strategies we use to establish or maintain distance from the people with whom we are interacting, either because we are not their friends, or, more commonly, because we wish to show them respect by not imposing on them. They include using more formal language and terms of address, trying to minimise the imposition, being indirect, apologising and trying to depersonalise the conversation (see Table A6.1).

These two kinds of face strategy correspond to two fundamentally and, in some ways, contradictory social needs that all humans experience: we all have the need to be liked (sometimes referred to as our **positive face**), and we all have the need to be respected (in the sense of not being imposed on or interfered with – sometimes referred to as our **negative face**). When we interact with others, we must constantly attend to their need to be liked and respected and constantly protect our own need to be liked and respected (Brown and Levinson 1987). How we balance and negotiate these needs in communication is fundamental to the way we show who we are in relation to the people around us.

In any given interaction, we are likely to use a combination of both of these strategies as we negotiate our relationships with the people with whom we are interacting. In section B, we will go into more detail about how we decide which of these strategies to use, when and with whom.

Table A6.1 Face strategies

Involvement strategies	Independence strategies
Using first names or nicknames (*Hey, Rodders!*)	Using titles (*Good afternoon, Professor Jones.*)
Expressing interest (*What have you been up to lately?*)	Apologising (*I'm terribly sorry to bother you.*)
Claiming a common point of view (*I know exactly what you mean.*)	Admitting differences (*Of course, you know much more about it than I do.*)
Making assumptions (*I know you love lots of sugar in your coffee.*)	Not making assumptions (*How would you like your coffee today?*)
Using informal language (*Gotta minute?*)	Using formal language (*Pardon me, can you spare a few moments?*)
Being direct (*Will you come?*)	Being indirect and hedging (*I wonder if you might possibly drop by?*)
Being optimistic (*I'm sure you'll have a great time.*)	Being pessimistic (*I'm afraid you'll find it a bit boring.*)
Being voluble (talking a lot)	Being taciturn (not talking much)
Talking about 'us'	Talking about things other than 'us'

Showing what we are doing: framing strategies

In order to understand one another, we have to interpret what other people say in the context of some kind of overall activity in which we are mutually involved. One could think of many examples of utterances whose meanings change based on what the people are doing when they utter them. The meaning of the utterance by a doctor of the phrase, 'please take off your clothes' is different if uttered in the context of a medical examination or in the context of his or her apartment. For different kinds of activities, we have different sets of expectations about what kinds of things will be said and how those things ought to be interpreted. We call these sets of expectations *frames*.

Goffman took his idea of frames from the work of the anthropologist Gregory Bateson (1972), who used it to explain the behaviour of monkeys he had observed at the zoo. Sometimes, he noticed, the monkeys displayed hostile signals, seemingly fighting with, or attempting to bite, one another. It soon became clear to him, however, that the monkeys were not actually fighting; they were playing. It then occurred to him that they must have some way of communicating to one another how a particular display of aggression should be interpreted, whether as an invitation to fight or an invitation to play.

We bring to most interactions a set of expectations about the overall activity in which we will be engaged, which Goffman called the **primary framework** of the interaction. When we are a patient in a medical examination, for example, we expect that the doctor will touch us, and we interpret this behaviour as a method for diagnosing our particular medical problem. When we attend a lecture, we do so with an idea of what the activities of delivering a lecture and of listening to a lecture involve.

Interaction, however, hardly ever involves just one activity. We often engage in a variety of different activities within the primary framework. While lecturing, for example, a lecturer might give explanations, tell jokes or even rebuke members of the audience if they are not paying attention. Similarly, medical examinations might include multiple frames. In the reading in D6, for example, Deborah Tannen and Cynthia Wallat analyse how a doctor uses a 'playing' frame while examining a young child, and then switches back to a 'consultation' frame when talking with the child's mother. These smaller, more local frames are called **interactive frames**. When we are interacting with people, we often change what we are doing within the broader primary framework and, like Bateson's monkeys, we need ways to signal these 'frame changes' and ways to negotiate them with the people with whom we are interacting. Gumperz called the signals we send to each other to show what we are doing 'contextualisation cues'. Contextualisation cues help to create the *immediate context* for our utterances. They can consist of linguistic cues, such as words or expressions (like 'let's get down to work') or choices about the language or register we use at a given movement in the conversation, or they can consist of **paralinguistic cues**, such as a change in our tone of voice, our facial expression or the position or posture of our bodies.

👁 **Look deeper into the work of Erving Goffman on the companion website.**

CONTEXT, CULTURE AND COMMUNICATION   A7

What is context?

By now it should be clear that what an utterance means and the effect it has on a hearer depends crucially on the circumstances under which it is uttered. The different approaches to spoken discourse we have considered so far all focus on different aspects of these circumstances. Pragmatics focuses on the intentions of speakers and the immediate conditions under which utterances are produced (including the knowledge, goals and status of those who produce them). Conversation analysis takes a rather narrower view, focusing on how talk occurring immediately before and immediately after utterances creates the circumstances for particular meanings to be produced. Finally, interactional sociolinguistics examines how utterances are interpreted based on the relationship of the participants and what they think they are doing, which are negotiated using *face strategies* and *contextualisation cues*. In this section, we will take a wider view of the circumstances in which conversations occur, taking into account broader aspects of the context as well as the 'cultural' norms and expectations of the people involved.

The idea that the meaning of utterances depends on the **context** in which they are produced can be traced back to the anthropologist Bronislow Malinowski and his 1923 paper 'The problem of meaning in primitive languages', in which he argued that we cannot understand the words spoken by members of societies very different from our own through mere translation. We must also have an understanding of the situation in which the words were spoken and the significance of various relationships and activities in that situation to the speakers. In other words, meaning is transmitted not just through words, but also through the ways words are embedded into social relationships, social goals and activities, histories, and the beliefs, values and ideologies of a particular cultural group.

The problem with this idea is determining exactly *which* aspects of the situation or of 'cultural knowledge' need to be taken into account in the production and interpretation of utterances. 'Context' could mean practically anything from the place and time of day of an utterance, to the colour of the clothing that the speakers are wearing, to speakers' political views or religious beliefs. How does the discourse analyst figure out which aspects of context are relevant to the production and interpretation of discourse and which are not? More to the point, how do people immersed in conversation figure this out?

Since Malinowksi, a number of scholars have proposed models to address this question. The linguist John Firth (1957), for example, proposed that context can be divided into three components:

1   the relevant features of participants, persons, personalities;
2   the relevant objects in the situation;
3   the effect of the verbal action.

Although Firth's formulation highlights what are undoubtedly central aspects of context, one nevertheless wonders why some elements are included and others are not.

Why, for example, is the setting or time not part of his model? Furthermore, while one of the most important aspects of Firth's model is his insight that only those things that are 'relevant' to the communication being analysed should be considered context, he does not fully explain how such relevance is to be established.

One of the most famous models of context is that developed by the linguist Michael Halliday, whose ideas about the structure of texts and the functions of language were discussed in units A2 and A4. Halliday, drawing heavily on the work of both Malinowski and Firth, also proposed a three-part model of context. For him, context consists of:

1   **field:** the social action that is taking place;
2   **tenor:** the participants, their roles and their relationships;
3   **mode:** the symbolic or rhetorical channel and the role that language plays in the situation.

It is these three aspects of context, Halliday says, that chiefly determine the *register* people use when they speak or write (see A4).

Halliday's model of context, however, suffers some of the same problems as Firth's: without clearer definitions of the three categories, the analyst is unsure where to fit in things such as the social identities of participants and their membership in certain social groups (are these subsumed under 'role' or can they be seen as part of field?), or why things such as the physical mode (or channel), the rhetorical form (or genre) and the role language plays in the situation should be subsumed under the same category (van Dijk 2008). Furthermore, like Firth, he fails to fully address the issue of exactly what makes some contextual features 'relevant' to speakers and others not.

Context and competence

Halliday explains context from an essentially linguistic point of view, seeing it as part of a language's system of 'meaning potential'. 'There is no need to bring in the question of what the speaker knows', he writes; 'the background to what he does is *what he could do – a potential*, which is objective, not a competence, which is subjective' (1978: 38, emphasis mine). In sharp contrast to this position is that of the linguistic anthropologist Dell Hymes, for whom the notion of 'competence' is central to a model of context he called **the ethnography of speaking**, or, as it is sometimes called, **the ethnography of communication**.

In his work, Hymes focuses on the interaction between language and social life – the ways using and understanding language are related to wider social and cultural knowledge. Knowledge or mastery of the linguistic system alone, he insists, is not sufficient for successful communication. People also need to know and master various rules, norms and conventions regarding *what* to say to *whom, when, where* and *how* – which he calls **communicative competence** (Hymes, 1987). He writes:

> The sharing of grammatical (variety) rules is not sufficient. There may be persons whose English I can grammatically identify but whose messages escape me. I may be ignorant of what counts as a coherent sequence, request, statement requiring an answer, requisite or forbidden topic, marking of emphasis or irony, normal

duration of silence, normal level of voice, etc., and have no metacommunicative means or opportunity for discovering such things.

(Hymes 1974: 49)

The question Hymes asks is: 'What kinds of things do participants in particular activities or **speech events** need to know in order to demonstrate that they are competent members of a particular *speech community*?'. What he means by *speech community* is a group of people who not only speak the same language but also share the rules and norms for using and interpreting at least one language variety *in particular contexts*.

Like Halliday and Firth, Hymes developed a model of what he considered to be the essential elements of context. Rather than just three components, however, Hymes's consists of eight, each component beginning with one of the letters of the word '**SPEAKING**':

❑ S stands for *setting* (where and when the speech event takes place);
❑ P stands for *participants* (who is involved and what their roles are);
❑ E stands for *ends* (the purpose or purposes of the speech event);
❑ A stands for *act sequence* (the order in which things normally occur);
❑ K stands for *key* (the 'mood' or 'tone' of the speech event);
❑ I stands for *instrumentalities* (the different 'tools' people use to communicate);
❑ N stands for *norms of interaction* (the shared expectations about how to communicate);
❑ G stands for *genre* (the form or structure of the communication; see unit A2).

One might point out that, although Hymes's model seems more 'complete', it suffers from the same fundamental problem as those of Firth and Halliday: why are some elements included and others not? Why are there only eight elements rather than nine or ten, and why are they divided up the way they are? The crucial difference between this model and the others is that, for Hymes, these elements do not represent *objective* features of context, but rather represent more subjective features of *competence*, the kinds of things about which speakers need to know to be considered competent communicators by other members of their group.

For Hymes, then, the 'subjective' nature of context is not the weakness of his model, but, in a way, the whole point of it. Even when the 'objective' aspects of context – the status of the participants, the nature of the activity and the semiotic modes being used – remain the same, expectations about who should say what to whom, when, where and how will still vary across different communities of speakers.

An understanding of the communicative competence necessary in a particular speech community in order to participate in a particular speech event cannot be acquired with reference to the linguistic system alone, or simply through the analysis of texts or transcripts of conversations. This is because what is of importance is not just the meanings people communicate and how they are communicated, but also the meaning *communication itself* has for them in different situations with different people. Understanding this requires a different approach to the analysis of discourse, an approach that is summed up in the word **ethnography**.

Ethnography is a research method developed in the field of anthropology that is concerned with describing the lived experiences of people in particular social groups.

It involves not just analysing the texts and talk that they produce from a distance, but also actually spending time with them, observing them as they use language, and talking to them at length about the meanings they ascribe to different kinds of utterance and different kinds of behaviour.

These methods are not just used in the approach to discourse developed by Hymes and his students. Many of the approaches to discourse discussed earlier have also begun to incorporate ethnographic fieldwork: genre analysts, for example, typically interview members of discourse communities about the kinds of text they use and how they use them; critical discourse analysts are increasingly focusing not just on how producers of texts express ideology and reproduce power relations, but also on how readers respond to and sometimes contest these ideological formations; and issues of cross-cultural pragmatics are increasingly being explored through ethnographic methods.

👁 **Look deeper into the question of context on the companion website.**

A8   MEDIATED DISCOURSE ANALYSIS

So far, this book has presented different methods for the analysis of written and spoken discourse. These methods include ways to understand how texts and conversations are put together and how people make sense of them, as well as how people use them to manage their activities and identities and to advance their ideological agendas. We have also explored how context, from the narrow context of the immediate situation to the broader context of culture, can affect the ways discourse is produced and interpreted.

In this unit, we will step back and attempt to answer a more fundamental question in discourse analysis: 'How do we determine what texts or conversations are worth analysing in the first place?'

We are literally surrounded by discourse. In the course of a single day, the number of words we speak and hear and the number of texts that pass before our eyes, from emails to advertising billboards to shop receipts, is mind-boggling. In the excerpt reprinted in D8, Ron Scollon talks about just some of the texts and spoken language involved in the simple act of having a cup of coffee at Starbucks. These include things such as conversations between customers and the cashier, the communication between the cashier and the person making the coffee, the chatting that occurs between the people sitting at tables and lounging on sofas throughout the shop, the writing on the paper cups out of which they are drinking their beverages, the menu posted on the wall above the counter, the name badges that the employees wear, the magazines and newspapers provided for patrons to read, and the various advertisements and posters hanging on the walls around the shop, to mention only a few. There is also a whole host of texts and conversations that have contributed to this moment of drinking coffee that are not immediately visible: training manuals and work schedules for employees, orders and invoices for bulk coffee beans, and conversations and text messages between friends planning when and where they might meet up for a cup of coffee.

Given this complex situation, the most important question for a discourse analyst is: where do I start? Which texts or utterances should I commence analysing? For most discourse analysts, the answer to this question is: 'Whatever *I* happen to be interested in'. Thus, analysts interested in casual conversation might focus on the talk that goes on between friends sitting at tables; analysts interested in promotional discourse might zero in on the advertising posters or menus that inform patrons of the 'drink of the month'; and those interested in the speech event of the 'service encounter' might want to record or observe people ordering and paying for their coffee.

In principle, there is nothing wrong with this 'analyst-centred' approach. From it we can learn quite a lot about things such as casual conversation, promotional discourse, and service encounters. What we might miss, however, is an understanding of what the *practice* of 'having a cup of coffee at Starbucks' is really like for the *actual participants* involved, what this practice means to them, how they go about performing it, and how it fits into their lives.

Mediated discourse analysis, the perspective on discourse that is the topic of this unit, approaches the problem of 'which discourse to analyse' by asking the simple question: 'What's going on here?' and then focusing on whatever texts, conversations or other things play a part in 'what's going on'.

Of course, the answer to that question might not be very simple either. For one thing, it is likely to be different depending on whom you ask: for a customer, it might be 'having a cup of coffee'; for a barista, it might be 'taking orders' or 'making coffee' or more generally 'making a living'; for a government health inspector, it might be determining whether the shop complies with government regulations when it comes to hygiene and food safety.

The focus of mediated discourse analysis is trying to understand the relationships between 'what's going on' for particular participants and the discourse that is available in the situation for them to perform these 'goings on'. Certain kinds of discourse make certain kinds of actions easier to perform and other kinds more difficult to perform. In other words, actions are mediated through discourse (as well as other tools like espresso machines and coffee cups), and the goal of mediated discourse analysis is to understand how this process of **mediation** affects what we are able to do and how we are able to do it. There is also a relationship between the actions we are able to perform and our *social identities*. It is not just that cashiers or customers in a coffee shop need to use certain kinds of tools to perform certain kinds of actions, but also that it is chiefly by using these different kinds of tools to perform these actions that they *enact* their identities as cashiers and customers and health inspectors. That is to say, we associate different kinds of actions and different kinds of discourse with different kinds of people. We might find it odd to see someone who is wearing a badge and uniform reading a newspaper and drinking a cup of coffee at one of the tables, or a customer inspecting the cleanliness of the espresso machine.

The point, then, is not that some discourse is more important than other discourse. Rather, it is that to really understand how discourse is relevant to 'real life', we have to try to understand how different texts and conversations are linked, sometimes directly and sometimes indirectly, to the concrete, real-time actions that are going on in coffee shops and classrooms and offices and on street corners at particular moments, and how these linkages work to create **social identities** (such as 'friends', 'colleagues', 'teachers', 'cashiers', and 'customers') and **social practices** (such as 'teaching a lesson' or 'having a cup of coffee').

Discourse and action

One of the definitions of discourse given in the very first unit of this book was that discourse is 'language in use' or, to put it another way, 'language in action'. Nearly all of the approaches to discourse analysis we have discussed are concerned in some way with the relationship between language and action. According to pragmatics (see A5 and B5), for example, people use language in order to accomplish particular actions such as requesting, apologising and warning; and according to genre analysis (see A3 and B3), the structure of genres is crucially determined by the actions that users are attempting to accomplish with them within particular discourse communities.

Mediated discourse analysis has a similar focus on action, but, whereas these other approaches start with the discourse and ask what kinds of social action speakers or writers can accomplish with it, mediated discourse analysis starts with *actions* and asks what role discourse plays in them.

This may seem to be a rather small distinction, but it is actually a crucial one, because it avoids the assumption that discourse (rather than other things such as espresso machines and coffee cups) is necessarily the most important **cultural tool** involved in the action. It also reminds us that just because a piece of discourse *might* be used to perform certain kinds of action, the way people *actually* use it may be to perform actions which we may not have expected. People might just as easily use a newspaper to wrap fish and chips as to find out about the latest news from Parliament. One's relationship status on Facebook might just as easily be used to *avoid* giving information about one's relationship status as to give it (as when someone chooses 'It's complicated' or jokingly pretends to be 'married' to a friend).

Thus, the unit of analysis in mediated discourse analysis is not the 'utterance' or 'speech act' or 'adjacency pair' or 'conversation' or 'text' but rather the **mediated action**, that is, the action that is *mediated* through discourse or other tools that may have nothing to do with language, such as espresso machines. Such an analysis, then, begins first with the question 'What is the action going on here?' and then asks 'What makes this action possible?'

The answer to the question 'What is the action going on here?' might have a very complex answer. As mentioned above, it might be different for different people, and even for the same person, it might depend on how broadly or narrowly they are focusing on what they are doing. The person operating the espresso machine at Starbucks, for example, might say she's 'working' or 'making a cappuccino' or 'steaming milk'.

What this tells us is that actions are always dependent on other actions that occur before them and are likely to occur after them, and that whatever one identifies as an action can always be divided up into smaller and smaller actions. In other words, actions are always related to other actions in complex patterns. Often, these patterns, such as the sequence of smaller actions and how they combine to make larger actions, become conventionalised in the same way that genres of written and spoken discourse can become conventionalised. When this happens, we refer to these patterns of actions as *social practices*.

Part of what a mediated discourse analyst focuses on is how small, discrete actions such as handing money to a cashier or steaming milk in a stainless-steel pitcher come to be habitually joined with other actions and regarded by participants as the social practices of 'having a cup of coffee' or 'making a cappuccino'. In particular, they are interested in the role discourse plays in creating and sustaining these social practices.

Like other analysts, then, mediated discourse analysts, through their interest in social practices, are concerned with the *ideological* dimension of discourse, or what James Paul Gee refers to as 'Discourses with a capital D'. When chains of actions occur over and over again in the same way in the same kinds of situation involving the same kinds of people, they become social practices and thus begin to exert control over the people who carry them out: people come to be expected to do things in a certain way, and the things that they do come to be associated with the kinds of social identities they are able to claim. Discourse of all kinds, from training manuals to health regulations to conversations, plays a crucial role in this process. In contrast to other approaches concerned with the ideological nature of discourse, however, mediated discourse analysis does not focus so much on how discourse itself expresses ideology but rather how it is used to help create and maintain the *practices* that come to exert control over us.

👁 **Look deeper into the idea of *social practices* on the companion website.**

MULTIMODAL DISCOURSE ANALYSIS   A9

In the first unit of this book, I said that one of the fundamental principles of discourse analysis is that discourse includes more than just language. It also involves things such as non-verbal communication, images, music and even the arrangement of furniture in rooms. I elaborated on this point a bit further in my examination of spoken discourse, first noting how non-verbal cues can serve to signal the 'frames' within which an utterance is meant to be interpreted, and later how the larger physical and cultural context, including such things as setting, participants and communication media, can affect how language is produced and understood. This point was taken even further in the last section in the discussion of mediated discourse analysis, in which I pointed out that language is only one of many *cultural tools* with which people take actions, and warned that focusing on language alone at the expense of these other tools can result in a distorted picture of 'what's going on'.

This unit introduces an approach to discourse called **multimodal discourse analysis**, which focuses more directly on these other tools or 'modes' of communication. Multimodal discourse analysts see discourse as involving multiple modes that often work together. In a face-to-face conversation, for example, people do not just communicate with spoken language. They also communicate through their **gestures**, **gaze**, facial expressions, posture, dress, how close or far away they stand or sit from each other and many other things. Similarly, 'written texts' rarely consist only of words, especially nowadays. They often include pictures, charts or graphs. Even the font that is used and the way paragraphs are arranged on a page or screen can convey meaning.

The point of multimodal discourse analysis is not to analyse these other modes *instead* of speech and writing but to understand how different modes, including speech and writing, work together in discourse. The point is also not to study some special kind of discourse – 'multimodal discourse' – but rather to understand how *all* discourse involves the interaction of multiple modes.

The idea of a **communicative mode** (sometimes called a **semiotic mode**) should not be confused with the notion of 'modality' in linguistics (the way we express possibility and obligation in language, discussed in B4), or with Halliday's use of the term 'mode' in his model of context (discussed in A7). What is meant by 'mode' in the context of *multimodal discourse analysis* is a system for making meaning. So we can speak, for example, of the modes of speech, writing, gesture, colour, dress, and so on. Any system of signs that are used in a consistent and systematic way to make meaning can be considered a mode.

Modes should also not be confused with **media**, which are the material carriers of modes. Telephones, radios and computers are all *media* that can carry the *mode* of spoken language. They can also carry other modes, such as music, and, in the case of computers and some mobile telephones, written text and pictures.

Multimodal discourse analysis can generally be divided into two types: one that focuses on 'texts' such as magazines, comic books, web pages, films and works of art, and one that focuses more on social interaction (sometimes referred to as **multimodal interaction analysis**).

Perhaps the most influential approach to the multimodal analysis of texts has grown out of the study of **systemic functional grammar** as it was developed by M.A.K. Halliday, whose work we have already discussed at length (see A2, A4). Halliday's view is that grammar is a system of 'resources' for making meaning shaped by the kinds of things people need to *do* with language. Those applying this framework to multimodal discourse analysis propose that other modes such as images, music and architecture also have a kind of 'grammar'. In other words, their components can be organised as networks of options that users choose from in order to realise different meanings.

The most famous application of this idea is the book *Reading Images: The Grammar of Visual Design*, first published in 1996 by Gunther Kress and Theo van Leeuwen, an excerpt from which is reprinted in D9. Before the publication of this book, most of those involved in the analysis of images assumed that their interpretation depended on their interaction with language – that images themselves were too 'vague' to be understood on their own. In contrast, Kress and van Leeuwen show that, while in many texts, images and language work together, images are not dependent on written text but rather have their own way of structuring and organising meaning – their own 'grammar'. This approach has also been applied to other modes such as music (van Leeuwen 1999), architecture (O'Toole 1994), colour (van Leeuwen 2011), hypermedia (Djonov 2007) and mathematical symbolism (O'Halloran 2005).

It is important to note, however, that this approach does *not* involve simply applying the 'grammatical rules' derived from the study of language to other modes. Instead, each mode is seen to have its own special way of organising meaning, and it is the task of the analyst to discover what that system is, independent of other systems.

The second approach to multimodal discourse analysis grows more out of traditions associated with the analysis of spoken discourse, especially conversation analysis (see A5), interactional sociolinguistics (see A6) and the ethnography of speaking (see A7). Some of the more recent work in what has come to be known as *multimodal interaction analysis* (Norris 2004) has also been influenced by meditated discourse analysis (see A8).

In analysing multimodality in interaction, analysts pay attention to many of the same kinds of things they do when they analyse spoken language, especially **sequentiality**, how elements are ordered in relation to one another; and **simultaneity**, how elements that occur at the same time affect one another. A multimodal discourse analyst, for example, might look for patterns in the ordering of non-verbal behaviour in a conversation, such as the role that things such as gaze play in the regulation of turn-taking, or at how the meanings of utterances are affected by non-verbal behaviour such as gestures or facial expressions, which often serve to contextualise utterances (see A6).

One of the key preoccupations of multimodal interaction analysis is the fact that when we are interacting, we are almost always involved in multiple activities. We might, for example, be chatting with a friend at the beauty salon, leafing through a magazine and checking the mirror to see what is going on with our hair all at the same time. Multimodal interaction analysis gives us a way to examine how people use different communicative modes to manage simultaneous activities and to communicate to others something about how they are distributing their attention.

It is important to mention that both of these approaches have been applied to both static texts and dynamic interactions. Approaches based on systemic functional grammar have been used to analyse things such as gestures and gaze, and multimodal interaction analysis has been applied to more static texts such as advertisements. Furthermore, with the increasing popularity of interactive text and image-based forms of communication such as instant messaging, social networking tools such as Snapchat and Instagram, and video-conferencing tools such as Skype and FaceTime, discourse analysts often find that they need to focus *both* on patterns and structures in the organisation of elements in texts/images *and* on the sequentiality and simultaneity of actions as people interact using these texts/images (see, for example, Jones 2005, 2009a, 2009b).

As new forms of media are developed that allow people to mix modes of communication in new ways over time and space, our whole idea of what we mean by a text or a conversation is beginning to change. If, for example, as we discussed in unit A2, *texture* is a result of elements such as clauses, sentences and paragraphs being connected together in various ways using *cohesive devices*, then it would make sense to consider not just a particular web page but also an entire website consisting of numerous pages joined together by hyperlinks as a kind of 'text'. We might also be tempted to consider as part of this text other websites outside of the primary site to which this text hyperlinks, and, before long, following this logic, we might end up with the idea that the entire Internet can on some level be considered a single text.

Similarly, our notion of conversations is changing. Not only do digitally mediated conversations often involve modes such as writing, emojis, images and animated gifs rather than spoken words, but also they may extend over days or even months on platforms such as Facebook or WhatsApp. Furthermore, conversations often travel across communication media and modes. You might, for example, begin a conversation with a friend over lunch, continue it later in the afternoon by sharing images using Snapchat, carry on chatting about the same topic over the telephone or WhatsApp in the evening, and resume the conversation the next morning over coffee at Starbucks.

These changes associated with multimedia and multimodality present challenges for communicators and discourse analysts alike. Because different modes and media alter the kinds of meanings we can make, we need to learn to adjust our discourse in different ways every time we move from one mode to another and from one medium to another. This phenomenon is known as **resemiotisation** – the fact that the meanings that we make change as they are shaped by the different modes we use as social practices unfold. The discourse analyst Rick Iedema (2001) gives as an example of *resemiotisation* the way meanings associated with the building of a new wing of a hospital changed as they were expressed orally in planning meetings, then later in the written language of reports, still later in the graphic language of architectural drawings, and finally in the materiality of bricks and mortar.

The most important point multimodal discourse analysts make is that modes can never really be analysed in isolation from other modes (although this is, as we have seen in this book, what most discourse analysts do with the modes of spoken and written language). Not only do modes always interact with other modes in texts and interaction, but also authors and conversational participants often shift from foregrounding one mode or set of modes to foregrounding other modes or sets of modes and, in doing so, alter the 'meaning potential' of the communicative environment.

A10   CORPUS-ASSISTED DISCOURSE ANALYSIS

So far, all of the approaches to discourse analysis we have considered involve analysing a relatively small number of texts or interactions at one time. In fact, the focus of most discourse analysis is on looking very closely at one or a small number of texts or conversations of a particular type, trying to uncover things such as how the text or conversation is structured, how writers/speakers and readers/listeners are constructed, how the text or conversation promotes the broader ideological agendas of groups or institutions, and how people actually use the text or conversation to perform concrete social actions.

Corpus-assisted discourse analysis is unique in that it allows us to go beyond looking at a small number of texts or interactions to analysing a large number of them and being able to compare them with other texts and conversations that are produced under similar or different circumstances. It also allows us to bring to our analysis some degree of 'objectivity' by giving us the opportunity to test out the theories we have formulated in our close analysis of a few texts or conversations on a much larger body of data in a rather systematic way.

A **corpus** is basically a collection of texts in digital format that it is possible to search through and manipulate using a computer program. There are a number of large corpora, such as the British National Corpus, which is a very general collection of written and spoken texts in English. You can also find general corpora of texts produced in different varieties of English and also other languages. There are also a large number of specialised corpora available, that is, collections of particular kinds of text such as business letters or academic articles. There are even multimodal corpora in which not just verbal data but also visual data are collected and tagged.

Normally, corpora are used by linguists in order to find out things about the grammatical and lexical patterns in particular varieties of language or particular kinds of text. A lot of what we know about the differences among the different varieties of English (such as British English, American English and Australian English) or among different registers (such as academic English and 'conversational' English) comes from the analysis of corpora. Corpora have also played an important role in **forensic linguistics** (the use of linguistics to solve crimes); linguists sometimes, for example, compare the features in a piece of writing to those in a corpus of texts by a particular author in order to answer questions about authorship.

Although the number of discourse analysts using corpora has increased dramatically over the past decade, there is a tension between corpus-assisted analysis and the kinds of close examination of situated texts that discourse analysts usually do. As I said at the beginning of this book, discourse analysts are not just interested in linguistic forms and patterns but also in how language is actually used in concrete social situations. Computer analysis using large corpora seems to go against this key aim: texts in corpora are taken out of their social contexts, and even the information we often get from the analysis, which usually consists of things such as lists of frequently used words or phrases, is often presented outside of the context of the texts in which these words and phrases occur.

Other than this, the analysis of corpora also presents other problems for discourse analysts. As we asserted at the beginning of our study of discourse analysis: 'People don't always say what they mean, and people don't always mean what they say'. A big part of discourse analysis, in fact, is figuring out what people mean when they do not say (or write) it directly. Any method that takes language and its meaning at face value is of limited use to discourse analysts. Words and phrases, as we have seen, can have multiple meanings depending on how they are used in different circumstances by different people, and just because a word is used frequently does not mean it is particularly important. Often the most important meanings that we make are implicit or stated indirectly.

Despite these potential problems, however, the *computer-assisted* analysis of corpora has proven to be an enormously valuable tool for discourse analysts. The key word in this phrase is *assisted*. The computer analysis of corpora cannot be used by itself to *do* discourse analysis. But it can *assist* us in doing discourse analysis in some very valuable ways.

First, it can help us to see the data that we are analysing from a new perspective. Often, seeing your data broken down into things such as concordances or frequency lists can help you to see things that you missed using more traditional discourse-analytical techniques.

Second, it can help us to see if we can generalise our theories or observations about certain kinds of text or certain kinds of interaction. If you find certain features in a WhatsApp conversation you are analysing, the most you can say is that this particular conversation has these features and that these features function in the particular social situation from which the conversation comes in a certain way. If, however, you have access to a large number of similar WhatsApp conversations, then you can start to make generalisations about the kinds of features that are common to these kinds of texts. This has obvious applications to *genre analysis*, in which the analyst is interested in identifying certain conventions of language use associated with particular kinds of communicative purposes.

Finally, and most importantly, the analysis of corpora can help us to detect what we have been calling 'Discourses with a capital D' – systems of language use that promote particular kinds of ideologies and power relationships. One of the biggest problems we have as discourse analysts is that, while we want to make some kind of connection between the texts and conversations that we are analysing and larger

'Discourses' – such as the 'Discourse of medicine' or the 'Discourse of racism' – we are usually just guessing about whether or not these Discourses actually exist and what kinds of ideologies, power relationships and linguistic strategies they entail. These are usually, of course, educated guesses that we make based on world knowledge, scholarly research, common sense and the analysis of lots of different texts over a long period of time. The analysis of large corpora, however, gives us a more empirical way to detect trends in language use – how words and phrases tend to reoccur – across a large number of texts, which might signal a 'Discourse', and also to detect if and how such language use changes over time (Baker 2005, 2006). Examples of this include Baker and McEnery's (2005) study of the portrayal of refugees and asylum-seekers in public discourse, Hardt-Mautner's 1995 study of British newspaper editorials on the European Union, Rey's (2001) study of gender and language in the popular US television series *Star Trek*, and Baker's (2005) study of the various 'Discourses' surrounding male homosexuality in Britain and America.

Of course, being able to detect 'Discourses' through the computer analysis of corpora requires the creative combination of multiple analytical procedures, and it also necessarily involves a large amount of interpretative work by the analyst. Corpus-assisted discourse analysis is not a science, it is an art, and perhaps the biggest danger of employing it is that the analyst comes to see it as somehow more 'scientific' than the close analysis of texts just because computers and quantification are involved. The computer analysis of corpora does not provide discourse analysts with answers. Rather, it provides them with additional information to make their educated guesses even more educated and their theory building more evidence based.

Theory or method?

One of the differences between corpus-assisted discourse analysis and the other approaches to discourse we have presented in this book is that, while approaches such as genre analysis, conversation analysis and the ethnography of speaking each explicitly advance a particular theory of discourse, corpus-assisted discourse analysis is often seen to be 'theory neutral'; that is, it is viewed more as a method for assisting in the application of different theories. Thus, one can use corpora in doing genre analysis, conversation analysis, pragmatics or critical discourse analysis.

Here, however, it would be useful to recall some of the points made in the discussion of *mediated discourse analysis* in unit A8 about the nature of *cultural tools*. Since all tools make certain kinds of action easier and others more difficult, there is really no such thing as an ideologically neutral tool. The computer-assisted analysis of corpora has certain *affordances* and *constraints* that make it more compatible with some approaches to discourse and less compatible with others. In particular, while it seems especially suited for approaches that concern themselves with the ways texts and conversations are structured or patterned (such as genre analysis and conversation analysis), it is perhaps less suitable for approaches that focus more on the social context of communication (such as the ethnography of speaking).

👁 **Look deeper into the applications of the analysis of corpora to discourse analysis on the companion website.**

Section B

DEVELOPMENT
APPROACHES TO DISCOURSE ANALYSIS

B1 THREE WAYS OF LOOKING AT DISCOURSE

Over the years, people have approached the study of discourse in many different ways, and in this section, you will explore some of these ways of analysing discourse and learn how to apply them to texts and conversations from your own life. People who analyse discourse have basically gone about it from three different perspectives, based on three different ideas about what discourse is.

Some have taken a **formal approach** to discourse, seeing it simply as 'language above the level of the clause or sentence'. Those working from this perspective often try to understand the kinds of rules and conventions that govern the ways we join clauses and sentences together to make texts.

Others take a more **functional approach**, defining discourse as 'language in use'. This perspective leads to questions about how people use language to do things such as make requests, issue warnings and apologise in different kinds of situations and how we interpret what other people are trying to do when they speak or write.

Finally, there are those who take what we might call a **social approach**, conceiving discourse as a kind of social practice. The way we use language, they point out, is tied up with the way we construct different social identities and relationships and participate in different kinds of groups and institutions. It is tied up with issues of what we believe to be right and wrong, who has power over whom and what we have to do and say to 'fit in' to our societies.

Although these three different approaches to discourse are often treated as separate and are certainly associated with different historical traditions and different individual discourse analysts, the position I will be taking in this book is that good discourse analysis requires that we take into account all three of these perspectives. Instead of three separate definitions of discourse, they are better seen as three interrelated aspects of discourse. The way people use language cannot really be separated from the way it is put together, and the way people communicate who they are and what they believe cannot be separated from the things people use language to do in particular situations.

Language above the clause

The use of the term 'discourse' to mean language above the level of the sentence or the clause originated with the linguist Zellig Harris, who, back in the 1950s, wanted to take the study of linguistics to a new level. Before this, linguists had come a long way in understanding how sounds are put together to form words and how words are put together to form sentences. What Harris wanted to do was to understand how sentences are put together to form texts.

The idea that texts could be analysed in terms of their formal structure was actually very popular in the early and mid-twentieth century, even before Harris invented the term 'discourse analysis', especially in the field of literature. One group of literary critics called the Russian Formalists, for example, tried to apply the same kinds of methods people used to analyse the grammar of sentences to analysing stories and novels.

Perhaps the most famous was Vladimir Propp, who tried to come up with a 'grammar of stories' by studying Russian folktales.

The method that Harris proposed for the analysis of discourse, which he called **distributional analysis**, was not much different from how people go about doing grammatical analysis. The idea is to identify particular linguistic features and determine how they occur in texts relative to other features, that is, which features occur next to other features or 'in the same environment' with them. However, as you will see from the excerpt from Harris's seminal paper reprinted in D1, his ambitions went beyond simply understanding how linguistic features are distributed throughout texts. He was also interested in understanding how these features correlate with non-linguistic behaviour beyond texts, that is, how the form that texts take is related to the social situations in which they occur. It was really left to discourse analysts who came after him, however, to figure out exactly how the relationship between texts and the social contexts in which they are used could be fruitfully studied.

When focusing on the formal aspect of discourse, we are mostly interested in how the different elements of texts or conversations are put together to form unified wholes. In this respect, we usually look for two kinds of things. We look for linguistic features (words and grammar), which help to link different parts of the text or conversation together, and we look at the overall pattern of the text or conversation. We can refer to these two things as: (1) *cohesion* – how pieces of the text are 'stuck together'; and (2) *coherence* – the overall pattern or sequence of elements in a text or conversation that conforms to our expectations about how different kinds of texts or interactions ought to be structured. We call these aspects of texts that make them recognisable as unified, coherent units *texture* (see A2).

Language in use

The second aspect of discourse that discourse analysts focus on is how people actually use language to get things done in specific contexts. In fact, as was pointed out in section A1, it is often very difficult to understand what a piece of language means without referring to the social context in which it is being used and what the person who is using it is trying to do.

This view of discourse grew out of the work of a number of important scholars including Michael Halliday, whose approach to the study of grammar differed markedly from earlier approaches by focusing less on the forms language takes and more on the social functions accomplished by language (see A2), and the work of the British philosophers John L. Austin and Paul Grice, who laid the foundation for what we call **pragmatics** (the study of how people do things with language) (see A5). Another important figure who promoted this view of discourse was the sociolinguist William Labov, whose main interest was the way variations in language use serve to mark people as belonging to different communities of speakers, but who was also interested in the practical ways people in these communities structure their language in particular ways to accomplish social goals (see D2).

There are a number of ways to study language in use. One way is to consider discourse itself as a kind of action, and to explore how, when we say things or write things, we are actually *doing* things such as apologising, promising, threatening or making requests (see A5). This notion of language as performing social actions extends from individual utterances (such as apologies) to complete texts. Genre analysts, for example, consider texts like news articles or dating site profiles as basically made up of collections of actions that people are performing with words, and Labov held the same view about the stories people tell each other, which he divided into parts based on what each part *accomplished* (see D2). The aim of these approaches is to understand how sentences or utterances are put together to perform coherent *communicative actions*.

Another way to consider language in use is to look at how people use discourse strategically to try to communicate *who they are* and *what they are doing* (see A6). Subtle aspects of our language use or non-verbal communication can signal to others whether we are 'serious' or 'joking', 'discussing' or 'arguing', and also how we feel about them (friendly, respectful, close or distant).

Finally, we might examine how different kinds of discourse make certain kinds of actions or activities possible in the first place. The 'like' button on certain social media sites like Instagram, for example, makes it possible to mean so many different things and accomplish so many different actions depending on what you are 'liking', who posted it, and what your relationship to them is (see A8).

Language and 'social practice'

The third aspect of discourse has to do with the role of language in 'social practice'. Language is seen not just as a system for making meaning, but as part of larger systems through which people construct social identities and social realities. Different people use language in different ways. An English teacher talks differently than a hip-hop artist, and a President (usually) talks differently than a reality TV host. These different ways of talking help to show who we are and also reflect our different ideas about the world, different beliefs and different values. These systems of identities, values and ways of talking are far from stable, and can sometimes be disrupted when, for example, English teachers suddenly start appropriating the language of hip-hop artists or Presidents start talking like reality TV hosts.

This view of discourse probably owes the most to the French philosopher Michel Foucault, who argued that discourse is the main tool through which we construct 'knowledge' and exert power over other people. Different kinds of discourse (or 'discourses') are associated with different kinds of people and different 'systems of knowledge'. Foucault spoke, for example, of 'clinical discourse, economic discourse, the discourse of natural history, (and) psychiatric discourse' (1972: 121). The American discourse analyst James Paul Gee uses a capital 'D' to distinguish this view of discourse from the others we have talked about. For him, Discourses are 'ways of being in the world, or forms of life which integrate words, acts, values, beliefs, attitudes and social identities' (1996: 127).

This aspect of discourse leads us to explore how people use language to advance certain versions of reality and construct certain relationships of power, and also how our beliefs, values and social institutions are constructed through and supported by discourse. A central principle of this view of discourse is that discourse is always *ideological*, meaning that discourse always has 'an agenda', that it always ends up serving the interests of certain people over those of others (see A4).

As stated above, it is difficult to look at discourse in any meaningful way from only one of these perspectives. Simply looking at how texts are put together, for example, while it may be interesting, has limited practical value. At the same time, you cannot really make broad statements about 'power' or 'ideology' in a text without first understanding some basic things about how the text is put together and how people are actually using it in specific social contexts to perform specific actions. The way people create 'versions of reality' with their discourse or use it to exert power over people depends on the kinds of words they use to describe things and the grammatical structures they use to communicate 'who is doing what to whom', as well as the way they formulate their words to accomplish particular social actions and create particular relationships with other people.

👁 **Look deeper into the different perspectives on discourse on the companion website.**

COHESION, COHERENCE AND INTERTEXTUALITY B2

One of the most basic tasks for a discourse analyst is to figure out what makes a text a text and what makes a conversation and conversation – in other words, to figure out what gives texts and conversations *texture*. *Texture*, as I said in unit A2, comes from *cohesion*, *coherence* and *intertextuality*. *Cohesion* mostly has to do with linguistic features in texts, *coherence* has to do with the kinds of expectations or 'interpretative frameworks' readers bring to texts, and *intertextuality* has to do with how texts form connections with other texts (the shopping list I talked about in A2, for example, might be linked to a recipe I have for rocket salad).

First, let's think about cohesion and coherence. When I say that cohesion is about the linguistic features in the text and coherence is about the expectations readers bring to the text about its structure I don't mean that, when it comes to cohesion, the reader doesn't have to do any work or, in the case of coherence, that the expectations in the mind of the reader are more important than what is actually in the text. In fact, what creates cohesion is not just the linguistic features within the text, but also the fact that these features lead readers to perform certain mental operations – to locate and take note of earlier or later parts of the text as they are going through it.

For example, if I were to say, 'Beyoncé doesn't appeal to Nimah, but my sister loves her', in order to understand the meaning of 'her' in the second clause, you have to do some mental work. Not only do you need to refer back to the first clause, you also have to be smart enough to know that 'her' refers to Beyoncé and not Nimah. Thus, cohesion is the quality in a text that forces you to look either backward or forward in the text in order to make sense of the things you read, and it is through your acts of looking backward and forward that the text comes to take on a quality of connectedness.

Similarly, to say that *coherence* is a matter of the 'frameworks' or sets of expectations that we bring to texts does not mean that what is actually in the text is any less important. Concrete features must exist in the text that 'trigger' those expectations.

For example, for me to interpret a text as a shopping list (see A2), it must have a certain structure (a list), certain kinds of words (generally nouns) and those words must represent things that I am able to purchase (as opposed to abstract things such as 'world peace' or unaffordable items such as the Golden Gate Bridge). And for me to interpret something as a 'story', the different parts of the story need to be arranged in a certain way so that the story has a clear 'beginning', 'middle', and 'end' (see D2).

Cohesion

Halliday and Hasan (whose work is excerpted in D2) describe two broad kinds of linguistic devices that are used to force readers to engage in this process of backward and forward looking that gives texts a sense of connectedness. One type depends on grammar (which they call **grammatical cohesion**), and the other type depends more on the meanings of words (which they call **lexical cohesion**).

Devices used to create grammatical cohesion include:

- ❑ **conjunction** (using 'connecting words');
- ❑ **reference** (using a pronoun to refer to another word);
- ❑ **substitution** (substituting one word or phrase for another word or phrase);
- ❑ **ellipses** (leaving something out).

Conjunction refers to the use of various 'connecting words' (such as conjunctions such as *and* and *but* and conjunctive adverbs such as *furthermore* and *however*) to join together clauses and sentences. Conjunction causes the reader to look back to the first clause in a pair of joined clauses to make sense of the second clause. The important thing about these 'connecting words' is that they do not just establish a relationship between the two clauses, but that they also tell us what kind of relationship it is.

'Connecting words' then, can be grouped into different kinds depending on the relationship they establish between the clauses or sentences that they join together. Some are called **additive**, because they add information to the previous clause or sentence. Examples are *and, moreover, furthermore, in addition, as well*. Others are called **contrastive** because they set up some kind of contrast with the previous sentence or clause. Examples are *but, however*. Still, others are called **causative** because they set up some kind of cause-and-effect relationship between the two sentences or clauses. Examples of these are *because, consequently, therefore*. Finally, some are called **sequential** because they indicate the order facts or events come in. Examples are *firstly, subsequently, then* and *finally*. In the two examples below, the first uses a contrastive connective and the second uses a causative connective.

He liked the exchange students. She, *however*, would have nothing to do with them.

He liked the exchange students. She, *therefore*, would have nothing to do with them.

All connecting words cause the reader to look back to a previous clause (or sentence) in order to understand the subsequent clause (or sentence), and the kind of connecting word used guides the reader in understanding the relationship between two clauses (or sentences). In the first example given above, the word *however* causes the reader to look back at the first sentence to find out what the difference is between her and him. In the second example, the word *therefore* causes the reader to look back at the first sentence to find out *why* she won't have anything to do with the exchange students. Similarly, in the example given above, 'Beyoncé doesn't appeal to Nimah, but my sister loves her,' the word *but* helps us to figure out that the pronoun *her* refers to Beyoncé (not Nimah) since the first clause is about somebody *not* liking *Beyoncé*, and the conjunction *but* signals that the second clause will give some contrasting information.

Another very common way we make our texts 'stick together' is by using words that refer to words we used elsewhere in the text. This kind of cohesive device is known as *reference*. The examples above, besides using connecting words, also use this device. The word 'them' in the second sentence refers back to 'the exchange students' in the first sentence, and so, to make sense of it, the reader is forced to look back. 'He' and 'she' are also pronouns and presumably refer to specific people who are probably named at an earlier point in the longer text from which these sentences were taken, though, as with the sentence about Beyoncé and Nimah, figuring out who or what a pronoun refers to sometimes requires that we pay attention to other cohesive devices. The word or group of words that a pronoun refers to is called its **antecedent**. What reference does, then, is help the reader to keep track of the various participants in the text as he or she reads (Eggins 1994: 95).

There are basically three kinds of reference:

1   **Anaphoric** reference – using words that point back to a word used before:

     After Lady Gaga appeared at the MTV Music Video Awards in a dress made completely of meat, *she* was criticised by animal rights groups.

2   **Cataphoric** reference – using words that point forward to a word that has not been used yet:

     When *she* was challenged by reporters, Lady Gaga insisted that the dress was not intended to offend anyone.

3   **Exophoric** reference – using words that point to something outside the text (reference):

     If *you* want to know more about this controversy, *you* can read the comments people have left on animal rights blogs.

The definite article ('the') can also be a form of *anaphoric* reference in that it usually refers the reader back to an earlier mention of a particular noun.

     Lady Gaga appeared in a dress made completely of meat. *The* dress was designed by Franc Fernandez.

Substitution is similar to reference except that, rather than using pronouns, other words are used to refer to an *antecedent*, which has either appeared earlier or will appear later. In the sentence below, for example, the word *one* is used to substitute for *dress*.

> Besides wearing a meat dress, Lady Gaga has also worn a hair *one*, which was designed by Chris March.

Substitution can also be used to refer to the verb or the entire predicate of a clause, as in the example below.

> If Lady Gaga was intending to shock people, she succeeded in *doing so*.

Ellipsis is the omission of a noun, verb or phrase on the assumption that it is understood from the linguistic context. In order to fill in the gap(s), readers need to look back to previous clauses or sentences, as in the example below.

> There is much to support the view that it is clothes that wear us, and *not we, them.*
>
> (Virginia Woolf)

All of the devices mentioned above are examples of *grammatical cohesion*, the kind of cohesion that is created because of the *grammatical relationships* between words. Lexical cohesion occurs as a result of the *semantic* relationship between words. The simplest kind of lexical cohesion is when words are repeated. But a more common kind is the repetition of words related to the same subject. We call these 'chains' of similar kinds of words that run through texts **lexical chains**. In the following text, for example, besides the use of reference (who, it, she), the clauses are held together by the repetition of the verb 'to wear' and of other words having to do with clothing and fashion ('bikini', '*Vogue*' – a famous fashion magazine, 'dress' and 'outfits').

> Lady Gaga, who came under fire recently for *wearing* a meat *bikini* on the cover of *Vogue* Hommes Japan, *wore* a raw meat *dress* at last night's VMAs. It was one of many *outfits* she *wore* throughout the night.
>
> (Oldenberg 2010)

Taken together, these words form a **lexical chain**, which helps to bind the text together. Lexical chains not only make a text more cohesive but also highlight the topic or topics (such as 'fashion', 'entertainment', 'technology') that the text is about – and so can provide context for determining the meaning of ambiguous words (such as 'rocket' in the example of the shopping list given in A2). In fact, searching for lexical chains is one of the main techniques used in computer-automated text categorisation and summarisation.

Halliday and Hasan (see D4a) call these devices 'ties'. Texts are made cohesive, they claim, usually through the use of a combination of different kinds of ties, and it is the job of the discourse analyst to reveal the 'patterns of ties' that give certain kinds of texts 'texture'. In other words, cohesion works not just because of cohesive devices, but also because these devices are deployed in particular kinds of *patterns*, something that we will explore in more detail in section C3.

Not all the texts we encounter, however, are cohesive in the ways described above. The shopping list I talked about in section B1, for example, contains no connecting words, and so readers need to figure out how the words are connected themselves, and sometimes speakers or writers make the relationships between different parts of a text ambiguous in order to confuse people or to create humour. The example Halliday and Hasan give in the excerpt reprinted in section D2 is the exchange:

A: Time flies.
B: You can't; they fly too quickly.

The humour in this exchange lies in the anaphoric reference B creates between 'they' and 'flies', which turns the latter word, which was originally intended as a verb, into a noun. Halliday and Hasan also point out that this exchange contains no less than *three* cohesive devices: reference, ellipsis and lexical repetition.

Sometimes people use cohesive ties in an ambiguous way to make it seem that certain things are logically connected when they are not. For example, US President Donald Trump, when talking to talk-show host Jimmy Kimmel about his proposed Muslim ban, gave the following answer in reply to the question, 'Isn't it wrong to discriminate against people because of their religion?: 'the *problem* – I mean, look, I'm for it. But look, we have people coming into the *country* that are looking to do tremendous *harm* … Look at what happened in *Paris*. I mean, these people, they did not come from Sweden, okay? Look at what happened in Paris. Look what happened last week in *California*, with, you know, 14 people *dead*. Other people are going to *die*, they're badly *injured,* we have a real *problem*'.

While Trump's answer, in many ways, does not seem particularly cohesive, what makes his answer oddly effective, at least for many listeners, is the way he creates ambiguity about what parts of the text are connected to other parts of the text. He begins by saying, 'look, I'm for it', but it is not clear what 'it' refers to (discriminating against people because of their religion, or it being wrong to discriminate against people because of their religion). He then goes on to mention 'people coming into the country that are looking to do tremendous harm'. He follows this by mentioning Paris and California, where terrorist attacks had recently taken place, though Paris is not in 'the country' he was referring to in his previous clause. He ties these two incidents together by repeating the phrase: 'Look at what happened …'. Then he says, 'other people are going to die', followed by, 'they're badly injured', but it is not clear who the 'they' in this clause refers to (the people in Paris, in California, elsewhere?). Trump's ambiguity in his use of reference actually makes it difficult to refute his statements, since is not entirely clear exactly who he means by 'it', 'they' and 'people'. By drawing loose connections between the terrorist attacks in Paris and California and 'people coming into the country' (who are not from Paris, California or 'Sweden'), he is able to imply that people from 'non-Western' countries immigrating to the United States are potential terrorists without saying that directly. The way the text is held together by a *lexical chain* of words related to violence (harm, dead, died, injured) also helps Trump create feelings of fear in his listeners.

Coherence

As the shopping list we discussed in A2 illustrates, what makes a text a text is often as much a matter of the connections people make between parts of the text *in the absence* of cohesive devices, using sets of expectations and interpretive frameworks that they bring to the reading of texts. The relationship between the words 'tomatoes' and 'rocket' becomes meaningful to a reader based on his or her understanding of what a shopping list is and what it is used for. In the same way, listeners are able to connect up 'Paris', 'California', people who 'are looking to do tremendous harm', and people who are 'coming into the country' because of the ideas about terrorism and terrorists that they bring to the text. This aspect of texture is known as *coherence*, and it has to do with our expectations about the way elements in a text ought to be organised and the kinds of social actions (such as shopping) that are associated with a given text.

The text in Figure B2.1 is a good example of how we sometimes need to apply our experience with past texts and with certain conventions that have grown up in our society in order to understand new texts we encounter. For most people, as soon as they see the words 'before' and 'after', a certain body of knowledge is 'triggered' based on texts they have seen in the past that contain these words, such as advertisements for beauty products. In such texts, 'before' is usually portrayed as 'bad' and 'after' is usually portrayed as 'good', and the product being advertised is portrayed as the 'agent' that causes the transformation from 'before' to 'after'. This structure is a variation on what Michael Hoey (1983) has called the 'Problem–Solution' pattern, which underlies many texts, from business proposals to newspaper editorials.

The challenge this ad presents for the reader is that there is no explicit information about what is meant by 'before' and 'after' other than a curved line drawn down the centre of the page. In order to interpret this line, we must make reference to the smaller words in the lower right corner, which give the name of the advertiser, Body Coach.Net, and the slogan: 'For a perfect body'. This information creates for readers an interpretive framework based on their knowledge of the kind of business such a company might be engaged in and cultural notions of what a 'perfect body' might look like. Once this framework is triggered, most readers have no trouble interpreting the space formed on the 'before' side of the ad as portraying the stomach of an overweight

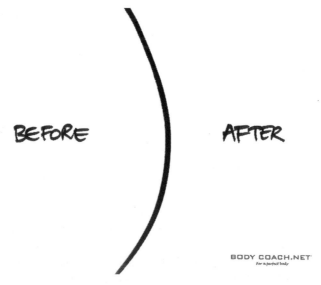

BEFORE   AFTER

BODY COACH.NET
For a perfect body

Figure B2.1 Advertisement for Body Coach.Net (Duval Guillaume, Brussels, Belgium).

person, and the space formed on the 'after' side as the 'hourglass' shape associated (at least in the culture in which this ad appeared) with female beauty, and of the company – Body Coach.Net and the product that it sells – as the agents of this transformation.

There are a number of different kinds of interpretative frameworks that we use to make sense of texts. One kind, which we will discuss further in the next section, we might call a **generic framework**. This kind of framework is based on the expectations we have about the kinds of information we expect to encounter in texts of different kinds and the order in which we expect that information to be presented, along with other kinds of lexical or grammatical features we expect to encounter. In the example above, for instance, it is partially our knowledge of the structure of 'before and after ads' that helps us to make sense of this particular ad.

Part of what forms such generic frameworks is that different parts of a text are not just grammatically and lexically related, but that they are also *conceptually* and *procedurally* related – in other words, they appear in a certain logical or predictable sequence. Texts following the 'Problem–Solution' pattern, for example, begin by presenting a problem and then go on to present one or more solutions to the problem. This idea that texts that to have a logical and predictable structure can also be seen in the analysis of oral narratives by William Labov (see section D2), who argued that the stories we tell tend to have predictable components that tend to be presented in a predictable order: we usually begin our stories with a short summary of what we're going to say, which he called an 'ABSTRACT'; then we 'set the scene' by telling when and where the story happened, which Labov called the 'ORIENTATION'; then we introduce the 'problem' or 'conflict' in the story, which he called the 'COMPLICATING ACTION'; then we tell how the problem or conflict was resolved, which he called the 'RESOLUTION'; and finally, we sometimes end with a statement about what the story meant or what the listener is supposed to learn from it, which Labov called a 'CODA'.

Just as people can create strategic ambiguity through their use of cohesive devices, they can also create ambiguity by playing with these patterns. Filmmakers, for example, might end a movie not with the resolution or coda but with the new complicating action, in order to prepare for a sequel, and Donald Trump is famous for exploiting the problem–solution pattern, frequently describing things or situations as 'big problems' but not offering a solution, thereby implying that he himself is a solution, that 'he alone can fix it'.

Not all of the knowledge we use to make sense of texts comes from our knowledge about the conventions associated with different kinds of text. Some of this knowledge is part of larger conceptual frameworks that we build up based on our understanding of how the world works. I will use the term **cultural models** to describe these frameworks. James Paul Gee (2010) calls cultural models 'videotapes in the mind' based on experiences we have had and depicting what we take to be *prototypical* (or 'normal') people, objects and events. To illustrate the concept, he points out that we would never refer to the Pope as a 'bachelor' even though the Pope, as an unmarried adult male, fulfils the conditions for the dictionary definition of the word, because he does not fit into our *cultural model* of what a bachelor is. Cultural models regarding both the kind of work 'coaches' do and about what constitutes a 'perfect body' are central to our ability to interpret the ad above, and especially for our understanding of the meaning of the two shapes formed by the line drawn down the centre of the page, while cultural models about 'terrorists', 'people who come into our country', and 'people who are not from Sweden' are important for listeners to understand the quote from Donald Trump above.

The important thing to remember about cultural models (and, for that matter, generic frameworks) is that they are *cultural*. In other words, they reflect the beliefs and values of a particular group of people in a particular place at a particular point in history. The ad reprinted above would be totally incomprehensible for people in many societies outside of our own because they would not share either the knowledge of 'before and after ads' or the beliefs about physical attractiveness that we have. It is even more important to remember that such texts do not just reflect such expectations, values and beliefs, but also *reinforce* them. Every time we encounter a text like the advertisement above or the quote from Donald Trump, these generic frameworks and cultural models and the habitual ways of looking at the world associated with them are strengthened.

Intertextuality

The third characteristic of texts that gives them texture is *intertextuality*, which refers to the connections that are formed between a text and other texts. The Soviet literary critic Mikhail Bakhtin (1981) argued that every time we speak or write, we are in some way 'borrowing' the words of others and making them our own. All texts, he said, somehow *make reference* to texts that have come before them and *anticipate* texts that will come after them, and so contribute to the formation of a larger *web of texts* of which they form a part. One way texts exhibit texture, then, is the way they form connections to these larger webs of texts.

Sometimes this borrowing from other texts is explicit: we might, for example, directly quote the words of someone else, as when a newspaper or magazine quotes someone or characterises what they have said. For example:

> President Trump defended the white nationalists who protested in Charlottesville on Tuesday, saying they included 'some very fine people.'
>
> (*The Atlantic*, Aug 15, 2017)

More often, however, we make reference to other people's words in more oblique or subtle ways, through paraphrasing them or by turning them into **presuppositions**, often failing to mention the texts or the people that were the source of these paraphrases or presuppositions. When Trump says, 'look at what happened in Paris', he is referring not so much to what happened as to the news reports about what happened, and presupposing that his listener has also read or heard those reports and has come to similar conclusions based on them. Presupposition is a particularly powerful form of intertextuality, because it does not just link a text with previous texts, but it also creates links between the speakers or writers and listeners or readers around a body of *shared knowledge* or assumptions. It also functions to make these words or ideas from other texts more difficult to challenge (see A4).

Sometimes texts are linked not to specific texts written or spoken in the past, but rather to certain kinds of texts that are associated with certain kinds of people or certain kinds of situations, or webs of texts which might be referred to as *Discourses*.

The discourse analysts Norman Fairclough refers to this kind of intertextuality as **interdiscursivity**: the borrowing of certain genres or styles or Discourses.

One of the most explicit ways people link their texts to larger *webs of texts* or *Discourses* nowadays is with the use of 'hashtags' in digital genres such as tweets and Instagram posts. When one of my students tweeted 'The worst way to be broken up with is when your boyfriend/girlfriend changes their relationship status without informing you first #savage #FirstWorldProblems', she used these two hashtags to link her tweet to other tweets with the same hashtag (intertextuality). But in doing this, she also linked her topic (breaking up on social media) with another Discourse, that of 'first world problems' (a phrase often used to remind privileged people not just that their problems are not as bad as those of less privileged people, but also that these problems are, in some respects, a *result* of their privilege).

Just as particular patterns of cohesive ties and particular generic frameworks are associated with particular kinds of texts (and the people that produce them), different kinds of texts exhibit different characteristics when it comes to intertextuality and interdiscursivity. For example, when journalists quote something that someone has said in news articles, they usually 'clean it up', that is, they take out the pauses, false starts and sounds like 'um' and 'ah', whereas when discourse analysts quote people's spoken words in academic articles they often leave these in – in fact, sometimes those are the features of the speech they are most interested in (See B6, C6). Similarly, when academics like discourse analysts use a fact or idea from another source, they are usually careful to cite the source and give a complete bibliographic reference, but journalists hardly ever do this.

👁 **Find more examples of cohesion and coherence on the companion website.**

ALL THE RIGHT MOVES   B3

Texts that are structured according to particular *generic frameworks* are called *genres*. But genres are more than just texts; they are means by which people *get things done*, and the way they are structured depends crucially on what the particular people using a genre want or need to do. In other words, what determines the way a particular genre is put together is its *communicative purpose*, and so this must be the central focus in analysing genres.

Usually, the overall communicative purpose of a genre can be broken down into a number of steps that users need to follow in order to achieve the desired purpose – rather like the steps in a recipe – and typically, the most important constraints and conventions regarding how a genre is structured involve: (1) which steps must be included; and (2) the order in which they should appear. In the field of *genre analysis*, these steps are known as **moves**.

John Swales, the father of genre analysis, illustrated the idea of *moves* in his analysis of introductions to academic articles. Instead of asking the traditional question 'how is this text structured?' Swales asked 'What do writers of such texts need to *do* in order to achieve their desired purpose?' (which, in the case of an introduction to an academic article, is mainly getting people to believe that the article is worth reading). In answering this question, Swales identified four *moves* characteristic of such texts. An introduction to an academic article, he said, typically:

1   *establishes the field* in which the writer of the study is working;
2   *summarises the related research* or interpretations on one aspect of the field;
3   *creates a research space* or interpretive space (a 'niche') for the present study by indicating a gap in current knowledge or by raising questions;
4   *introduces the study* by indicating what the investigation being reported will accomplish for the field (adapted from Swales 1990).

Of course, not all introductions to academic articles contain all four of these moves in exactly the order presented by Swales. Some article introductions may contain only some of these moves, and some might contain different moves. Furthermore, the ways these moves are *realised* might be very different for articles about engineering and articles about English literature. The point that Swales was trying to make, however, was not that these moves are universal or in some way *obligatory*, but that these are the *prototypical* moves one would expect to occur in this genre, and understanding these default expectations is the first step to understanding how 'expert users' might creatively flout them. At the same time, it is important to remember that not all genres are equally 'conventionalised'; while some genres have very strict rules about which moves should be included and what order they should be in, other genres exhibit much more variety.

Some genres, such as the oral narratives described by Labov (see section D2), are familiar to most people, and so few would have trouble reproducing them using the appropriate move structure. In fact, it is difficult to think of oral narratives as being associated with any particular *discourse community* (see D3a). Certain kinds of narratives, however, are more specialised, and while their structures may resemble or draw upon the more 'universal' structure Labov outlined, they are different enough in both *form* and *communicative purpose* that being able to reproduce them successfully shows that one is a member of a particular group.

One example of a more specialised genre of oral narrative that has been circulating on YouTube since 2010 is the genre of the 'It Gets Better' video, a form of digital storytelling in which older LGBTQ people share their experiences of being bullied when they were younger with teenagers who might be experiencing bullying themselves. The genre began when a famous online columnist named Dan Savage and his husband, Terry White, shocked by a highly publicised news story of a 15-year-old boy who had hung himself as a result of anti-gay bullying, posted a video on YouTube (https://youtu.be/7IcVyvg2Qlo) in which they talk about their own experiences when they were younger in order to send a message to 'at risk' teens that 'it gets better'. Within weeks, hundreds of videos from other LGBTQ adults appeared on the website Savage had set up (http://www.itgetsbetter.org), and now the number exceeds 100,000, including videos made by a number of celebrities and politicians.

When they posted their video, Savage and White presented something like a 'template' or 'model' for this genre, and people who posted videos after them almost universally followed this structure, even though it was never written down or 'prescribed' in any way. In many ways, the stories told in 'It Gets Better' videos are not that different from the oral narratives that Labov analysed: they usually begin with an ABSTRACT; include an ORIENTATION, which sets the scene; present some kind of COMPLICATING ACTION; move on to a RESOLUTION; and often end with a CODA, telling the purpose of the story. At the same time, because 'It Gets Better' videos have a particular *communicative purpose*, the way their narrative structure is realised as *moves* – or *actions* that the narrators take in relation to their listeners – is different from other stories. And this is really the main difference between Labov's approach to the genre of narrative and the way genre analysts approach it: whereas Labov is interested in the *structure* of the genre (what makes it *coherent*), genre analysts are more interested in the genre as a series of *actions*. In most of the 'It Gets Better' videos you can find on the campaign's website, narrators arrange the genre into six *moves*:

1   *Announcing the purpose of the video (to tell you that 'it gets better')*

Hi, my name is David from Orange County and I'm making this video so that you know whoever watches that it gets better.

Hi, my name is Taylor, and I'm just here to make this video to tell you guys that it does get better.

2   *Explaining the problems I had when I was young*

I grew up in a small town, conservative Wisconsin ... there were many incidents of homophobia in my school and community.

So I started telling other kids that I was gay, launching what was probably the worst year of my life. I was harassed; I was followed; I was threatened; kids wanted to kill me. I couldn't go from class to class without being accosted. Kids would throw desks and chairs at me in class and the teachers would just pretend that they didn't see what was going on.

3   *Explaining how those problems were resolved*

It wasn't until college that things began to get clearer, that I began to realise that there was a truer me, within the me that everyone else knew.

It was so refreshing to suddenly have someone to count on. I had been keeping this secret my whole life, and I was finally able to experience what it was like to be completely honest with another person.

4   *Comparing your situation to my situation*

None of this would have happened if I were not here. If I had ended my life, I would not have been able to meet so many wonderful people. I would not have experienced the togetherness and belonging that comes from truly deep friendships. I would not have been able to fall in love. I would not have known what it feels like to be embraced by a community. I would not have been able to see that life does get better.

It is too late for me to speak to my own sixteen-year-old self, so instead I want all of the misfits and weirdos and artists and queer kids to know a couple of things I wish someone had told me back then.

5   *Offering encouragement and advice*

If you are being bullied, say something. Supportive adults can be your allies.

Don't take your own life. It's not worth it. If you take your own life, they win. And if you take your own life, that's one less gay person of color, or white, or disabled, or multi-abled, or whatever, that isn't here, able to show them the truth. So please love yourself. Please be strong. And you'll be all right. That I do promise you.

6   *Reminding you that 'it gets better'*
> Guys don't be scared because no matter what, like I said, at the end of the day it's gonna get better.
> Just remember, no matter what, it does get better.

This is not to say that all of the 'It Gets Better' videos uploaded to the campaign's website contain all of these moves (or *only* these moves) in exactly this order. At the same time, most of the moves in the list above are pretty much *essential* if narrators want to achieve the communicative purpose of the genre (to illustrate to watchers that 'it gets better' through the example of their own life experiences), and to show themselves to be members of the *discourse community* associated with this genre (which is related to, but not the same as, the 'LGBTQ community').

Genres are not just distinguished by the set of moves they employ. They also often use particular kinds of words or phrases (such as the repetition of the phrase 'it gets better'), or they are written, spoken or performed in a particular style (for example, nearly all 'It Gets Better' videos consist of narrators sitting in domestic settings (such as a bedroom), looking directly at the camera and speaking in a casual, conversational style). Genres also often are associated with different *modes* (see A9) and *media* (see A10), and so, for example, an 'It Gets Better' video must be a video (rather than, say, a conversation in a bar), and it must be uploaded onto the Internet (either to YouTube or to the campaign's dedicated site). In the same way, the genre of a 'Snapchat story' must involve images of some kind and must be broadcast using the Snapchat app (see C3), and a scientific article must be written down and usually appears in either the print or online version of an academic journal.

Communicative purpose

Above, I talked about how moves and move structures are associated with the *communicative purpose* of a genre, and how certain moves delivered in a certain order are essential for achieving this communicative purpose. The idea of communicative purpose, however, is not as simple as it might seem. Since many genres have *multiple authors* and *multiple audiences*, genres might have multiple purposes. The genre of a 'rental contract' has different purposes for the landlord, the tenant, the rental agent, the solicitor who helps to make sure that it conforms to legal requirements, and the civil servant at the government office where it might be filed.

Similarly, the genre of the 'It Gets Better' video might have different purposes for different people who make them and different people who watch them. For young people struggling with bullying and their sexual or gender identities, the videos are meant to inspire them and prevent them from attempting suicide as well as to 'give voice' to the indignities that they are suffering, and we might say that these young people are the main audience of these videos. But sometimes genres are designed with multiple audiences in mind, which in this case which might include the parents or teachers of LGBTQ teens, their friends, school or government officials and even the people who now or in the past were involved in bullying other people. For parents and teachers, the communicate purpose of the videos might be to arouse concern and to help them to understand what the young people under their care might be going through; for policy makers, it might be to alert them to a problem and urge them to take some kind of action; and for bullies and those who enable them, it might be to shame them and get them to stop treating others badly

The different people who make 'It Gets Better' videos may also have different purposes for doing so. Most of the people who appear in these videos are just ordinary LGBTQ adults who presumably remember the difficulties they faced when they were young and wish to help others who might be going through the same thing. But not all of them are 'ordinary people', and some of them are not even members of the LGBTQ community. Posters include famous singers, actors, politicians and even companies like Google and Microsoft:

> I don't know what it's like to be picked on for being gay. But I do know what it's like to grow up feeling that sometimes you don't belong.
>
> (Barack Obama)

> My name is Boris Erickson I'm a gay man and a program manager and software designer here at Microsoft but actually my job title is the Xbox Live enforcement unicorn ninja and if that's not proof that it gets better I don't know what to tell you.
>
> (Microsoft G.L.E.A.M.)

Although people like President Obama and corporations like Microsoft clearly wish to send a positive message to 'at risk' teens, they also have other purposes (and other audiences) in mind. By making an 'It Gets Better' video, for example, President Obama is making a *political statement* and sending a message both to his constituents and to other politicians (such as lawmakers considering legislation related to school bullying or LGBTQ issues) about policy matters, and Microsoft's 'It Gets Better' video serves not just to show support to its LGBTQ employees, but also to portray Microsoft as a 'progressive' company and to recruit new employees.

In fact, the 'It Gets Better' genre is so flexible that it can even be used by bullies to apologise for their bullying:

> I saw the program *It Gets Better* and I was on the other end of it growing up. I was the bully, one of the bullies. There was like three or four of us, and we were fucking bad. People got beat up, kicked, punched, put the boots to. It was bad growing up. Um … It was a very small-minded town, very small-minded people. If you didn't fit in, if your skin was the wrong color, if you had the wrong hairdo, you got beat up, pretty much that's how it was … I'm sorry. I cried many nights. Even being a bully. It was hard. I don't know why it happened, or what twisted screwed up thoughts were going through my head … I have no excuses … It's kind of embarrassing … I just hope you all get through whatever you're going through. That's it.

Discourse communities

If so many people, including LGBTQ adults and teens, singers, actors, politicians, tech companies and even former bullies can use the genre of the 'It Gets Better' video for a range of communicative purposes, can we identify one particular 'discourse community' to which this genre belongs? Clearly, the community of people who use this genre is not synonymous with the 'LGBTQ community', since there are members of this larger community who have never watched or made such a video, and people who watch and make 'It Gets Better' videos who are not gay, lesbian, bisexual, transgender or queer.

To answer this question, we need to consider the function that genres serve in discourse communities beyond helping members accomplish the very concrete goals (in this case, encouraging 'at risk' young people from harming themselves). First, genres have the function of promoting the *values* of the community. They might do this explicitly, or they may do it implicitly through the kinds of social actions and social relationships that they make possible among members. 'It Gets Better' videos, for example, promote values like openness, honesty, tolerance and resilience by giving those who make them a way to share personal experiences of resilience and by giving those that watch them the opportunity to be exposed to examples of tolerance and diversity.

Another important function genres play in discourse communities is to bring new members into the community. Sometimes this includes attracting new members. But it always includes *socialising* new members into the ways of acting and thinking associated with the community. For members who have already been socialised, genres serve as a way of portraying themselves as competent members of the community. In other words, what is important about the various 'rules' and conventions and constraints associated with genres is not only that they make communicative actions more efficient, but also that they demonstrate that the person who uses them knows 'how we do things' and is therefore a 'person like us'. This process of socialisation is particularly evident in 'It Gets Better' videos, as the people who watch them become inspired to make their own videos following the templates provided by those made by others, thus taking up and passing on a kind of 'tradition' of discourse production. And by participating in this tradition, they are able to participate in the political project of promoting the values embedded in this genre. The desire to be part of this tradition and contribute to this political project is not limited to those in the LGBTQ community but extends to others as well, partly because of their desire to support their LGBTQ friends and family members, and partly because the stories of suffering and redemption told in these videos are something that everyone can relate to.

And so the best answer to the question of what is the 'discourse community' that 'It Gets Better' videos support might be 'The It Gets Better Community', the people who congregate on the project's website and on YouTube, watch and produce these videos, and give one another feedback and encouragement. This online community shares all of the qualities Swales (see D3) identified with 'discourse communities': it has 'expert' and 'novice' members, members have ways of communicating with one another and providing feedback, they share a special vocabulary or 'jargon' (the most obvious example being the catchphrase 'it gets better'), and they share a common goal – to stop people from being bullied and to promote equal rights for LGBTQ people. In fact, we might even say that, apart from giving hope to bullied teens, a key purpose of 'It Gets Better' videos is to 'grow' this community and to promote its political agenda by 'gathering together' likeminded people. But this is not just the case for activist videos like this. *All genres* have political or ideological dimensions because their main functions are to create and maintain communities and to serve as the means through which people in those communities learn how to be 'legitimate members'. Although this political dimension is rather explicit in 'It Gets Better' videos, it is as true for other genres like job application letters and Snapchat stories. Understanding the political dimension of genres tells us a lot not just about how genres work, but also about how politics works. It's not just that discourse communities invent genres in order to accomplish communicative purposes and reach common goals; genres themselves help to *create* discourse communities by gathering people around them and inviting them to engage in shared actions and shared goals.

👁 **Find more examples of the creative use of genres on the companion website.**

CONSTRUCTING REALITY   B4

In unit A4, I argued that no text is ideologically 'neutral' – that all texts promote certain kinds of beliefs about the world and certain kinds of power relationships between people. The main ways authors of texts promote ideologies is by constructing versions of reality in which certain kinds of *participants* are excluded, and those that are *included* are linked to each other in certain relationships, often based on the actions (*processes*) they are portrayed as engaging in. They also construct reality by creating a certain kind of *relationship* between the producers of texts and those that read them through the resource of *modality*, or through the use of particular styles or *registers*. Finally, another thing that contributes to the way texts create versions of reality is the way they portray the *circumstances* in which these processes are taking place and these relationships are being formed. *Circumstances* are usually expressed through **circumstantial adjuncts**: phrases or clauses that tell the reader *when*, *where*, *how* or *why* an action is taking place. All of these strategies for constructing reality can be seen in a simple sign that I saw on a bus from Reading to Heathrow airport that said:

> For your comfort and peace of mind during your journey CCTV is fitted to this bus.

There are a number of different participants in this sentence: there is 'CCTV' (which stands for closed circuit television, referring to the surveillance cameras on the bus), there is the bus, and there is the reader of this sentence, 'you', the passenger. What is interesting is that the most important participant, the one that has actually carried out the action of fitting the camera to the bus, is *excluded*. One strategy made possible by passive verb forms such as 'is fitted' is to allow writers to leave out the *agents* of processes.[1] So passengers don't know who is watching them; is it the bus company, the government or some shadowy unknown entity? This makes a difference because when we are unaware of who is watching us, we are less able to adjust our behaviour accordingly, and we begin to be careful about *everything* we do.

Another important aspect of the version of reality constructed by this sign is the reason that is given for *why* CCTV has been fitted to the bus, expressed in the circumstantial adjunct: 'For your comfort and peace of mind during your journey'. While the presence of surveillance cameras (fitted by some unknown agent) might make passengers uncomfortable, this circumstantial adjunct aims to make them feel that this surveillance is not such a bad thing, though it is not explained exactly how being surveilled would make them more 'comfortable' or give them 'peace of mind'. The answer to this lies in the *relationship* that the sign creates between the writer and the reader using the *interpersonal* resources of the language. First, by speaking directly to readers using the pronoun 'you', the writer creates a feeling of intimacy with the reader. This strategy, which is used in a lot of advertising texts, is known as **synthetic personalisation** (Fairclough, 2001); it's a way of giving the impression that the reader and the writer have a personal relationship, but of course, this relationship is 'synthetic' or 'fake', entirely constructed by the text. Another interpersonal resource that the sign uses is the 'style' of luxury advertising; the phrase 'For your comfort and peace of mind ...' is the kind of phrase one would expect to see in an advertisement for a posh hotel or expensive mattress.

The combined effect of all of this is that the sign does not just depict a certain kind of situation involving busses with cameras fitted to them, but also *constructs the reader as a certain kind of person* who has a certain kind of relationship with the bus, the cameras, and the people who fitted them. In other words, the text has created for the reader a particular **reading position** (Kress, 1989), a particular way to read and interpret the information about the cameras. More importantly, though, this positioning of the reader also has the effect of creating *another* kind of participant, people who may attempt somehow to disturb the comfort of the passengers by robbing or assaulting them, or who might break the rules of the bus by smoking or not wearing their seatbelts, people whom 'normal' passengers ought to be afraid of. Even more interesting is the fact that, when you think of it, it is *these* participants, the potential pickpockets and smokers and terrorists, that are the *real* intended readers of this text, though they are never mentioned or addressed.

Another example of the way signs related to surveillance cameras create different kinds of readers and different ways for them to read the text can be seen in the sign I saw in the supermarket where I shop, which says:

> Images are being monitored and recorded for the safety of our customers and colleagues and to detect crime.
>
> Sainsbury's will prosecute shoplifters and use the civil recovery scheme to recover its expenses due to theft and damage.
>
> Sainsbury's is looking out for you.

In this sign, the participants include a number of **concrete** objects and people such as 'images', 'customers', 'colleagues', and 'shoplifters', as well as a number of **abstract** participants, participants that represent states of affairs such as 'safety', and those that represent **nominalised processes,** actions that are expressed as nouns such as 'theft'. Interestingly, all of these participants are portrayed as having things done to them: 'images' are monitored, 'customers' and 'colleagues' are made safe, 'crime' is detected, and 'shoplifters' are prosecuted. The only participant in the text that is presented as an agent is Sainsbury's, which is presumably responsible for all of these actions, though the way its responsibility is represented is different in different parts of the text.

The most striking thing about this text is that, like the aspirin bottle Gee analyses in section D3, it is **heteroglossic**, that is, it contains different 'voices', in this case, two distinct voices, each of which constructs a different kind of reader. The first sentence of the text is directed towards 'innocent' customers and colleagues and is designed not just to inform them that images of them are being monitored but to explain to them that it is for their own good. In fact, surveillance is portrayed almost as a form of customer service or, in the case of the colleagues, a workplace benefit. Sainsbury's, the presumed agent of this monitoring, is not explicitly named; rather, the monitoring is construed as simply 'happening'. The only clue that Sainsbury's is an agent in this sentence is the pronoun 'our' before 'customers' and 'colleagues', which serves to align Sainsbury's with these other participants in a kind of protective, caring relationship.

The second sentence, on the other hand, is directed towards a different kind of reader – potential shoplifters, and it is strikingly different both in tone and in grammar. In this sentence, there is no ambiguity about who the agent is and what they will do to shoplifters if they catch them, and the language they use to portray this threat is distant and legalistic rather than caring and paternal. Sainsbury's in this case is not a protective ally but an uncompromising enforcer of the law.

Perhaps the most interesting sentence in the whole text is the last sentence, 'Sainsbury's is looking out for you', in which both kinds of reader is addressed simultaneously, with the phrase 'looking out for' taking on a different meaning for each of them.

As we can see in the above example, producers of text use the lexical and grammatical resources of the language (whos doing whats) as well as interpersonal resources such as 'social languages' not just to create different versions of reality, and not just to construct particular relationships with their readers, but also sometimes to create *different* versions of reality for *different* readers. In doing so, they reinforce certain ideological assumptions not just about the benefits of surveillance but also about the different kinds of people that exist in the world and how they should be treated. The world created by the Sainsbury's sign analysed above is world of 'good guys' and 'bad guys', one in which shoplifters could never be customers or colleagues or vice versa, and in which social or contextual factors associated with shoplifting (such as poverty or the high price of food) are irrelevant.

Ideology and indexicality

The texts above work to create particular versions of reality and promote particular ideologies not just through the way they *represent* the world, but also through the way they *interact* with it. In the last section, as well as in section A1, I said that one of the main things that makes texts meaningful (and gives them texture) is through the connections that they create with the world outside of them, which includes connections both to other texts (intertextuality) and to the *physical and social environments in which they are found*. The sign that says that 'this bus is fitted with CCTV' doesn't make much sense if the sign itself is not fitted to a bus, and signs that say 'Sainsbury's will prosecute shoplifters' only constitute warnings if they are actually placed in a

Figure B4.1 Sign at US-Mexico border (photo credit: AT2663-commonswiki).

Sainsbury's. The relationships texts create with the external world also represent one of the main things that makes texts ideological; a surveillance camera or a sign put in a particular place does not just say 'This place is under surveillance' but also 'This is the *kind of place* that *should* be under surveillance' or 'The *kinds of people* who might inhabit or move through this place need to be watched'.

The sign in Figure B4.1, for example, is found near the border between the United States and Mexico (on the US side) and says: *Caution! Do not expose your life to the elements. It's not worth it.* The literal meaning of this sign depends on the connection it makes with the 'elements' in the environment in which it is placed, a connection that is reinforced by pictures of these elements appearing on the sign (the hot sun, mountains, a desert, rattlesnakes, a drowning man and an icon that says 'No potable water'). It depends for its ideological meaning on the fact that it is written in Spanish (rather than English) and that it appears in a place in which illegal border crossings between Mexico and the United States occur. Through these connections to a particular place, a particular practice and a particular group of people, the sign becomes more than just piece of friendly advice about the dangers of nature; it becomes a warning to those who have entered the United States illegally that they will face consequences.

Texts also interact with the physical world in the way they exclude or include, label or classify people who interact with them. A sign in front of a Chinese restaurant in Reading, the United Kingdom, that says (招聘, 'Help wanted') only in Chinese excludes readers who don't read Chinese and sends the message that the restaurant would prefer that a Chinese person apply for the job. Similarly, in the picture below (Figure B4.2) of a currency exchange booth in Hong Kong International Airport, the surveillance cameras are pointing towards the cashier, sending the message that the cashier (rather than the customer) is the person who should be watched. Although the cameras here are not conventional 'texts' in the way the signs analysed above are,

Figure B4.2 Currency exchange booth (photo credit: author).

they function as texts by communicating something though what they are *pointing* at, and this is actually a feature of all texts: part of their meaning comes from the way they *point to* things in the physical or social world.

The kind of meaning that texts create not through the words that they contain but though the way they point to things in the physical or social world is called *indexical meaning*. An **index** is a kind of sign that points to some aspect of **context** (see section A7). Some words are always dependent for their meaning on their context: words like 'this' as in 'this bus' or 'you'[2] in 'Sainsbury's is looking out for you'. Linguists call these kinds of words **deictic expressions**: expressions (words or phrases) that refer to something that exists in the *context* in which a text occurs. Examples are 'this', 'that', 'here' and 'there'. But indexical meaning doesn't always require deictic expressions. Sometimes it is created simply by placing a text in a particular place; so, a STOP sign placed at an intersection does not just mean 'stop', it means 'stop *here*.'

Indexical meaning is created not just through connections with the physical world, but also through the connections that are made with the broader social and cultural worlds in which texts appear. In the excerpt reprinted in section D4, for example, Jan Blommaert talks about a sign on the outside of a chocolate shop in Tokyo that says 'Nina's Derrière'. The meaning of this sign is indexical in three ways: it points to the establishment on which it is affixed and says 'This chocolate shop is called Nina's Derrière'. It uses the French language in which the sign is written and says 'This is a French chocolate shop'. And it points to the 'Frenchness' of the shop and says 'Buying chocolate here shows that you are engaging in a chic, cosmopolitan lifestyle'. It doesn't matter that the literal (or *semantic*) meaning of the sign is 'Nina's rear end'; to the non-French speaking potential customer, the sign is an invitation to engage in a certain kind of lifestyle by buying overpriced chocolate from a shop with a French name.

Figure B4.3 Sign in luxury hotel (photo credit: author).

A similar kind of 'layering' of meaning can be seen in the sign in Figure B4.3, which I found in the lobby of an expensive hotel in the United Kingdom. Like other surveillance signs, it points to the place under surveillance ('This area') and to the reader who is the person under surveillance. But by using the term 'strike a pose' and a picture of two hands framing a photograph, it indexes the world of fashion photography and intimates that the person being photographed is like a fashion model. Finally, this world of fashion and this identity of a fashion model indexes a broader lifestyle of luxury and privilege, so that being filmed by a CCTV camera, rather than communicating suspicion, is made to seem like it is part of the luxurious experience of staying at this fashionable hotel.

The American linguistic anthropologist Michael Silverstein (2003) calls these different levels of indexical meaning **indexical orders**. A simple way to think of these levels in the context of the signs we have been looking at in this chapter is that the 'first order' of indexicality points to a particular person, place, thing or practice in the physical environment in which the index occurs; the 'second order' of indexicality links these physical things to ideas about particular *types* of people, places, things or practices that are part of 'models' about the way the world is or should be that we carry around in our heads – what Gee (see section D4) calls *cultural models*;

and 'third order' indexicality links these *types* of people to broader 'theories' about lifestyle, morality, identity and knowledge, which we could call 'ideologies' but we might also, using the term that I introduced in section B1, call 'Discourses' with a capital D.

These three levels can also be seen in the sign I analysed above placed on the border between the United States and Mexico warning people about the danger of rattlesnakes and undrinkable water. The 'first order' of indexicality refers to the place where the sign is placed (the border) and the dangers in that place, as well as to 'you', the potential reader. The 'second order' of indexicality refers to the kinds of practices that people expect to occur in that place (illegal border crossing) and the kind of people who engage in that practice (undocumented migrants from Mexico). And the 'third order' of indexicality points to a whole set of ideas about undocumented migrants from Mexico and how they should be treated. The most important thing about these three indexical orders is that they interact with one another to promote a particular 'Discourse' of illegal immigration that depends not just on what the sign says but also on it being placed near the border and being written in Spanish. Furthermore, as with the sign in Sainsbury's above, it speaks to different audiences differently: to potential undocumented migrants, it is as much of a threat as a warning ('If the snakes don't get you, we will!'). To English-speaking US citizens who don't understand the Spanish, it might serve to remind them about the 'problem' of 'illegal immigrants' or even to suggest that they are somehow associated with dangerous or unpleasant things like rattlesnakes, cacti and drowning.

This last observation brings us to the final point about indexicality – that indexical meaning can change when texts are read by different people or placed in different social environments. The sign 'Nina's Derrière' would have different literal and ideological meanings if it were placed outside the Moulin Rouge, a strip club in Paris, and the sign warning of the dangers of the snakes and treacherous mountains would have different literal and ideological meanings if it were placed on a hiking trail in the Peruvian Andes. Blommaert (see section D3) argues that beyond the indexical orders explained above, we also need to take into account what he calls **orders of indexicality**, which are not just conventional ways of pointing to certain kinds of people or practices or invoking certain ideologies, but also systems of *valuing* people, practices and ideologies that exist in different social contexts. The sign 'Nina's Derrière' only works as an index of chic cosmopolitism because of the way French is *valued* in Japanese society (as opposed to other languages like Romanian). Orders of indexicality also tend to enforce power and inequality through the kinds of people who are included, excluded or 'erased' from texts. The invitation to 'strike a pose' on the hotel sign, for example, is clearly not directed at employees of the hotel such as cleaners and desk clerks, who might read the sign as a warning that they are being watched by the boss. Systematic patterns of indexicality, then, to use Blommaert's words (see D3), are also 'systemic patterns of authority, of control and evaluation, and hence of inclusion and exclusion'. Thus, understanding the ideological effect of texts requires an understanding not just of the 'versions of reality' that texts construct, but also of the social, political and economic contexts in which these texts appear.

👁 **Find more examples of critically analysing texts on the companion website.**

B5

THE TEXTURE OF TALK

In the analysis of how people make sense of written texts (see A2 and B2), I introduced the concept of *texture*. Texture, I said, basically comes from two things: the
ways different parts of a text are related to one another, and the various expectations
that people have about texts. Making sense of conversations also involves these two
aspects of communication: the structure and patterning of the communication and
the broader expectations about meaning and human behaviour that participants bring
to it. Generally speaking, *conversation analysis* focuses more on the first aspect, and
pragmatics focuses more on the second.

The basis of pragmatics is the idea that people enter into conversations with the
assumption that the people they are conversing with will behave in a logical way. The
philosopher Herbert Paul Grice called this assumption the **cooperative principle**.
When people engage in conversation, he said, they do so with the idea that people will:

> Make (their) conversational contribution such as is required, at the stage at which
> it occurs, by the accepted purpose or direction of the talk exchange in which you
> are engaged.
>
> (Grice 1975: 45)

What he meant by this was that when people talk with each other, they generally cooperate in making their utterances understandable by conforming to what they believe
to be reasonable expectations about how people usually behave in conversation. Most
people, he said, have four main expectations about conversational behaviour:

1   what people say will be true (the maxim of quality);
2   what people say will be relevant to the topic under discussion (the maxim
    of relevance);
3   people will try to make what they mean clear and unambiguous (the maxim
    of manner);
4   people will say as much as they need to say to express their meaning and not say
    more than they need to say (the maxim of quantity).

Grice called these four expectations **maxims**. Maxims are not rules that must be followed; rather, they are general statements of principle about how things are done.
In actual conversations, however, people often violate or 'flout' these maxims: they
say things that are not true; they make seemingly irrelevant statements; they are not
always clear about what they mean; and they sometimes say more than they need
to or not enough to fully express their meaning. The point that Grice was making
was not that people always follow or even that they 'should' follow these maxims, but
that when they *do not* follow them, they usually do so for a reason; the very fact that
they have flouted a maxim itself *creates meaning*, a special type of meaning known
as **implicature**, which involves implying or suggesting something without having to
directly express it. When people try to make sense of what others have said, they do so
against the background of these default expectations. When speakers do not behave

as expected, listeners logically conclude that they are trying to imply something indirectly and try to work out what it is.

For example, if you ask your partner what they want for their birthday, and they say 'Is my birthday coming up? I totally forgot', you would probably conclude that they are not telling the truth – violating the maxim of quality (it is unlikely that they really forgot about their birthday). They would also be violating the maxim of relevance (not answering your question) as well as the maxim of quantity (not giving enough information). If you want to continue your relationship with them, however, you probably want to examine why they are doing this, which would probably lead you to infer that they take their birthday seriously and that you'd better get them something good.

The obvious question is, why do people do this? Why don't they simply communicate what they mean directly? One reason is that implicature allows us to manage the interpersonal aspect of communication. We might, for example, use implicature to be more polite or avoid hurting someone's feelings. Or we might also use implicature to avoid making ourselves too accountable for what we have said – in other words, to say something without 'really saying' it.

Of course, the fact that someone says something that is not true or is not entirely clear does not necessarily mean they are creating implicature. Sometimes people simply lie. In this case, you have not created any indirect meaning. Your meaning is very direct. It is just not true. Another example can be seen in the often-quoted exchange below from *The Pink Panther Strikes Again* (1976 United Artists):

> A: Does your dog bite?
> B: No.
> A: [Bends down to stroke it and gets bitten] Ow! I thought you said your dog did not bite.
> B: That is not my dog.

Here, A has violated the maxim of quantity by saying too little, but in doing so, he has *not* created implicature. He has simply said too little. And so for the flouting of a maxim to be meaningful, it must be done within the overall framework of the cooperative principle. The person flouting a maxim must expect that the other person will realise that they are flouting the maxim and that the meaning created by this is not too difficult to figure out.

How we do things with words

Another important aspect of pragmatics concerns how people accomplish various social actions when they talk, such as requesting, promising and threatening. The philosopher John Austin pointed out that certain utterances, when they are spoken, have the effect of actually performing some action in the physical world. When the officiant at a wedding ceremony, for example, says, 'I now pronounce you husband and wife', it is by this *pronouncement* that the couple becomes married, and when a judge says, 'I sentence you to five years in prison', it is by this utterance that the person to whom this is uttered is *sentenced*. Austin called these kinds of utterances **performatives**.

The more Austin thought about this idea of performatives, the more he realised that many utterances – not just those containing phrases such as 'I pronounce ...' and 'I declare ...' and 'I command ...' – have a performative function. If somebody says to you, 'Cigarette smoking is dangerous to your health', for example, he or she is usually not just making a statement. He or she is also *doing* something, that is, *warning* you not to smoke. In fact, Austin concluded, whenever we talk, we are almost always trying to do something with our words – such as to inform, apologise, console, explain, request, threaten or warn.

While Austin's insight might seem rather obvious now, it was quite revolutionary at the time he was writing, when most philosophers of language were mainly focused on analysing sentences in terms of whether or not they were 'true'. Austin pointed out that, for many utterances, their 'truth value' is not as important as whether or not they are able to perform the action they are intended to perform.

Austin called these utterances that perform actions **speech acts**. The important thing about these kinds of utterances, he said, is not so much their 'meaning' as their 'force', their ability to perform actions. All speech acts have three kinds of force: **locutionary force**, the force of what the words actually mean; **illocutionary force**, the force of the action the words are intended to perform; and **perlocutionary force**, the force of the actual effect of the words on listeners.

One of the problems with analysing speech acts is that, for many of the same reasons that speakers express meanings indirectly by flouting conversational maxims, they also express speech acts indirectly. In other words, the *locutionary force* of their speech act (the meaning of the words) might be very different from the *illocutionary force* (what they are actually doing with their words). We have already discussed a number of examples of this, such as the question 'Do you have a pen?' uttered to perform the act of requesting (see A1).

And so the problem is, how do we figure out what people are trying to *do* with their words? For Austin, the main way we do this is by logically analysing the conditions under which a particular utterance is produced. He called the ability of an utterance to perform a particular action the 'felicity' (or 'happiness') of the utterance, and in order for speech acts to be 'happy', certain kinds of conditions must be met, which Austin called **felicity conditions**.

Some of these conditions relate to what is said. For some speech acts to be felicitous, for example, they must be uttered in a certain conventional way. The officiant at a wedding must say something very close to 'I now pronounce you husband and wife' or 'I now pronounce you spouses for life' in order for this to be a pronouncement of marriage. Some of the conditions have to do with who utters the speech act – the kind of authority or identity they have. Only someone specially empowered to do so, for instance, is able to perform marriages. If a random person walked up to you and your companion on the street and said, 'I now pronounce you spouses for life', this would not be considered a felicitous pronouncement of marriage. Some of these conditions concern the person or people to whom the utterance is addressed. They must generally be able to decipher the speech act and comply with it. People under a certain age, for example, cannot get married, and so the pronouncement of marriage given above would not succeed as a speech act. Similarly, if the two people to whom this pronouncement is uttered are not willing to get married, the pronouncement would also lack felicity. Finally, some of these conditions may have to do with the time or place the utterance is issued. Captains of ships, for example, are only empowered to make pronouncements of marriage aboard their ships.

And so, according to Austin and his followers, the main way we figure out what people are trying to do when they speak to us is by trying to match the conditions in which an utterance is made to the conditions necessary for particular kinds of speech acts. So, when somebody comes up to me in a bar and says, 'Hey mate, I suggest you leave my girlfriend alone', I use my logic to try to figure out what he is doing and what he is trying to get me to do. At first, I might think that he is making a suggestion to me. But, when I consider the conditions of the situation, I realise that this utterance does not fulfil the necessary conditions of a suggestion, one of which is that whether or not I follow the suggestion is optional. I can tell quite clearly from the expression on this fellow's face that what he is 'suggesting' is not optional. I also realise that there will probably be unpleasant consequences for me should I fail to comply. Given these conditions, I can only conclude that what he is doing with his words is not making a suggestion but issuing a threat.

The important thing about this example is that I must use both of the tools introduced above. I must make use of the cooperative principle to realise that he is flouting the maxim of quality (he is not making a suggestion) and that there must be some reason for this, and I must be able to analyse the conditions in which this utterance is made to figure out what the speaker is actually trying to do.

Sense and sequencing: conversation analysis

Whereas pragmatics begins with the assumption that conversations are logical, *conversation analysis* begins with the assumption that they are *orderly*. What *orderly* means is that they follow a certain predictable pattern, with some kinds of utterances necessarily coming before or following other kinds of utterances.

Conversation analysts also see utterances as *actions*. Where they differ is in their ideas about how we interpret these actions – what gives 'force' to our words. Whereas followers of Austin consider the speaker's intentions and the conditions under which the words are uttered to be the most important things, conversation analysts consider the utterance that occurred *prior* to the utterance in question, and the one that occurs *afterwards* to be more important. In other words, they believe we interpret utterances chiefly based on how they 'fit' sequentially with other utterances in a conversation.

The core of conversation analysis, then, is the exploration of the sequential structure of conversation. According to Schegloff and Sacks (1973), social interaction is often arranged in pairs of utterances – what one person says basically determines what the next person can say. They call these sequences of 'paired actions' **adjacency pairs**. Examples of common adjacency pairs are 'question/answer', 'invitation/acceptance', and 'greeting/greeting'.

The most important thing about the two utterances that make up an adjacency pair is that they have a relationship of **conditional relevance**. In other words, one utterance is dependent on (*conditioned by*) the other utterance. The first utterance determines what the second utterance can be (e.g. a question should be followed by an answer, and a greeting should be followed by a greeting). In the same way, the second utterance also determines what the first utterance has been understood to be. If I have given you an answer, this provides evidence that I have taken your preceding utterance to be a question. This is a big difference between conversation analysis and the speech act theory of Austin. For speech act theory, the conditions for whether or not an utterance constitutes a particular speech act include things such as the intentions and identities of the speakers and the context of the situation. For conversation analysts, the conditions that determine how an utterance should be interpreted must exist *within the conversation itself*.

At the same time, conversation analysis also focuses on how speakers make use of the default expectations people bring to conversations in order to make meaning. The main difference is that the kinds of expectations they are concerned with are not so much about the *content* of utterances (whether or not, for example, they are 'true' or 'clear'), but rather about the *structure* of conversation and particularly the ways that utterances should 'fit' with previous utterances. The idea behind adjacency pairs is that when one person says something, he or she creates a 'slot' for the next person to 'fill in' in a particular way. If they fill it in in the expected way, this is called a **preferred response**. If they do not fill in this slot in the expected way, their interlocutor 'hears' the preferred response as being **officially absent**. As Schegloff (1968: 1083) put it:

> Given the first, the second is expectable. Upon its occurrence, it can be seen to be the second item to the first. Upon its non-occurrence, it can be seen to be officially absent.

Take, for example, the following exchange between a couple:

A: I love you.
B: Thank you.

The reason this exchange seems odd to us, and undoubtedly seems odd to A, is that the preferred response to an expression of love is a reciprocal expression of love. When this response is not given, it creates *implicature*. Thus, the most important thing about B's response is not the meaning that he expresses (gratitude), but the meaning that is *absent* from the utterance.

All first utterances in adjacency pairs are said to have a 'preferred' second utterance. For example, the preferred response to an invitation is an acceptance. The preferred response to a greeting is a greeting. What makes a preferred response preferred is not that the person who offered the first utterance would 'prefer' this response (the preferred response for an accusation, for example, is a denial), but rather that this is the response which usually requires the least additional conversational work. So the preferred response is the most *efficient* response. When we issue **dispreferred responses**, we often have to add something to them in order to avoid producing unintended implicature. For example, if you ask me to come to your party and I accept your invitation, all I have to do is say 'Sure!'. But if I want to refuse the invitation, I cannot just say 'No!' If I do, I create the implicature that I do not much like you or care about your feelings. If I want to avoid communicating this, I have to supplement it with other things such as an apology ('I'm really sorry ...') and an excuse or account of why I cannot come to your party ('I have to do my discourse analysis homework'). I might even try to avoid saying 'No' altogether and just offer apologies and excuses, leaving it to you to infer that I will not be attending.

You can divide almost any conversation into a series of adjacency pairs. Sometimes, though, adjacency pairs can be quite complicated, with pairs of utterances overlapping or being embedded in other pairs of utterances. Nevertheless, for conversation analysts, it is this underlying 'pairwise organisation' of utterances that helps us to make sense of our conversations and use them to accomplish actions in an orderly way.

Apart from being organised in pairs of utterances, conversations also tend to have predictable overall structures. They can be divided into 'stages' or 'phases' based on the kind of 'conversational work' people are doing. The two 'phases' conversation analysts are most concerned with are **openings** – in which people generally ratify their relationship by greeting each other and engage in ritual exchanges such as A: 'How are you?' B: 'I'm fine, and you?' as a way to ease into the conversation and negotiate what they are going to be talking about by opening up **slots** for the other person to introduce a topic – and **closings** – which are usually prepared for with some kind of 'preclosing' comments like, 'Anyway, I've got to get to class' as well as 'empty' adjacency pairs like A: 'Okay', B: 'Okay', which are designed to make sure that the other person does not want to introduce a new topic before goodbyes are exchanged. Sometimes closings are particularly difficult due to the 'back-and-forth' nature of conversation, which makes it difficult to resist filling in a slot created by the other person. In the case of the adjacency pair: A: 'Goodbye', B: 'Goodbye', this is particularly tricky since the second part of the pair can also function as the first part of a new pair. In other words, even seemingly simple exchanges like openings and closings can be quite complicated and usually require more than one adjacency pair to complete. An example is the section below of one part of the closing of a phone conversation between Charles, Prince of Wales and his girlfriend Camilla Parker Bowles (from Channell 1997: 168–169)

> *A:* Love you.
> *B:* Don't want to say goodbye.
> *A:* Neither do I, but we must get some sleep.
> *B:* Bye.
> *A:* Bye, darling.
> *B:* Love you.
> *A:* Bye.
> *B:* Hopefully talk to you in the morning.
> *A:* Please.
> *B:* Bye.
> *A:* I do love you.
> *B:* Night.
> *A:* Night.
> *B:* Night.
> *A:* Love you forever.
> *B:* Night.
> *A:* G'bye.
> *B:* Bye my darling.
> *A:* Night.
> *B:* Night, night.

A: Night.
B: Bye bye.
A. Going.
B: Bye.
A: Going.
B: Gone.
A: Night.

There is, of course, a lot more to both pragmatics and conversation analysis than has been covered in this brief summary. Pragmatics, for example, has much more to say about the various cognitive models that people bring to interaction, and conversation analysis has much to say about how people manage things such as turn-taking, topic negotiation, openings and closings and repair in conversations. What we have focused on here is primarily how each of these approaches addresses the problem of ambiguity in spoken discourse – the problem that people do not always say what they mean or mean what they say.

⊚ **Find more examples of the texture of talk on the companion website.**

B6 NEGOTIATING RELATIONSHIPS AND ACTIVITIES

Power and politeness

Whenever we interact with others, we always communicate something about our relationship with them. We do this by using various discursive strategies, which, as I said in unit A6, we can divide into two categories: *involvement strategies* and *independence strategies*. *Involvement strategies* are strategies people use to communicate friendliness or solidarity, and *independence strategies* are strategies people use to communicate respect or deference.

In many cases, both parties in an interaction share a fairly clear idea about how close they are and whether one has more power than the other, but in other cases, participants in interaction need to negotiate their relationship. Such negotiations are common, for example, as people move from more distant to closer relationships, or when one person wishes to challenge another person's assertion of power or dominance.

Regardless of whether or not a relationship is seen as 'negotiable', we always approach interactions with certain sets of expectations about how independence and involvement strategies will be used to communicate information about power and intimacy. We call these expectations **face systems**. Although expectations about when *independence* and *involvement strategies* are appropriate and what they mean vary across cultures and groups, most people enter interaction with three basic ideas: (1) In interactions where the parties are socially distant but relatively equal, both parties are likely to use independence strategies (**deference face system**); (2) in interactions where people are close and relatively equal, they are likely to use involvement strategies (**solidarity face system**); and (3) in interactions in which one person has more power than the other (regardless of their social distance), the more powerful one is more likely to use involvement strategies and the less powerful one is more likely to use independence strategies (**hierarchical face system**).

Like the conversational maxims we discussed in the last section, these 'systems' should not be treated as 'rules' but rather as broad sets of expectations people draw on to decide how to act towards other people and how to interpret others' behaviour towards them. Since power and distance are relative rather than absolute, and because interaction often involves the sometimes subtle use of power and distance, people usually employ both independence and involvement strategies, mixing them tactically depending on the situation and what they are trying to accomplish.

An example of the way participants strategically mix independence and involvement strategies can be seen in the following conversation between a senior engineer (Martin) and his subordinate (Ollie) reported in Ladegaard (2011):

Martin:	happy birthday or (0.2) whatever it is (laughing)
Ollie:	thank you (0.2) it's actually a while ago
Martin:	okay eh: Ollie//
Ollie:	//there's Danish pastry over there if you're interested (0.2)
Martin:	thanks ah: (0.6) (talks about tape recorder)
Martin:	okay well to cut a long story short Sam called (0.2) and I'm not sure how busy you are or what you're doing right now (0.4)
Ollie:	ah: we're just about to launch the [name] project and ah:
Martin:	okay
Ollie:	so this is where we are [xxx] quite busy (0.5) but Sam called you said
Martin:	yes (0.2)
Ollie:	and he? (0.3)
Martin:	he needs some help here and now (0.2) he needs someone to calculate the price of rubber bands (0.3) for the [name] project in India
Ollie:	okay
Martin:	they expect the customer to sign today (1.3)
Ollie:	okay

(Ladegaard 2011: 14–15)

In this example, Martin, the more powerful participant, begins using involvement strategies, wishing Ollie happy birthday (although it is not his birthday) and laughing. Ollie, on the other hand, though friendly, uses more independence strategies, accepting the inappropriate birthday wish and then using words such as 'actually' and 'a while' to soften his revelation that it is not his birthday, and then offering Martin some pastry in a way which is designed not to impose on him ('if you're interested'). Were Martin and Ollie equals and friends, the inappropriate birthday wishes might have been answered in a more direct way, such as, 'What are you talking about? My birthday was ages ago!' and the offer of pastry might have been more insistent (Have some Danish!). In other words, the configuration of involvement and independence strategies in the beginning of the conversation conforms with what one might expect in a hierarchical face system.

What happens next in the conversation, however, is rather interesting. Martin, the more powerful person, changes to independence strategies, asking Ollie how busy he is and making it clear that he does not wish to impose on him. In fact, he acts so reluctant to make the request that Ollie practically has to drag it out of him ('but Sam called you said … and he?'). This, in fact, is the opposite of what one might expect in a hierarchical relationship. Of course, this shift in politeness strategies, with the more powerful participant using independence strategies and the less powerful one showing more involvement, does not really reflect a shift in power. Rather, it is a clever strategy Martin has used to make it more difficult for Ollie to refuse the request by putting him in the position of soliciting it.

The point of this analysis is that, even though our expectations about face systems form the background to how we communicate about relationships, people often strategically confound these expectations to their own advantage.

One further factor that determines which strategy a person will use to communicate his or her relationship with another person is the topic of the conversation he or she is engaged in. In cases in which the topic of the conversation is serious or potentially embarrassing for either party, or in which the weight of imposition is seen to be great, independence strategies will be more common, whereas in situations where the topic is less serious, the outcome more predictable and the weight of imposition seen to be relatively small, involvement strategies are more common.

As can be seen in the example above, rather than as simple reflections of *a priori* relationships of power and distance or the 'weightiness' of a particular topic, face strategies can be regarded as *resources* that people use to negotiate social distance, enact power relationships and sometimes manipulate others into doing things that they may not normally be inclined to do. A person might use involvement strategies with another not *because* they are close, but because he or she wants to *create* or strengthen the impression that there is a power difference. Similarly, a person might use independence strategies not to create a sense of distance from the person they are interacting with, but rather to endow the topic under discussion with a certain 'weightiness'. In other words, face strategies are not just reflections of the expectations about relationships that people bring to interactions but *resources* they make use of to manage and sometimes change those relationships on a moment-by-moment basis.

Framing and contextualisation cues

As we have seen above, conversational strategies such as involvement and independence are not just ways that we communicate and manage our relationships with other people, but also ways that we communicate something about what we are doing (e.g. the degree to which we think we are imposing on other people). We also have other ways of signalling to people what we think we are doing in an interaction, whether we, for example, are arguing, joking, commiserating or making small talk. Whenever we speak, in fact, we communicate not just the message contained in (or implied by) our words, but also information about what we think we are doing and, therefore, how our words should be interpreted. We call the signals we use to communicate this information **contextualisation cues**.

In unit A6, I said that there are basically two kinds of *frames*: broader *primary frameworks*, which consist of the relatively stable sets of expectations we bring to particular situations (such as lectures or medical consultations); and smaller, more dynamic *interactive frames*, which consist of our negotiated ideas about what we are doing moment by moment in a conversation, ideas that often change rapidly in the course of an interaction. Although *contextualisation cues* are often important in signalling *primary frameworks*, they are particularly important in the role they play in helping us to manage and negotiate *interactive frames*.

Sometimes contextualisation cues are verbal. We might, for example, use specific words to explicitly signal that we are shifting frames. One of the most obvious ways we signal frame shifts verbally is through what are known as **discourse markers**. These are words or phrases that often rather explicitly mark the end of one activity and the beginning of another. A lecturer, for example, might move from the pre-lecture chatting and milling around frame to the formal lecture frame with words such as '*Okay, let's get started …*'. Similarly, a doctor might move from small talk to the more formal medical examination by saying something such as '*So, how are you feeling?*' Discourse markers typically consist of words such as *okay, so, well* and *anyway*, as well as more formal connectors such as *first, next* and *however*. It is important to remember that discourse markers do not *always* signal a shift in frame – sometimes they signal other things, such as the relationship between one idea and another (see B2).

We also might signal frame shifts through our choice of topic, vocabulary, grammar or even the language that we use. For example, in her analysis of the talk of teachers in bilingual classrooms, Angel Lin (1996) has pointed out that when English teachers in Hong Kong are focusing on teaching, they tend to use English, but when they are engaged in reprimanding their students, they tend to switch to Cantonese.

Sometimes these verbal cues involve adopting a particular register or social language (see A4 and B4) or certain genres (see A3 and B3) associated with particular kinds of activities.

A doctor, for example, might begin a consultation with a period of small talk in which the language might be extremely informal and the topic might range from the weather to a local sports team before he or she 'shifts gears' and starts 'talking like a doctor'. Tannen and Wallat's (D6) example of the doctor who is examining a child while at the same time explaining the child's condition to the mother and addressing a group a medical students who will watch the interaction on video is a good example of how people use shifts in register to signal shifts in frame. In the excerpt below, Tannen and Wallat label the different registers the doctor is using: *teasing register* (addressed to the child), *reporting register* (addressed to the students) and *conversational register* (addressed to the mother):

[Teasing register]
Doctor: Let's see. Can you open up like this, Jody. Look.
            [Doctor opens her own mouth]
Child: Aaaaaaaaaaaaaah.
Doctor: Good. That's good.
Child: Aaaaaaaaaaaah.

[Reporting register]
Doctor: /Seeing/ for the palate, she has a high arched palate
Child: Aaaaaaaaaaaaaaaaaaaaaaaaah.
Doctor: But there's no cleft,
            [maneuvers to grasp child's jaw]

[Conversational register]
> ... what we'd want to look for is to see how she ... moves her palate ... Which may be some of the difficulty with breathing that we're talking about.

(Tannen and Wallat 1987: 209)

These verbal strategies are not the only ways, or even the most common ways, people signal what they are doing when they talk. *Contextualisation cues* also include *non-verbal* signals delivered through things such as gestures, facial expressions, gaze or use of space; and *paralinguistic* signals delivered through alterations in the pitch, speed, rhythm or intonation of our voices. For this reason, people who study frames and contextualisation cues often pay a lot of attention to marking things such as stress, intonation and pausing and even facial expressions, gestures and other movements when they produce transcripts of the conversations they are studying.

These non-verbal and paralinguistic contextualisation cues are sometimes much more subtle than verbal strategies and so are more easily misunderstood. The way they are used and interpreted might also vary considerably from group to group or even person to person. In one of his most famous studies, Gumperz (1982: 173–174) found a mismatch between the way South Asian servers in a staff canteen in a British airport used intonation as a contextualisation cue and the ways their British customers interpreted it. The South Asian servers used falling intonation when asking customers if they wanted gravy on their meat (consistent with the conventions of their variety of English), but the British customers, expecting the rising intonation they associated with a polite offer, interpreted the servers' behaviour as rude. What this example tells us is that contextualisation cues do not in themselves contain information about what we think we are doing – rather, they *activate* culturally conditioned assumptions about context, interactional goals and interpersonal relationships that might be different for different people.

There are many reasons why someone might shift frames in an interaction. They might do so simply to manage multiple tasks or multiple audiences. But sometimes they might use reframing strategically, changing the 'definition of the situation' (Goffman, 1974) as a way of getting the upper hand or delegitimising something their interlocutor is trying to do. Sometimes participants in an interaction will experience disagreement regarding 'what's going on'. The way one person frames the conversation, for example, may be at odds with the other person's wishes, expectations or interpretation of the situation. In some cases, they may simply accept the framing that has been imposed by the other person, or they may contest or resist it by either attempting to reframe the conversation using their own contextualisation cues or by breaking the frame altogether and engaging in a 'meta-conversation' about 'what's going on'.

In an early debate when he was running for president, Donald Trump was asked a question by moderator Megyn Kelly about the way he had talked about women in the past. 'You've called women you don't like "fat pigs", dogs and animals', she noted. 'How will you answer the charge ... that you are a part of the war on women?' Trump answered this question not by justifying or explaining his past comments, but by reframing the discussion from one about his own behaviour to one about 'political correctness':

> I think the big problem this country has is being politically correct. I've been challenged by so many people and I don't, frankly, have time for total political correctness. And to be honest with you, this country doesn't have time, either.

By 'reframing' the conversation as a conversation about how other people talk rather than how he has talked about women, Trump was able to deflect the question.

Reframing can also be used as a way to manage *face* (see above). In a famous article called 'Talking the Dog', Deborah Tannen (2004) shows how people sometimes use the frame of playfully talking to their dogs as a way to talking to other people who might be present without confronting them directly. In the example below, Clara uses playful talk with her dog Rickie to communicate to her husband her displeasure at him having left the door open:

> *Clara:*   You leave the door open for any reason?
>   ((short pause, sound of door shutting))
>   —> <babytalk> Rickie,
>   — > he's helpin' burglars come in,
>   —> and you have to defend us Rick.>
>
> (Tannen 2004: 413)

👁 **Find more examples of how people use face strategies and framing strategies on the companion website.**

THE SPEAKING MODEL   B7

Speech acts, speech events and speech situations

The main unit of analysis for the ethnography of speaking is the *speech event*, which can be defined as a communicative activity that has a clear beginning and a clear ending and in which people's shared understandings of the relevance of various contextual features remain fairly constant throughout the event. Examples of speech events are such things as religious ceremonies, lessons, debates and conversations. Speech events occur within broader speech situations and are made up of smaller *speech acts* of the type we have already discussed (including such things as greeting, questioning, promising and insulting, see B5). For example, a university lecture can be considered a *speech event* that occurs within the **speech situation** of a school day and is made up of smaller *speech acts* such as asking and answering questions, giving explanations and illustrations of certain concepts, and even joking or threatening. Similarly, the *speech event* of a conversation may occur within the larger *speech situation* of a party and may include smaller *speech acts* such as joking. Notice that the same speech act – joking, for example – can take place in many different kinds of speech events, and that different speech events – conversations, for example – can occur in many different kinds of speech situations.

What distinguishes a *speech event* from a *speech situation* is not just its size and the fact that speech events tend to have clearer boundaries. The main distinction is *coherence* (see B2): participants tend to approach speech events with consistent sets of expectations that remain the same throughout the speech event, whereas participants' expectations about the relevant features of context may undergo dramatic changes throughout a speech situation; students eating lunch at the university canteen during a school day, for example, are likely to pay attention to different sorts of things than they do in a lecture during the same day. The way to distinguish between a speech situation and a speech event, then, is to ask if the same rules of SPEAKING apply *throughout* the phenomenon. If so, it can be regarded as a speech event.

SPEAKING

One potentially confusing aspect of the ethnography of speaking is that it does not, as its name implies, focus so much on rules and expectations about *speaking* as on rules and expectations about the *circumstances* in which certain kinds of speaking takes place (or does not take place). In fact, one of the most famous studies using this approach, Keith Basso's examination of silence among the Western Apache in the United States (Basso, 1970), explored the conditions under which, for members of this speech community, *not speaking* is considered the most appropriate behaviour.

Ron and Suzanne Scollon have used the term 'the Grammar of Context' to refer to a model very much like Hymes's SPEAKING model (Scollon *et al.*, 2012). Their reasons for comparing the rules and expectations associated with context to the kinds of rules and expectations associated with the grammar of a language are twofold: first, to highlight that the same difference between competence and performance that we see in grammar also occurs in rules and expectations associated with context; and second, to introduce the notion of **markedness** into the analysis of context, the acknowledgement that not everyone performs in particular speech events exactly in accordance with how people in their speech community (including themselves) think they should.

The idea of 'unmarked' (the usual or normal way of saying or doing something) versus 'marked' (an unusual or deviant way of saying or doing something) was introduced into structural linguistics by the Prague School of linguists, which included such figures as Roman Jakobson (see Jakobson 1990: 134–40). Although the concept is quite complex, the general idea is that when people deviate from the default or expected way of using language, the result is often the expression of some special, more precise or additional meaning. This is an idea we have already encountered in our discussion of the *cooperative principle*. When it is applied to 'context', it reminds us that communicative competence does not refer to a set of 'rules' that must be followed, but rather to a set of expectations that experienced speakers can sometimes manipulate in order to strategically manage the meanings of speech acts, the relationships among participants or the outcomes of the speech event.

The components of the SPEAKING model devised by Hymes, therefore, are not meant to provide an objective list of those elements of context which need to be taken into account by the analyst, but rather a set of guidelines an analyst can use in attempting to find out what aspects of context are important and relevant *from the point of view of participants*. In other words, in any given speech event, different elements will be afforded different weight by participants, and some might be regarded as totally unimportant.

The first component in the model is **setting**, which refers to the time and place of the speech event as well as any other physical circumstances. Along with the physical aspects of setting, Hymes included what he called the 'psychological setting' or the 'cultural definition' of a scene. The unmarked setting for a particular speech event, for example, might be in a church. A church has particular physical characteristics, but it is also likely to have certain associations for people in a particular culture so that when they enter a church they are predisposed to speak or behave in certain ways. Thus, the component of setting can have an effect on other components such as *key* and *instrumentalities* (see below).

The second component in the SPEAKING model is **participants**. Most of the approaches to spoken discourse we have looked at so far, including conversation analysis and pragmatics, begin with the assumption of an essentially dyadic model of communication in which the participants are the speaker and the hearer. Ethnographic work, however, indicates that many, if not most, speech events involve many kinds of participants, not just speakers and hearers but also participants such as audiences and bystanders. Furthermore, groups differ in their ideas of which participants in speech events are considered legitimate or relevant (for example, domestic helpers, pets, supernatural beings). Besides identifying the relevant participants, the different kinds of identities, roles and rights different participants have are also important. These aspects, of course, will depend on things such as the *genre* of the speech event and may change over the course of the speech event in accordance with a particular *act sequence* (see below).

The third component of the model is **ends**, which refers to the purpose, goals and outcomes of the event, which, of course, may be different for different participants (e.g. the goals of a teacher are not always the same as the goals of his or her students); and the fourth component is **act sequence**, the form the event takes as it unfolds, including the order of different speech acts and other behaviours. Both of these components are intimately connected not just with expectations about participant roles, but also with the *genre* of the speech event.

The fifth component in the model is **key**, by which is meant the overall 'tone' or mood of the speech event. Key is important because it provides an attitudinal context for speech acts, sometimes dramatically altering their meaning (as with sarcasm). At the same time, key is often signalled in very subtle ways using resources like tone of voice, facial expression and bodily posture. We have already explored some of these signals in our discussion of *contextualisation cues* in B6.

The sixth component is **instrumentalities**, meaning the 'message form' – the means or media through which meaning is made. Speech, for example, might be spoken, sung, chanted or shouted, and it may be amplified through microphones, broadcast through electronic media or written down and passed back and forth between participants. Typically, speech events include complex combinations of instrumentalities that interact with one another and with the other components in the model. In the next unit on mediated discourse analysis, we will explore in more detail the effect different instrumentalities can have on speech acts and speech events.

The seventh component is **norms**, which can be divided into **norms of interaction** and **norms of interpretation**. These are the common sets of understandings that participants bring to events about what is appropriate behaviour and how different actions and utterances ought to be understood. The important thing about norms is that they may be different for different participants (a waiter versus a customer, for example) and that the setting of norms is often a matter of power and ideology (see A4).

Finally, the eighth component is genre, or the 'type' of speech event. We have already dealt at length with the concept of genre (see A3, B3) and, although Hymes's understanding of genre is slightly different from that of genre analysts like Swales and Bhatia, much of what was said before about community expectations, form and communicative purpose applies here. The most important aspect of this component is the notion that certain speech events are *recognisable* by members of a speech community as being of a certain type, and as soon as they are 'labelled' as such, many of the other components of the model such as ends, act sequence, participant roles and key are taken as givens.

It should be clear from this brief rundown of the components of the SPEAKING model that none of them can really be considered alone; each component interacts with other components in multiple ways. The most important job of an analyst using this model, then, is not just to determine the kinds of knowledge about the different components that members of speech communities need to successfully participate in a given speech event, but also to determine how the different components are linked together in particular ways for different speech events. For it is in these *linkages*, the ways, for example, different kinds of participants are associated with different genres, or different settings are seen as suitable for different purposes, or different forms of discourse or media are associated with different keys, that the analyst can begin to get an understanding of deeper *cultural assumptions* about people, places, values, power and communication itself that exist in a particular speech community.

> 👁 **Find examples of how the SPEAKING model can be applied to different speech events on the companion website.**

B8   MEDIATION

Cultural tools

The starting point for mediated discourse analysis is the concept of *mediation*. The traditional definition of mediation is the passing of a message through some *medium*, which is placed between two or more people who are communicating. When we think of *media*, we usually think of things such as newspapers, television and computers. Lots of people have pointed out that when messages pass through media, they change fundamentally. Different kinds of media favour different kinds of meanings. The kinds of meaning people can make in a newspaper article, for example, are different from those they can make in a television broadcast. This fact led the media scholar Marshall McLuhan (1964/2001) to make the famous pronouncement: 'the medium *is* the message'.

Mediated discourse analysis is also interested in how different media such as televisions and computers affect the way people use discourse, but it takes a rather broader view of media and mediation. This view comes from the work of the Russian psychologist Lev Vygotsky. Vygotsky (1981) had the idea that *all* actions that people take in the world are somehow mediated through what he called *cultural tools*. Cultural tools can include technological tools such as televisions, computers and megaphones, but also include more abstract tools such as languages, counting systems, diagrams and mental schema. Anything an individual uses to take action in the world can be considered a cultural tool.

The important thing about cultural tools is that they make it easier to perform some kinds of actions and communicate some kinds of meanings, and more difficult to take other kinds of actions and communicate other kinds of meanings. In other words, all tools come with certain **affordances** and **constraints**. Writing a letter or an email, for example, allows us to do things that we cannot do when we are producing spoken discourse in the context of a conversation, things such as going back and deleting or revising things we have written before. But it is more difficult to do other things such as gauge the reaction of other people to what we are writing as we are writing it (as we can do with spoken language in face-to-face conversations). A microphone makes it easier to talk to a large group of people, but more difficult to say something private to a person standing next to you (as some politicians have rather painfully learned). Messaging applications like WhatsApp make it easy to have a real-time conversation using writing, but more difficult to interrupt one's conversational partner in the middle of an utterance the way we can do in face-to-face conversations.

What this idea of *affordances* and *constraints* means for discourse analysis is that the kinds of discourse and other tools we have available to us affect the kinds of actions that we can take. Different genres (see A3, B3), for instance, such as dating site profiles, Facebook status updates and job application letters make some kinds of actions easier and others more difficult. It might be more difficult to convince an employer to hire you using the genre of a dating site profile, and it might be more difficult to attract a sexual partner using the genre of a job application letter. Different modes and media also allow us to do different things: we can perform different actions with pictures and gestures than we can with words (see A9, B9), and we can do different things with mobile telephones than we can with landlines.

When we perform mediated discourse analysis, we first identify the *actions* that are important to a particular social actor in a particular situation and then attempt to determine how the *cultural tools* (such as languages and other modes, media, genres and social languages) contribute to making these actions possible and making other kinds of actions impossible or more difficult. Of course, we also have to recognise that many of the cultural tools we use to perform actions are *not* discursive. If you want to put together a piece of furniture you have bought at Ikea, while some discourse such as the instructions for assembly or the conversation you have with your spouse or roommate while putting the furniture together might be very important, if you lack access to *technological tools* such as a hammer and a screwdriver, no amount of discourse can make it possible for you to perform the actions you need to perform.

This simple idea that having access to different kinds of tools makes it easier or more difficult to perform social actions has important implications. Earlier, for example, we discussed how people sometimes try to use discourse to advance certain ideologies or versions of reality in order to try to affect what people think. Mediated discourse analysis highlights the fact that discourse does not just have a role in affecting what we think, but also, in a very practical way, in affecting what we can do. If we do not have the proper tools available to us, there are certain things that we simply cannot do. And so people who have access to particular tools (such as languages, genres, electronic media) can often exert certain power over people who do not in very concrete ways. If we also consider that our social identities are *created* through the actions that we can take, we come to the conclusion that the tools we have available to us and how we use them help to determine not just what we can do, but also who we can be.

At the same time, human beings are extremely creative in their use of tools. If I do not have a screwdriver to put together my Ikea table, I might try using a butter knife. If the genre of the résumé does not allow me to showcase my talents, I might try to bend that genre or blend it with another genre. In fact, one important focus of mediated discourse analysis is exploring the *tension* that exists between the affordances and constraints built into different cultural tools and the ways people creatively *appropriate* and *adapt* those tools into different situations to achieve different goals.

Context revisited: sites of engagement

Mediated discourse analysts call the situations into which tools are appropriated **sites of engagement**. Sites of engagement are moments when different kinds of social actors, different kinds of cultural tools and different kinds of social relationships come together to make certain actions possible.

Previously we have explored the importance of 'context' in the production of meaning (see A7, A8). The problem with the idea of 'context' from the point of view of mediated discourse analysis is that it takes 'texts' as its reference point. The concept of *sites of engagement* takes social actions as its reference point. Instead of making an artificial distinction between discourse and everything else, it considers all cultural tools (texts, furniture, objects, machines) that are available to social actors at a particular time in a particular place and explores how they contribute to making possible certain kinds of actions.

Ron and Suzanne Wong Scollon (2004) say that all social actions occur at the *nexus* or 'coming together' of three crucial elements: (1) the discursive resources and other cultural tools that people have available for action (which they call **discourses in place**); (2) the social relationships among the people involved (which they call the **interaction order**); and (3) the knowledge, abilities and experiences of the individual social actor (which they call the **historical body**).

To illustrate how these three elements come together to form the *site of engagement* of a social action we can take the example of crossing a busy city street (see Figure B8.1). There is normally a lot of discourse available to people in this situation. There are things such as street signs, traffic signals and zebra stripes painted on the pavement to assist pedestrians in crossing the street; there is also a lot of discourse such as shop signs and advertisements that might actually interfere with the action of successfully crossing the street. And so one of the most important things for people engaged in performing this action is determining which discourse to attend to and which discourse to ignore.

The second element is the interaction order, the relationships people have with the people with whom they are crossing the street. If we are crossing the street alone, for example, we might take extra care in checking for oncoming traffic, whereas if we are part of a large crowd of people, we might pay more attention to the actions of other pedestrians to decide when to cross simply by following them. If we are with someone

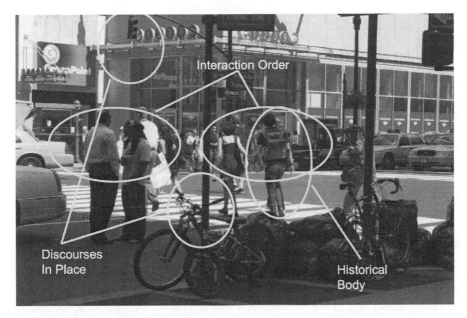

Figure B8.1 Crossing the street.

else, we might find we need to distribute our attention between the action of crossing the street and some other action such as carrying on a conversation or making sure our companion (e.g. if they are a small child) gets across the street safely.

Finally, the action of crossing the street depends on people's knowledge and experience of crossing city streets, the habits and mental models they have built up around this social practice, which the Scollons refer to as the historical body. Most of the time we do things such as crossing the street in a rather automatic way. When we find ourselves in unfamiliar situations, however, our habitual ways of doing things sometimes do not work so well. Most of us have found ourselves having some difficulty crossing streets in cities where conventions about which discourses in place pedestrians ought to attend to or what kind of behaviour is expected from drivers are different from those in the city in which we live.

And so the main differences between the ideas of 'site of engagement' and 'context' are, first, that while 'contexts' take 'texts' as their points of reference, sites of engagement take *actions* as their points of reference; and second, that while contexts are usually considered to be external to the social actor, sites of engagement are a matter of the *interaction* among the texts and other cultural tools available in a social situation, the people that are present, and the habits, expectations and goals of those people.

Discourse itineraries

It should be obvious from the above example that the people (historical bodies), relationships (interaction orders) and discourse in place are not stable; they change over time. They have their own histories, and these historical trajectories also affect how they interact at sites of engagement. The street signs or even the physical configuration of an intersection may change over time in response to traffic patterns: our under-standing of the best strategy to use for crossing at a particular intersection is different the first time we cross there and the hundredth time, and our relationship with the people we are with also changes; a parent, for example, will cross the street differently with a five-year-old child and a fifteen-year-old child.

Scollon (2008) calls these historical trajectories 'discourse itineraries'; they are the paths people, texts and relationships travel along, accumulating different meanings along the way. One problem with these itineraries is that often they are invisible to us when we are actually using texts, which sometimes makes it difficult for us to use them in ways that help us to meet our goals. In the excerpt reprinted in D8, for example, Jones talks about the difficulty he has in interpreting the label on a box of microwave popcorn without understanding the 'discourse itineraries' that have contributed to it being written the way it is.

👁 **Find more examples of mediated discourse analysis on the companion website.**

B9   MODES, MEANING AND ACTION

As discussed in unit A9, *multimodal discourse analysis*, the analysis of how multiple modes of communication interact when we communicate, can be divided into two broad approaches, one that focuses on 'texts' (such as magazines and web pages) and one that focuses on 'real time' interactions. One important concept that is common to both of these approaches is the idea that different modes have different *affordances* and *constraints*. Different modes have different sets of 'meaning potential' and allow us to take different kinds of actions.

In written text and spoken language, for example, we must present information in a sequential way governed by the logic of time. Thus, an author or speaker can manipu-late the order and speed at which information is given out, perhaps withholding cer-tain facts until later in the text or conversation for strategic purposes. Images, on the other hand, are governed by the logic of space. The producer of the image presents all of the elements in the image all at once and has limited control over the order in which viewers look at those elements. At the same time, whereas images allow for the com-munication of very fine gradations of meaning when it comes to things such as shape and colour – the exact shade of pink in someone's cheeks, for example – language forces us to represent things in terms of *types* – the word 'pink', for example, cannot represent an exact colour, but only a range of colours within a particular class.

The fact that different modes make some kinds of meaning more possible and others less possible is one of the reasons why people strategically mix different modes when they are communicating, so that the constraints of one mode are balanced out by the affordances of others. While there are some things that 'just cannot be expressed in words', it might be possible to express them with a carefully timed facial expression or a carefully placed image.

Communicative functions of modes

In A4, I introduced Halliday's idea that language has three basic functions: it is used to represent our experience of the world; it is used to communicate something about the relationship between us and the people with whom we are communicating; and it is used to organise ideas, representations and other kinds of information in ways that people can make sense of. Halliday calls these three functions the *ideational function*, the *interpersonal function* and the *textual function*. Although these three functions were originally conceived of as a model for understanding language, Kress and van Leeuwen insist that they provide a useful starting point for studying all modes. In their book *Reading Images: The Grammar of Visual Design*, they explore how images also fulfil these three functions but do so in a rather different way than language (see D9).

Ideational function

As noted in A4, the ideational function of language is accomplished through the linking together of *participants* (typically nouns) with *processes* (typically verbs), creating what Gee (2010) calls 'whos doing whats'. In images, on the other hand, participants are generally portrayed as *figures*, and the processes that join them together are portrayed visually.

Images can be **narrative**, representing figures engaged in actions or events; **classificatory**, representing figures in ways in which they are related to one another in terms of similarities and differences or as representatives of 'types'; or **analytical**, representing figures in ways in which parts are related to wholes.

In narrative images, *action processes* are usually represented by what Kress and van Leeuwen call **vectors**, compositional elements that indicate the directionality of an action. In Figure B9.1, for example, the arm of the boxer on the left extending rightward towards the head of the other boxer portrays the process of 'hitting'. There are also other processes portrayed. For example, the upward gazes of the figures in the background create vectors connecting the spectators with the fighters.

Like this image, many images actually represent multiple processes simultaneously. Figure B9.2, for example, also involves action processes: the process of taking a photograph and the process of 'posing' for a photograph. At the same time, the expressions on the faces of the people in the photo represent mental processes: the look on the woman's face suggesting a concentrated focus on the act of taking the picture, and the look on the man's face communicating amiable confidence. That is not to say that he really is amiable or confident. Whether we are communicating with photographs or with our bodies, we are always using the resources available to send a certain kind of message to others.

Interpersonal function

Another important function of any mode is to create and maintain some kind of relationship between the producer of the message and its recipient. As discussed in units A4 and B4, in language these relationships are usually created through the language's system of modality, as well as through the use of different *social languages* or *registers*.

Figure B9.1 Warriors (photo credit Claudio Gennari).

Figure B9.2 Selfie (credit Robert Couse-Baker).

Figure B9.3 Child (photo credit Denis Mihailov).

In images, viewers are placed into relationships with the figures in the image and, by extension, the producers of the image, through devices such as perspective and gaze. The image of the child in Figure B9.3 illustrates both of these devices. The camera angle positions the viewer above the child rather than on the same level, creating the perspective of an adult and the child's direct gaze into the camera creates a sense of intimacy with the viewer, though the expression on the child's face does denote some degree of uncertainty. Another important device for expressing the relationship between the viewer and the figures in an image is how close or far away they appear. Long shots tend to create a more impersonal relationship, whereas close-ups tend to create a feeling of psychological closeness along with physical closeness.

Cell phones with cameras in the front have created a range of new possibilities for the creation of interpersonal meaning and perspective. In Figure B9.4, for example, the photographer is able to create multiple perspectives for the viewer. The image is of the photographer taking a selfie. The direct gaze of a selfie, however, is slightly different from the direct gaze of the image above, since the figure in the photograph is looking simultaneously at the viewer and at him or herself. This image, however, also includes the shadow of another figure taking a photo of the first figure, which creates for the viewer the perspective of being a photographer documenting someone taking a selfie. Finally, the hand holding the phone on which the picture is displayed creates a third perspective for the viewer, the perspective of someone looking at a selfie after it has been taken.

'Modality' in images is partially realised by how 'realistic' the image seems to the viewer. Photographs, for example, generally attest more strongly to the 'truth' of a representation than drawings or paintings. However, this is not always the case. Scientific diagrams and sketches, for example, are often regarded as having even more 'authority' than photographs, and black-and-white photographs like those often found in newspapers are often regarded as more 'realistic' than highly saturated colour images in magazine advertisements. The 'filters' that are now part of most standard photo apps can also affect the modality of images. Changing a colour photo to black and white,

Figure B9.4 Selfie II (photo credit hannesdesmet).

for example, might make it seem more 'real' because of the association with traditional news photography, and sepia tones can give the image a nostalgic or 'retro' feeling.

Textual function

As I said above, while texts are organised in a linear fashion based on sequentiality, images are organised spatially. Figures in an image, for example, can be placed in the centre or periphery of the image, on the top or the bottom, the left or the right, and in the foreground or in the background. Although producers of images have much less control than producers of written texts over how viewers 'read' the image, they can create pathways for the viewer's gaze by, for example, placing different figures in different places within the frame and making some more prominent and others less prominent.

One obvious way to do this is by creating a distinction between foreground and background, with the figures that seem closer to the viewer generally commanding more prominence. Another way is to place one or more figures in the centre of the image and others on the margins. Many images make use of the centre/margin distinction to present one figure or piece of information as the centre or 'nucleus' of the image and the marginal figures as somehow dependent upon or subservient to the central figure (Kress and van Leeuwen 2006).

Two other important distinctions in the composition of images, according to Kress and van Leeuwen (2006), are the distinction between the left side and the right side of the image, and the distinction between the upper part and the lower part. Taking as their starting point Halliday's idea that in language, 'given' information (information that the reader or hearer is already familiar with) tends to appear at the beginning of clauses, and new information tends to appear closer to the end of clauses, they posit that, similarly, the left side of an image is more likely to contain 'given' information and the right side to contain 'new' information. This is based on the assumption that people tend to 'read' images in the same way they read texts, starting at the left and moving towards the right. This, of course, may be different for people from speech communities that are accustomed to reading text from right to left or from top to bottom.

The distinction between the upper part of an image and the lower part is related to the strong metaphorical connotations of 'up' and 'down' in many cultures (Lakoff and Johnson 1980). According to Kress and van Leeuwen, the top part of the image is often used for more 'ideal', generalised, or abstract information, and the bottom for 'real', specific and concrete information. They give as an example advertisements in which the upper section usually shows 'the "promise of the product", the status of glamour it can bestow on its users' and the lower section tends to provide factual information such as where the product can be obtained (2006: 186).

The strategic use of the textual function can often be seen in the way information is arranged in 'infographics,' texts that often combine narrative, classificatory and analytical genres. Figure B9.5, for example, is divided into two halves, each populated with human-like figures meant to represent different kinds of people (men, women, those who have and have not been sexually assaulted, false rape accusers and rapists).

The information in this chart is strategically arranged so that as we move our eyes from left to right we move from the 'given' (more familiar) information (women → women who have been sexually assaulted) to the 'new' (less familiar) information (men who have been sexually assaulted), creating the message: 'just as women are victims of sexual assault, so are men'. At the same time, the text at the top part of the

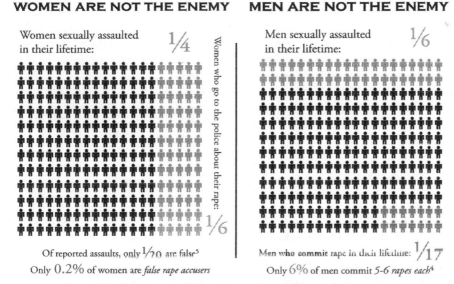

Figure B9.5 Rape infographic (photo credit Snipegirl).

image talks about 'ideal' men and women who 'are not the enemy', and the text at the bottom of the image informs us who the 'real' enemy is.

Multimodality in interaction

Modes in face-to-face interaction such as gaze and gesture also fulfil these three functions. The mode of gaze, for example, has an obvious *interpersonal* function, creating a relationship between the gazer and whomever or whatever is the object of the gaze. It also carries *ideational* meaning, conveying that the gazer is looking at, watching or paying attention to something. Finally, gaze is often an important *textual* resource, helping people to manage things such as turn-taking in conversations.

While the 'inter-modal' relationships (the ways multiple modes work together) in static texts such as those analysed above can be complicated, they can be even more complicated in dynamic interactions. One of the problems with analysing real-time, face-to-face interactions is that participants have so many modes available to them to make meaning. There are what Norris (2004) calls 'embodied' modes such as gaze, gesture, posture, head movement, proxemics (the distance one maintains from his or her interlocutor), spoken language and prosody (features of stress and intonation in a person's voice). And there are also 'disembodied' modes such as written texts, images, signs, clothing, the layout of furniture and the architectural arrangement of rooms and other spaces in which the interaction takes place. All of these different modes organise meaning differently. Some, such as spoken language and gaze, tend to operate *sequentially*, while others, such as gesture and prosody, tend to operate *globally*, often helping to create the context in which other modes such as spoken language are to be interpreted (see section B6). Not all of these modes are of equal importance to participants at any given moment in the interaction. In fact, different modes are likely to take on different degrees of importance at different times. How, then, is the analyst to determine which modes to focus on in a multimodal analysis?

Norris (2004) solves this problem by adopting the practice of *mediated discourse analysis* (see A8 and B8) and taking *action* as her unit of analysis. Thus, in determining which modes to focus on, the analyst begins by asking what actions participants are engaged in and then attempts to determine which modes are being used to accomplish these actions.

As I said in unit A8, actions are always made up of smaller actions and themselves contribute to making up larger actions. Norris divides actions into three types: **lower-level actions**, the smallest pragmatic meaning units of communicative modes (including things such as gestures, postural shifts, gaze shifts and tone units); **higher-level actions** (such as 'having a cup of coffee'); and **frozen actions** (previously performed actions that are instantiated in material modes – e.g. a half-eaten plate of food or an unmade bed).

One of the goals of multimodal interaction analysis, then, is to understand how participants in interaction work cooperatively to weave together lower-level actions such as gestures, glances and head and body movements into higher-level actions and, in doing so, help to create and reinforce social practices, social relationships and social identities (see C9).

Transduction

The whole point of multimodality is that we rarely use only one mode together, and meaning is not just made through exploiting the resources of particular modes, but also in the way modes work together. Text, for example, is often used together with images to explain the image or comment on it, and lecturers commonly project writing on a screen behind them to clarify or summarise their spoken words.

Sometimes people try to communicate or 'translate' the meanings of one mode using a different mode. Kress (1997) calls this process **transduction**. For example, verbs in a verbal description of an action might be translated into vectors in a drawing of that action, or we might attempt to communicate the taste of a sandwich we are eating through the sounds we make when we are chewing. Shifting across modes can be tricky. It requires us to use different semiotic resources but, at the same time, to retain consistency of meaning. One particular *genre* where transduction is particularly evident is in what is known as ASMR videos on YouTube. ASMR stands for *autonomous sensory meridian response*, and it refers to a kind of physical sensation that is triggered by certain kinds of sounds or images. In these videos people try to use sound effects and representations of action to communicate things like textures and physical feelings.[3]

👁 **Find more examples of the communicative functions of different modes and how they work together on the companion website.**

PROCEDURES FOR CORPUS-ASSISTED DISCOURSE ANALYSIS

B10

Conducting a corpus-assisted discourse analysis requires a number of steps, which include building a corpus, cleaning and tagging the corpus, analysing the corpus with computer tools using a number of procedures and, finally, interpreting the data. These last two steps tend to be cyclical and recursive. That is, usually the results of several procedures need to be combined when we are interpreting the data, and often our interpretations lead us to re-performing these procedures or performing other procedures.

The first step in building a corpus is deciding what kinds of texts you want to include in it and making sure that you can include a representative sample of those kinds of texts. For very specialised corpora, such as the works of a particular author, this is easy since there are a limited number of texts and you can simply include them all. This is more difficult the less specific the corpus is. For example, if you want to build a corpus of business letters, you need to decide what kind of letters (sales letters, complaint letters, etc.) you want to include and what kinds of company these letters will come from. You might choose texts based on some predetermined criteria such as topic or the inclusion of some keyword. Baker, in his study on the representation of Muslims in British newspapers reprinted in section D10, for example, chose the texts for his corpus on the basis of whether or not they contained the words referring to Muslims or Islam.

Another important decision is how many texts you are going to include in your corpus. Generally, with corpus-assisted analysis, the bigger the corpus, the easier it will be for you to make generalisations from your results. However, it is also possible to have very small corpora.

You will probably also need a **reference corpus**. A reference corpus is another corpus that you will compare your primary corpus with. It is usually made up of a broader spectrum of texts or conversations than the corpus you are analysing.

You might, for example, use one of the large corpora such as the British National Corpus, or you might choose another specialised corpus with a broader sample of texts.

Nowadays it is actually quite easy to build a corpus since so many texts are already in electronic format on the Internet. But it is important that you go through these texts carefully and take out any HTML code or formatting that might have been attached to them, which might interfere with your analysis. You also might want to attach new code to certain parts of the text or to certain words to aid your analysis. This latter process is called *tagging*. Analysts, for example, sometimes insert code to indicate different parts of a text (such as introduction, body and conclusion), and others tag individual words based on their grammatical function so they can detect grammatical patterns in their analysis along with lexical patterns. It is important that each text in your corpus is saved in a separate text file.

The analysis of the corpus is carried out with a computer program, and there are a number of such programs available from the Internet. The most widely used commercial programs are called WordSmith Tools (http://www.lexically.net/wordsmith/index.html) and Sketch Engine (https://www.sketchengine.co.uk/), but there is also a very good free program available called AntConc, developed by Laurence Anthony, which works on both Windows and Macintosh operating systems (http://www.laurenceanthony.net/software/antconc/). In the explanations and examples below, I will describe how to perform the relevant procedures using AntConc.

After your corpus has been cleaned and tagged, you need to import it in the form of text files into your analysis program. In AntConc, this is done by using the commands File < Open File(s) (or Ctrl F). You may choose as many files as you wish. If you would like to open a directory of files, choose Open Dir (or Ctrl D).

While there are a whole host of different operations that can be performed on corpora using this software, the six most basic procedures useful for discourse analysis are as follows:

1   generating word frequency lists;
2   calculating type token ratio;
3   analysing concordances;
4   analysing collocation;
5   analysing keywords;
6   creating dispersion plots.

Most of these procedures can be performed on their own, but it is usually a good idea to perform them together with the other procedures since the results from one procedure can often inform your interpretation of the results from the others.

Word frequency and type token ratio

One of the most basic pieces of information you can get from a computer-aided analysis of your corpus is information about the frequency with which different words occur. In AntConc, a **word frequency** list for a corpus can be generated by clicking on the Word List tab and then clicking the Start button. Unless you have a good reason to treat words in different cases (e.g. 'selfie' versus 'Selfie') as separate words, you should tick 'Treat all data as lower case' in the Display Options. Words in frequency lists can be sorted by rank, frequency or word, so an analyst can easily determine not just the most or least frequently occurring words, but also check the frequency of specific words.

After a word list is generated, the information necessary to calculate **type token ratio** appears at the top of the AntConc window. Type token ratio is basically a measure of how many different kinds of words occur in the text in relation to the total number of words, and so can give some indication of the lexical complexity of texts in a corpus. It is calculated by dividing the number of types by the number of tokens. A low type token ratio generally indicates a relatively narrow range of subjects, a lack of lexical variety or frequent repetition. A high type token ratio indicates a wider range of subjects, greater lexical variation and/or less frequent repetition. In the British National Corpus, the type token ratio for the corpus of written texts is 45.53, whereas the type token ratio for the corpus of spoken texts is 32.96. This confirms a number of things we already know about the differences between speech and writing, in particular that writing tends to involve a much more varied and complex vocabulary, and that speech tends to involve frequent repetition.

Usually the most frequent words in any text are **function words** (articles, prepositions, pronouns and other grammatical words) such as 'the' and 'a'. While looking at function words can be useful in helping you to understand grammatical patterns, style and register in the corpus, **content words** such as nouns, verbs and adjectives are usually more relevant to finding evidence of 'Discourses'.

Concordances

Concordances show words in the context of the sentences or utterances in which they were used. Usually, we use frequency lists to give us an idea of what some of the important words in a corpus might be, and then we do a concordance of those words in order to find out more information about them. Concordances can be sorted alphabetically based on the words either to the right or left of the word that you searched for, and playing around with this sorting system is often a good way to spot patterns in word usage.

In AntConc, concordances are created by typing a word or phrase into the Search Term box, generating a list of instances in which this word appears in the corpus listed in their immediate contexts. The search word appears in the concordance in the centre of the page highlighted in blue, with what occurs before and after appearing to the left and the right of the word. The Kwic Sort dialogue can be used to sort the concordance alphabetically based on the word that comes one, two, three (etc.) places to the left or the right of the search term.

Collocation analysis

Collocation has to do with the fact that certain words tend to appear together. Often words take on a negative or positive meaning based on the kinds of words they are most often grouped with. As Firth (1957) put it, 'You shall know a lot about a word from the company it keeps'. For example, the verb 'commit' is nearly always associated with negative words such as 'crime'. We don't 'commit' good deeds, we 'perform' them. Thus, we find phrases such as 'commit random acts of kindness' humorous.

Analysing the kinds of words that appear together with other words is an especially useful way to understand the 'Discourses' that are expressed in a corpus because they can reveal patterns of association between different kinds of words or concepts. In their study of the portrayal of refugees in the British press, for example, Baker and McEnery (2005) note not just that the word 'stream' is used frequently in their corpus to describe the movement of refugees, but also that in the British National Corpus this word frequently collocates with the words 'tears', 'blood', 'sweat', 'water', and 'rain', giving it a generally negative connotation. Baker (2006) refers to the situation where patterns can be found between words and various sets of related words in ways that suggest a 'Discourse' as **discourse prosody**. Others (see for example Sinclair 1991) refer to this as **semantic prosody**.

Some programs have additional tools to analyse collocates. In the excerpt in D10, for example, Baker uses the Word Sketch function in the Sketch engine to determine the most statistically salient adjective and verb collocates of extreme belief words (such as *fanatic* and *extremist*). Word Sketch provides a summary of the grammatical and collocational behaviour by categorising collocates by grammatical relations (e.g. words that function as the subject or object of the word in question).

Unfortunately, AntConc does not provide such sophisticated tools, but, in most cases, simple collocation analysis is sufficient. In order to perform a collocation analysis with AntConc, click the Collocate tab and enter your chosen search term. You will also need to determine the **span** to the left or right of the search term within which you want to check for collocates. This can be set from any number of words to the left of the search term to any number of words to the right of the search term using the Window Span dialogue. The result will be a list of collocates, their rank, their overall frequency and the frequency with which they occur to the left of the search term and to the right of the search term.

Keyword analysis

Word frequency lists can only tell you how frequently certain words occur in the corpus. Some words, however, such as articles, occur frequently in nearly every text or conversation. The frequency with which a word occurs in a corpus is not in itself necessarily meaningful. What is more important is whether or not a word occurs more or less frequently than 'normal'. This is what **keyword analysis** is designed to determine.

The difference between keywords and frequent words is that keywords are words that appear with a greater frequency in the corpus that you are studying than they do in a 'reference corpus'. Reference corpora usually consist of a broader sampling of texts or conversations. Many people, for example, use large publicly available corpora such as the British National Corpus.

In order to generate a list of keywords for your corpus with AntConc, it is first necessary to load your reference corpus. This is done using the Keyword List preferences (Tool Preferences < Keyword List). The reference corpus can be loaded either as a list of files or as a directory. Once it is loaded, the keyword list is generated by choosing the Keyword List tab and clicking Start. The result will be a list of keywords, their rank, their frequency and a number measuring their **keyness**. The *keyness* value indicates the degree to which the word occurs more frequently than expected in your primary corpus (taking the reference corpus as representing a 'normal' pattern of frequency). Some programs also allow you to calculate **negative keyness**, that is, to determine which words occur *less* frequently than expected.

Dispersion plots

Dispersion plots, referred to in AntConc as 'concordance plots', can give you information about where words occur in texts. This can be particularly useful if an analyst is interested in the structure of texts or conversations. A genre analyst, for example, might be interested in the kinds of words or phrases that occur in a section of a text associated with a particular move, or a conversation analyst might want to explore the kinds of words that occur in different parts of a conversation, such as the opening or the closing.

In AntConc, concordance plots are generated by clicking the Concordance Plot tab, typing in a search term and clicking Start. The result is a series of bars, each representing a text in the corpus with lines representing where the search term has appeared.

👁 **Find examples of these and other procedures for corpus analysis on the companion website.**

NOTES

1 When people use the passive voice, they don't always leave out the agent, and when the agent is included, the passive voice can actually have the effect of *emphasising* the agent, as in the sentence: 'The cameras were installed by the Government'.
2 Here, 'you' is a deictic pronoun. **Deictic pronouns** refer to entities that must be identified according to the context of utterance rather than referring to an antecedent in another part of the utterance or text (See B2).
3 For examples of ASMR videos, see the work of Heather Feather: https://www.youtube.com/watch?v=xppnzlkpLzg&feature=youtu.be

Section C
EXPLORATION
ANALYSING DISCOURSE

C1 DOING DISCOURSE ANALYSIS: FIRST STEPS

As discussed in unit B1, there are basically three different ways of looking at discourse: discourse as language beyond the clause, discourse as language in use and discourse as social practice. Each of the three different ways of looking at discourse can lead us to ask different kinds of questions about the texts and interactions that we encounter in our everyday lives. A view that sees discourse as language above the level of the clause or the sentence leads us to ask: what makes this text or conversation a *text* or *conversation* rather than just a random collection of sentences or utterances? What holds it together so that people can make sense of it? A view that sees discourse as language in use leads us to ask: what are people trying to do with this text and how do we know? Finally, a view that sees discourse as a matter of social practice and ideology leads us to ask: what kinds of people are the authors of this text or the participants in this conversation trying to show themselves to be, and what kinds of beliefs or values are they promoting?

Consider, for example, the text that I found posted above the urinal in the men's lavatory in my university (Figure C1.1). This may seem like an odd text to perform discourse analysis on, but even seemingly trivial texts can tell us a lot about how people construct their messages strategically to accomplish particular goals, and they can also reveal something about the social relationships and ideologies in the societies in which these texts are found.

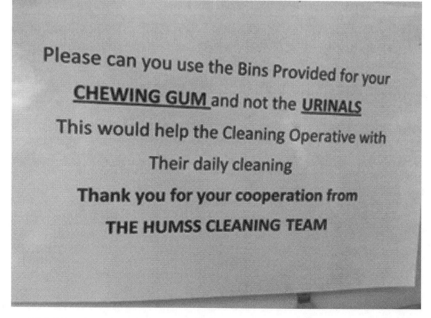

Please can you use the Bins Provided for your
CHEWING GUM and not the **URINALS**
This would help the Cleaning Operative with
Their daily cleaning
Thank you for your cooperation from
THE HUMSS CLEANING TEAM

Figure C1.1 Sign from men's lavatory, University of Reading.

Although this text seems to be rather straightforward, if we apply the three perspectives on discourse that were discussed in B1, we can start to see how complex it really is. We might start by looking at how this text is put together in a formal way. First of all, we can notice that there are three different sections, each distinguishable from the other both grammatically and typographically. The first clause asks readers not to put their chewing gum in the urinals, with CHEWING GUM and URINALS written in a different font, perhaps for emphasis. The second clause tells the reason why. It is connected to the first clause in two ways. First with the pronoun 'This', which refers back to not putting gum in the urinals, and second by the fact that the two clauses reproduce a common pattern we see in all sorts of texts in our daily lives that we might call *directive-justification*, in which a message is issued with a two-part structure, the first part telling us what to do, and the second part explaining why. Another example of this pattern is 'Caution – Slippery Floor' (see sections A2, B2). The third part of the message is also connected to the other two parts in a similar way. The 'you' in 'Thank you' connects it to the 'you' in the first clause, and THE HUMSS CLEANING TEAM presumably refers back to the 'Cleaning Operatives' mentioned in the second clause. The placement of this section also follows a particular pattern that we are familiar with from other texts: the ending of a message with an expression of gratitude and the identification of the sender of the message. This is the same way we often end emails or letters: 'Thank you for your attention … Sincerely, Rodney Jones'.

While we are paying attention to the formal aspects of this text, we might also notice that it does not conform to the conventions of capitalisation and punctuation that we might have learnt in school. 'Bins Provided' is capitalised, although it is not a proper noun, as is 'Cleaning Operatives'. And, as I mentioned above, some words are written in all capital letters, like CHEWING GUM. There is also no punctuation in the entire message; instead, line breaks are used to organise the message, a bit like poetry. This doesn't necessarily mean that the writer of this message is bad at English or didn't pay attention in school. As you probably know from your own writing, we often use unconventional capitalisation and punctuation to express special meanings. For example, the writer might have capitalised 'Bins Provided' to give these bins the 'status' of a proper noun, that is, a noun that refers to a particular 'named' thing.

After considering the formal features of the text, we might then go on to consider what exactly the authors of this text are trying to do. We might notice that the first clause of the text is written in the form of a question ('can you …) about the reader's ability not to put his chewing gum in the urinal, but, of course, most people would interpret this as a request rather than a question based on the context of this message. It makes a difference, however, that the writer decided to formulate the request as a question rather than a directive ('Don't put your chewing gum in the urinal'). One reason people do this is to 'soften' a directive, to make it seem more polite. At the same time, the capitalisation of CHEWING GUM and URINALS signals a kind of urgency, which makes the clause seem more like an order than a request. The use of the word 'Please' at the beginning of the clause is particularly interesting; although please is usually associated with requests (such as, 'Can you please lend me a pen?'), it can also be used to issue orders, especially when it is placed at the beginning of an utterance, as when the invigilator at the end of an examination says,

'Please stop writing'. And so, the writer of this message is using language in a very subtle way to formulate a message that can simultaneously be considered a polite request and a direct order.

It is when we consider this text from the third perspective – discourse as social practice – that it really starts to get interesting, and issues we considered above like the unconventional capitalisation and the difference between requests and directives start to make more sense. The kinds of social practices and social identities associated with this text are all familiar to us: practices of janitorial work, and identities such as cleaners and users of public lavatories, in this case mostly university students and professors, though you might need to belong to the particular 'discourse community' (see section A3) of the University of Reading to understand some of the sign, such as the fact that HUMSS means 'Humanities and Social Sciences Building'. The important thing is the way these identities and practices are described: cleaners are referred to as 'cleaning operatives' who work as part of a 'team', and users of the lavatory are asked to take responsibility for 'helping them in their daily cleaning'. Behind these word choices is an ideology that insists that janitorial work is a kind of 'profession' rather than just a job and that the 'cleaning operatives' are equal in social status to the professors and students who might throw their gum in the urinal. There is also evidence of a kind of managerial 'big D Discourse' that is popular in many workplaces these days that emphasizes 'teamwork'. Whether or not the cleaners at the University of Reading really have the same social status as the professors and students or feel that they are part of a 'team', this sign, for one reason or another, promotes this 'version of reality'. In fact, such discursive expressions of equality may in part allow management to avoid doing things that really would make the cleaning staff more equal, such as paying them more money.

Another 'way in' to discourse analysis might be to apply the four principles of discourse discussed in unit A1 to a particular text or interaction. Look at the text above and consider the following questions:

1   Is there anything about the language that is ambiguous? What kinds of **inferences** do you need to make to understand it?
2   How is the meaning of the text dependent on the way it is situated in the physical and social world?
3   How do the authors of the text use language to talk about social identity?
4   Does the text involve more than one 'mode' of communication (e.g. verbal, visual, material)? How do the different modes work together?

As it turns out, people like to put signs above urinals in men's lavatories, and often the meaning of these signs has some kind of relationship to where they have been placed. Look at the sign below, which I found in the men's lavatory at Paddington Station, and conduct a similar kind of analysis to the one I conducted above, looking at the text from the *three perspectives on discourse*, and then considering it using *the four principles of discourse analysis* (Figure C1.2).

C2

Figure C1.2 Sign from men's lavatory, Paddington Station.

 Find more activities on the companion website.

ANALYSING TEXTURE

C2

As I noted in unit B2, not only is *texture* (*cohesion*, *coherence* and *intertextuality*) neces-sary to turn a collection of words or sentences into a *text*, but different kinds of texts – such as shopping lists, newspaper articles and 'before and after ads' – have specific kinds of texture associated with them.

First, different kinds of texts tend to use different kinds of cohesive devices. Descriptive texts that give information about people or things such as encyclopaedia articles often make heavy use of pronoun reference, since pronouns allow writers to refer to the person or thing being talked about without repeating his, her or its name. Advertising texts, on the other hand, which describe products, are more likely to use repetition, since there are benefits to repeating the name of the product in this context. Legal texts also prefer repetition to reference, since repeating a word rather than refer-ring to it with a pronoun avoids ambiguity. Analytical and argumentative texts often make heavy use of *conjunction*, since making logical connections between ideas is usu-ally central to the process of making an argument.

I also mentioned in B2 that different kinds of texts are also based on different kinds of *generic frameworks* – they present information or actions in certain predictable sequences – and they trigger different kinds of *world knowledge*.

Finally, while nearly all texts exhibit *intertextuality* of some kind, they tend to make connections to different kinds of texts in different ways (using devices such as quotations, presuppositions and hashtags).

In order to explore these ideas further, consider the newspaper article in Text C2.1.

Text C2.1: *From* The Independent

Baby dolphin dies after being passed around for selfies with tourists

Marine rescue group condemns 'selfish' holiday-makers who poked and took photos of 'terrified' calf after it washed up at beach
　　Chris Baynes, Wednesday 16 August 2017 14:29 BST 105 comments.

Figure C2.1 One of the photos shows a child appearing to accidentally cover the dolphin's blowhole (from Equinac's Facebook page).

1　A baby dolphin died after being passed around and photographed by tourists who found it stranded at a busy Spanish beach.

2　Curious holidaymakers flocked to examine the calf – some of them taking selfies with the creature – after it washed up in Mojácar, Almería.

3　They were criticised by a marine wildlife rescue group, which said the dolphin would have been "terrified" and may have been saved if beach-goers been quicker to alert authorities.

4　Pictures emerged of bathers stroking the tiny mammal, young enough to still need breast-feeding, as it floated "frightened and weak" in the shallows after being separated from its mother.

5　"Once again we find that the human beings are the most irrational species that exists," wrote conversation group Equinac in an impassioned statement.

6   "Many are unable to feel empathy for a living being alone, scared, starving, without his mother and terrified because many of you, in your selfishness, only want to photograph and touch it, even if the animal suffers from stress."

7   The non-profit group said "hundreds" of people had mobbed the dolphin and were "obsessed" with touching and photographing the calf.

8   One picture appeared to show a child inadvertently covering the young animal's blowhole as they stroked it.

9   Equinac rescuers rushed to help the dolphin after a concerned beach-goer called Spain's 112 emergency number. But it was already dead by the time they arrived 15 minutes later.

10   "Cetaceans are animals very susceptible to stress and ... crowding them to take pictures and touch them causes them a very strong shock that greatly accelerates a cardiorespiratory failure, which is what finally happened," said the marine rescue organisation.

11   Rescuers retrieved the dolphin's corpse and are to conduct an autopsy.

12   Equinac also warned disturbing a protected species of dolphin could be a criminal offence.

13   Four species of dolphin are found off the coast of Almería, along with porpoises and six species of whale.

Cohesion

Many of the cohesive devices that we discussed in section B2 can be found in this article. Perhaps the most prevalent are *substitution* and *reference*. The noun 'baby dolphin' used the headline, for example, is later substituted with 'the creature' (paragraph 2), and 'the tiny mammal' (paragraph 4). Pronouns are also used to refer back to participants that were mentioned earlier. 'They' in the beginning of paragraph 4 refers to the 'curious holidaymakers' in the previous paragraph. Connecting words such as conjunctions and conjunctive adverbs seem to be used much less frequently as cohesive devices in this text, but words referring to time, such as 'after', sometimes play an important role in connecting clauses, as in paragraph 2 ('Curious holidaymakers flocked to examine the calf ... *after* it washed up in Mojácar, Almería). Lexical cohesion, in the form of 'chains' of words having to do with particular 'semantic domains', also appears to play a role in giving this text 'texture'. One example is words having to do with negative emotions such as 'terrified' (paragraph 3), 'frightened' (paragraph 4), 'irrational' (paragraph 5), and 'scared', 'terrified' and 'stress' (paragraph 6).

Use these observations as a starting point for *mapping* the cohesion in this text.

❑   Circle all of the examples of substitution you can find and use lines to connect the words together with the words that they stand for.

❑   Put a rectangle around all of the pronouns and use lines to connect them to their **antecedents**.

❑   Underline any connecting words you can find (including conjunctions and conjunctive adverbs, such as *and, but, after, before, also*).

❑   Choose one 'semantic domain' that you think is important in the text and list all of the words you can find that are related to this domain.

C2

□   What role does the picture at the beginning of the article take in contributing
    to the overall cohesion of the text? Can you find places in the article that refer
    specifically to objects and actions in the photograph or to the photograph itself?
□   Discuss:
    •   What are the most common cohesive devices in this text? What are the least
        common? Why do you think some devices are used more than others?
    •   In what ways are types of cohesive devices used in this text typical of newspa-
        per articles? Can you find similar patterns in other newspaper articles?

Coherence

The rich texture created by the combination of cohesive devices described above is not
the only thing that holds this text together. It is also held together by the fact that we,
as readers, recognise it to be a certain kind of text – a news article – and along with this
recognition comes a set of expectations about what the purpose of the text is and how
it will be structured. Most newspaper articles are structured based on what journalists
have come to refer to as the 'inverted pyramid' (Pöttker 2003), a structure in which the
main points of the story are summarised in the first paragraph (known as the 'summary news lead'), and the rest of the article is used to elaborate on these main points
and give details. As in this article, quotations from people involved in the incident
being reported on often appear near the end of stories.

At the same time, news stories are also 'stories', and so often share characteristics with
the oral narratives described by Labov in the excerpt reprinted in D2; the 'news lead'
functions somewhat like a combination of the ABSTRACT and the ORIENTATION,
summarising the incident and 'setting the scene'; there is a set of COMPLICATING
ACTIONS (the dolphin is manhandled by the tourists, a child accidentally covers its
breathing hole) and a RESOLUTION – though not a happy one – (representatives
from Equinac arrive to try to save the dolphin but find it dead); and finally, there is a
kind of CODA in the form of a 'lesson' that readers should learn from this story (people should not touch or harass beached dolphins, and they should treat animals with
respect and consideration).

Finally, there is also a certain amount of *world knowledge* that you need to have
in order to interpret this article as the authors intended. In particular, you have to
share with the authors *cultural models* having to do with things like dolphins, tourists and selfies, models which, for example, characterise dolphins not just as 'good'
animals that ought to be protected, but also as cute and cuddly, worthy subjects of
tourists' snapshots; and models that see the taking of selfies both as a normal practice
of holidaymakers and something that is sometimes associated with self-indulgence
or self-absorption.

A good example of how coherence works can be seen in the headline. We expect
newspaper headlines to give us a short and pithy summary of the contents of the article. In fact, we sometimes feel that the information we get in headlines is sufficient
to tell us 'what happened' so that we don't have to read the rest of the article. Most
importantly, headlines provide us with a kind of framework or **schema** for navigating
through the information in the article.

The headline in the article above: 'Baby dolphin dies after being passed around
for selfies with tourists' tells us the most important information about the story, in

particular, what happened, why it happened and who was involved. Many news stories also have secondary headlines, such as:

> Marine rescue group condemns 'selfish' holiday-makers who poked and took photos of 'terrified' calf after it washed up at beach.

When we see such secondary headlines, we are likely to treat them as elaborations of the information that we learned in the primary headline. In this case, for example, the secondary headline contains a *commentary* on what happened by the marine rescue group Equinac.

Consider the following questions:

❑ What is the overall order of information in the article? Does the order in which information appears reveal some sort of overall pattern or 'logic'?

❑ One of the particularly striking features of this text is that the paragraphs tend to be very short. Why do you think this is the case?

❑ In what ways is the overall structure or 'shape' of the article similar to other news articles you have read? Why do you think news articles are structured in this way? How are news stories structured differently from other kinds of stories?

Intertextuality

Another important aspect of 'texture' is *intertextuality*: the way texts are connected to other texts through quotations from and paraphrases of other texts. The text above, for example, achieves texture through the connections that it creates with a number of other texts: things people said, things Equinac posted on its Facebook page, and printed regulations about the treatment of wildlife. The main questions we need to ask about intertextuality are: whose voices are represented in this text? How are they represented? And whose voices are left out?

In the 'secondary headline' discussed above, for example, the words of the marine rescue group Equinac, taken from the press release it posted on its Facebook page, are *appropriated* into this text: the group is characterised as *condemning* the holiday-makers, calling them 'selfish' and saying that the dolphin was 'terrified'. This sentence illustrates some of the choices writers have to make when they use the words of others. Sometimes they can paraphrase them, for example, characterising the statement by the marine rescue group as a *condemnation* of the tourists; and sometimes they can quote the words of others verbatim, as when the words 'selfish' and 'terrified' are put in quotes. There are many reasons why authors might make such choices. Direct quotes, for example, might lend an air of authority to a text by linking it more directly to its primary source. At the same time, such cases of intertextuality can also function to create links *within* a text. For example, the words quoted in the secondary headline are repeated in the article in the context of longer quotations in paragraphs.

❑ Go through the article above and identify all the instances of intertextuality that you can find. Whose 'voices' are represented in this text? Whose voices are left out?

❑ Identify when the author of the article uses paraphrase and when he uses direct quotations. What do you think motivated these choices?

The main text that the article cites is Equinac's Facebook page, but if you go to that page, you find that there are actually several postings related to this incident posted before this article was published on August 16, 2017. Two posts appeared on August 12, the first[1] with a picture of an Equinac member holding the dead dolphin along with text reporting many details about the incident that never made it into the news story, for example, the fact that the lifeguard was unable to control the crowd that gathered around the animal. The second[2] post on that day includes the photo that *The Independent* reprinted of a child covering the dolphin's breathing hole, with an angry statement condemning the people involved (Figure C2.1). This was the post that many of the quotes for the newspaper article came. One thing you will notice is that this post is in Spanish, and so the author of the *Independent* article did not appropriate the *actual* words but *re-presented* those words in English (Figure C2.2).

Figure C2.2 From Equinac's Facebook page.

On the next day, August 15, the organisation re-posted[3] a news story from another organisation called Partido Animalista (PACMA), which recounts the same events detailed in the *Independent* article using similar words. The first paragraph of that story (translated from Spanish) reads:

> A small dolphin was stranded on a beach in Mojácar (Almeria), and was subjected to harassment by bathers, who took pictures with him and manipulated him to death.[4]

Another source of the article might have been a later posting by Equinac of an 'official statement' on August 16,[5] which covers most of the information contained in the article.

At the same time, just as this text borrowed from a dense web of other texts, it itself also became part of a web of texts from which other texts – including other newspaper articles – inevitably borrowed, paraphrasing, interpreting and evaluating the events in different ways, as, for example, the story posted on a website called *True Activist*, whose headline reads: 'Baby Dolphin Dies After Selfie-Obsessed Humans Surround It, Take Photos', or the one posted on the site *Carbonated TV*, whose headline reads: 'Horrible Humans Kill Baby Dolphin After Passing It Around For Selfies'. Regular readers like you and me also have a hand in weaving these dense intertextual webs when we share and comment on such stories from our own social media accounts.

The main point I'm trying to make here is that it is often difficult to tell whose voices are represented in texts since the writers of many kinds of texts (including newspaper articles) are not always explicit about their sources. The information in the *Independent* article could have come from a range of different texts mentioned above, including other newspaper articles about this incident.

❑ Do an Internet web search for '*baby dolphin* and *tourists* and *selfies*' and find as many articles about this incident as you can. Can you find differences between the ways different voices are represented in these different texts? Can you find any intertextual links between these texts?

*****

The text reproduced in Text C2.2 is a very different kind of text about a similar phenomenon, the abstract of an academic article published in the journal *Social Psychology and Personality Science*. Look at this text and try to conduct the same kind of analysis we conducted above. Specifically, attempt to answer the following questions:

❑ What are the main cohesive devices used in the text? How are they different from those in the text analysed above? Can you think of any reason for the difference?
❑ What sorts of expectations do readers bring to texts like this in terms of both the structure of the text and the world knowledge needed to interpret it, and how are these expectations reflected in the text?
❑ How does the text draw on other texts (or the 'voices' of other people), and how are these texts/voices represented? Is there a difference between the way voices are represented in this text and the way they are represented in the text above?

Text C2.2: From social psychology and personality science

Selfie Indulgence: Self-Favouring Biases in Perceptions of Selfies

Daniel E. Re, Sylvia A. Wang, Joyce C. He, Nicholas O. Rule
  Social Psychology and Personality Science

People often perceive themselves as more attractive and likable than others do. Here, we examined how these self-favouring biases manifest in a highly popular novel context that is particularly self-focused—selfies. Specifically, we analysed selfie-takers' and non-selfie-takers' perceptions of their selfies versus photos taken by others and compared these to the judgments of external perceivers. Although selfie-takers and non-selfie-takers reported equal levels of narcissism, we found that the selfie-takers perceived themselves as more attractive and likable in their selfies than in others' photos, but that non-selfie-takers viewed both photos similarly. Furthermore, external judges rated the targets as less attractive, less likable, and more narcissistic in their selfies than in the photos taken by others. Thus, self-enhancing misperceptions may support selfie-takers' positive evaluations of their selfies, revealing notable biases in self-perception.

🏅 **Do more activities on the companion website.**

C3 **ANALYSING GENRES**

Analysing genres involves more than just analysing the 'moves' in particular types of text. It involves understanding how these text types function in social groups, how they reinforce and reflect the concerns of and social relationships in these groups, and how they change over time as societies and the groups within them change. Therefore, analysing genres requires as much attention to *social context* as it does to texts.

Part of this context includes other genres to which the genre under consideration is related. Genres are related to other genres in a number of different ways. First, actions or 'communicative events' associated with genres are usually part of larger **chains** of events that involve different genres. The videos we looked at in unit B3, for example, might be followed by comments from viewers and might inspire viewers to engage in genres like 'coming out' discussions with their parents or friends. And so, just as moves in a genre are often arranged in a kind of sequential structure, genres themselves are also often related to one another in sequential chains based on the ways they are employed by people as they work to achieve larger communicative purposes.

Genres are also related to other genres in non-sequential relationships that are called **networks**. A job application letter, for example, is related to the job ad that prompted it; the applicant's résumé, which might accompany the letter; and any letters of reference former employers or teachers of the applicant might have written in support of the application. The letter is also related to the letters of all of the other applicants who are applying for the same job. Genres are said to be linked together in *networks* when they have some sort of *intertextual* relationship with one another, that is, when one genre makes reference to another genre, or when the users of a genre need to make reference to another genre in order to realise the communicative purpose for which the genre is intended.

Genres can also be seen as existing in larger **genre ecologies** in which texts that are not directly related to one another in chains or networks can nevertheless affect one another in sometimes subtle and sometimes dramatic ways. Like natural ecologies, genre ecologies are not static: conditions change; old discourse communities dissolve and new ones form; and genres themselves change and evolve as users creatively *bend* or *blend* them, or else become extinct if they can no longer fulfil the communicative goals of their users.

Genre analysis, therefore, must account not just for the way a particular genre is structured and its function in a particular discourse community, but also the dynamic nature of the genre, how it has and continues to evolve in response to changing social conditions, the relationships it has to other genres past and present, and the multiple functions it might serve in multiple discourse communities.

One example of a genre that has evolved from earlier genres and also exists a complex relationship with other genres are online restaurant reviews of the kind you might find on sites like Trip Advisor.

Consider the review of a restaurant in New York City called *Ninja* in Figure C3.1.

Figure C3.1 Review from Trip Advisor I.

The first thing we might notice about online restaurant reviews such as this one is that although they are related to the kinds of restaurant reviews written for newspapers and food websites by professional restaurant reviewers and share some of the same features (such as a rating system), they are also very different in both structure and style. For one thing, they tend to be much shorter and written in a more informal style. They also tend to include more personal details about the writers.

If we were to do a 'move analysis' of this review, we might start with the notion that the purpose of a restaurant review is to *recommend* that people either go to the restaurant or do *not* go to the restaurant. The review above begins with a 'headline' ('Memorable') which, along with the 4-star rating, summarises the recommendation of the review. The first part of the review *describes* the circumstances in which the restaurant was visited and the overall experience of dining there. The second part *informs* about the quality and prices of particular dishes. The last part gives an *overall evaluation* ('A good time was had by all').

But this review is also connected to other genres. It is connected to the menu of the restaurant, for example, from which information about prices and dishes can be discerned, and it might be connected to genres like restaurant guidebooks, which the writer may have used when deciding what restaurant to eat at. It is also connected to other reviews on Trip Advisor of this restaurant (and the rating given in this review will be aggregated with that of other reviews to produce an overall rating of the restaurant). This review might also lead to future genres such as comments or questions to 'Lisa R' who wrote the review, and positive reviews like this are sometimes incorporated into genres like advertisements for restaurants.

Understanding what *discourse community* is implied in this review is also complex. An easy answer might be the discourse community of Trip Advisor users or the wider community of 'restaurant goers'. But there are other discourse communities that are 'gathered' by this particular review, such as the discourse community of parents looking for a suitable restaurant to take their children to.

Now look at another review of this restaurant and answer the following questions:

❏ In what ways is the 'move structure' of this review similar to the one above? In what ways does it differ? Can you account for these differences?
❏ What other genres does this review link to? What is the nature of these links? (Figure C3.2).

Figure C3.2 Review from Trip Advisor II.

YouTube genres

Genres on YouTube are particularly good examples of new media genres that imitate old media genres that came before them and adapt to the affordances and constraints of digital media. They are also good examples of people trying to *do* specific things with language, showing themselves to be members of particular *discourse communities*, and using the genre to 'gather' members of these communities around them to interact with the texts they've created by 'liking' them and leaving comments. Finally, YouTube genres are often good examples of what Bhatia, in the excerpt reprinted in D3, calls 'creative interdiscursivity'. In other words, they often 'blend' different genres together or 'bend' the rules of existing genres, often because they have multiple audiences or multiple communicative purposes. Consider some of the YouTube genres you are familiar with and fill in Table C3.1. You might visit YouTube and search for these genres by name to get some ideas.

Table C3.1 Analysing YouTube genres

Genre	Beauty/ makeup videos	Unboxing/ 'haul' videos	Gaming videos	'Coming out' videos
What is are/the communicative purpose/s of the genre?				
What discourse community or communities does the genre 'gather around' it?				
What are the characteristic features of the genre? Does it follow a particular 'move structure'?				
Does the genre mix together different genres? Which ones? Why?				

 Find more activities on the companion website.

COMPETING IDEOLOGIES   C4

In sections A4 and B4, I discussed some of the main ways we can analyse texts in order to understand the kinds of ideologies they are promoting. These included:

❏ Examining how the text creates a certain 'version of reality' by representing people, things, and what they do to one another in certain ways ('whos doing whats').

❏ Examining how the text creates a relationship between the reader and the writer – how it makes available certain 'reading positions' for the reader or 'hails' the reader as a certain kind of person, often through the use of different 'voices' or what Gee calls 'social languages'.

❏ Examining how authors of texts *appropriate* and *represent* the words of other people.

❏ Examining how certain features in texts 'point to' or *index* things in the social world (such as certain kinds of people, certain kinds of relationships and certain kinds of situations), thus invoking particular 'Discourses'.

Two good sources of texts for **critical discourse analysis** are newspapers and websites where people representing different political ideologies or social positions describe or comment on the same social event or situation. The newspaper commentary below is from the local paper of the British borough of Tower Hamlets. In it, the mayor of the borough talks about the use of CCTV surveillance cameras in the town.

Text C4.1: Lutfur Rahman, Mayor of Tower Hamlets

In Tower Hamlets, the council has been making effective use of CCTV to tackle crime and make the borough a safer place to live, work and visit.

Live 24-hour monitoring of the CCTV system by council operators resulted in 837 proactive arrests in 2012, and 907 in 2011.

A proactive arrest happens when a council CCTV operator either alerts the police to an incident, or leads the police to a suspect after hearing a call out on the police radio and identifies the suspect using CCTV at the time of the incident.

Hundreds more arrests take place as a result of police officers reviewing video and suspects being identified at a later date.

CCTV is one of the most powerful tools to be developed during recent years to assist with efforts to combat crime and disorder.

One way to approach this text is to explore what kind of 'world' it is portraying, what kinds of people and things inhabit this world, what kinds of actions these people or things take and who or what exerts *agency* in these actions.

The most prominent participant in the text is the town council and 'council operators', which 'make use' of CCTV cameras, 'monitor CCTV systems', 'alert the police', 'lead the police to suspects', and 'make the borough safe'. In almost all cases, the council or 'council operators' are portrayed as *agents* in the clauses in which they appear (they are *doing the action* with which they are associated). Moreover, most of these actions are *material processes* ('physical' actions). Another prominent actor is the CCTV camera itself, which is portrayed as a 'tool' that the council uses to 'combat crime and disorder'. Other participants include 'suspects', a generic class of people about which little information is given (including what they are suspected of or why they are suspicious); and the broad abstract noun 'crime', which is similarly undefined. These participants are never in agentive positions. Versions of reality are defined as much by the participants that are *left out* as by those that are included. One important class of participants that *does not* appear in this text is 'citizens', the residents of the borough who are not 'suspects' and whom the cameras are intended to protect (but who also might feel that they violate their privacy).

This text also contains many 'voices', that is, words and ideas taken from other texts. What is striking is none of these words or ideas are attributed to anyone other than the author of the text. For instance, the statistics 'Live 24-hour monitoring of the CCTV system by council operators resulted in 837 proactive arrests in 2012, and 907 in 2011' must have come from somewhere, but the source of these statistics is not provided. Moreover, some of the words used in this text *index* broader Discourses. Words such as 'crime' and 'disorder', for example, index a Discourse that might be called a 'law and order Discourse', one that promotes a worldview in which obeying authority is seen as a key feature of a successful society and not doing so makes someone a dangerous 'suspect', and in which any action taken to maintain 'order' is seen as justified, even when it involves comprising other social values like privacy.

Now look at the commentary below by an opponent of the CCTV cameras and perform a similar analysis, exploring what kind of 'world' this writer portrays and what kinds of people and things are included or excluded. Consider the following questions:

❑ Which participants are construed as agents, and what kinds of processes are they represented as performing?
❑ Whose voices are represented in this text? How are they represented and how does this representation serve to position the author (and reader) in relation to these voices?
❑ Do any of the words *index* particular kinds of people or particular Discourses?
❑ What can you say about how these two texts reflect the different ideologies and the different social agendas of the writers?

Text C4.2: Tahmeena Bax, a volunteer at the newham monitoring project

Whilst most of us at Newham Monitoring Project (NMP) would agree that safety is a priority, we have doubts that increased CCTV is the way to deliver this. The cost to the community, both financial and in terms of intrusion, is potentially high. The question, therefore, is do the benefits outweigh the risks? Through our work at a community level, we come across divided views.

Support for cameras tends to come from those frustrated with inaction over antisocial behaviour. However, Newham already has 959 cameras – more than Birmingham and Liverpool combined.

Despite this high figure, of the 32,809 crimes recorded in Newham in 2012, less than one per cent of arrests resulted from this network. These statistics suggest that CCTV is neither an effective deterrent nor a quick-fix solution.

Any decision to extend the surveillance of citizens erodes the basic right to privacy. A common argument in favour of CCTV is: 'If you are doing nothing wrong, you have nothing to worry about.'

However, this does not answer the question: 'If you are doing nothing wrong, why are you being watched at all?'

Some may argue cameras don't discriminate in whom they film.

However, at NMP, we receive frequent complaints that cameras are installed in areas where communities already feel unfairly targeted by police or authorities and CCTV only serves to exasperate tensions and increase alienation.

Indexicality and cultural models

One of the most important uses of *indexicality* is that it allows people to *invoke* certain cultural models or stereotypes very efficiently without having to spell them out. The French writing on the sign discussed in B4, for example, allows shop owners to efficiently invoke sophistication and cosmopolitanism to passers-by without having to 'spell it out' (even though the sign would invoke something very different for people who actually understand French).

One place where people have to be very efficient in invoking cultural models is online dating advertisements. In an analysis of such advertisements, Fullick (2013) talks about a website that asks users to list 'five things I can't live without'. Fullick quotes one user who listed: 'My Mac/The next bottle of wine/Business cards/My passport/ A dinner companion (hate eating alone!)'. She analyses this list as a list of indexicals that 'point to' certain stereotypes about gender and class and certain 'cultural models' about lifestyle and romance. She writes:

> Within a single line, (the poster) makes references that indicate an affiliation with and reliance on particular forms of technology (a trendy laptop); an appreciation for wine (as opposed to beer, which may be viewed as less "classy" and also more "male"); the importance of work and international travel; and a "place" for a partner within a particular vision of urban living. Compare this with the items listed by (another poster), who in the same category included "Crockpot / Guitar / Microphone / A Man (unfortunate but true …) / Spices." This demonstrates a concurrence with traditional gender norms for women—not only is "a man" listed as an object among others; he is also indispensable.
>
> (Fullick, 2013: 555–556)

❑ Look at the way people describe themselves on online dating sites or apps like Tinder, or in profiles on social media sites such as Twitter. How do the kinds of words they use and objects and activities they include 'point to' certain kinds of stereotypes or cultural models?

 Do more activities on the companion website.

C5 ANALYSING SPEECH ACTS AND IMPLICATURE

In this unit, we will consider how principles from pragmatics and conversation analysis can be applied to understanding how people make sense of potentially ambiguous contributions in social interaction. The kinds of contribution we will focus on are **orders** and **refusals** (as well as the opposite of refusals: agreement or **consent**). Orders are potentially ambiguous because, although they are often accompanied by rather explicit language such as 'Would you please [do x]', it is sometimes difficult to distinguish them from **requests** or even just observations (such as 'Wouldn't it be nice if this were done'). Refusals are also often delivered in an indirect fashion: because refusals constitute a *dispreferred* response to a request, people usually try to 'soften' or 'mitigate' their refusals or even avoid refusing altogether and instead use some other means to 'hint' that they do not wish to carry out a request. Refusals can be particularly important speech acts in certain situations that might involve negotiations of power or a person's ability to maintain their personal autonomy, freedom of choice or integrity, as we will see below. Related to refusals is consent the speech act by which people agree to do something or give permission for something to happen. Consent is a particularly tricky speech act since in many situations, consent is inferred when there is the lack of refusal, and in other situations, consent is 'coerced' through the employment of various strategies that make it difficult for people to understand exactly what they are consenting to, as when Internet companies ask you to 'Agree' to 'Terms and Conditions' that you couldn't possibly understand and don't have the time to read.

'Will no one rid me of this meddlesome priest?'

Requests and orders belong to a family of speech acts called **directives**, speech acts in which we use our words to get someone to do something. What distinguishes different kinds of directives (for example, orders, suggestions, requests) from one another, however, is sometimes unclear.

On the face of it, the felicity conditions for a request are rather straightforward:

1   it involves the hearer doing some future act;
2   this act is something that the hearer can do;
3   the hearer might not normally do it without being asked;
4   the speaker really wants the hearer to do it.

The problem is that the felicity conditions for an order are very similar, except that whereas carrying out a request is voluntary, and carrying out an order is compulsory. In order to understand whether a directive is voluntary or compulsory, however, the hearer needs to consider *who* is issuing the request (his boss, his girlfriend, his mother) and the *conditions* under which it is issued (the workplace, the home, a social occasion).

Another problem is that often people make requests or issue orders in very indirect ways, not even stating directly what action they wish the other person to take. The classic example of this is the utterance 'it's hot in here', used as a request for the hearer to open the window or turn on the air conditioner. Of course, if this statement is uttered by the most powerful person in the room, it might be heard as an order rather than just a request. Powerful people often exploit this grey area between requests and orders when they want to get people to do things but do not want to take responsibility for ordering them to do them, or when they want to test the loyalty of their subordinates.

One famous example of this is contained in the June 8, 2017 Senate testimony of former US FBI director James Comey about a conversation he had with President Donald Trump, which later became an important piece of evidence in building a case that the president tried to obstruct justice by trying to get the FBI director to abandon an investigation into his former National Security Advisor, Michael Flynn. According to Comey, during a meeting in the Oval Office, Trump asked everyone else to leave the room, and then told Comey that Flynn was a good man who didn't deserve to be under investigation. 'I hope', he said, 'you can let this go'.

Of course, the important question here is whether or not 'I hope you can let this go' constituted an order to suspend the investigation and therefore an attempt to obstruct justice. Trump supporters insisted that the president was just expressing his mental state, that 'hope' in this case means exactly what the dictionary says it means: 'the desire for something to happen'. Comey, on the other hand, interpreted it as an order. Below is an excerpt from Comey's Senate testimony in which he is being questioned about the incident by Senator Jim Risch (R-Idaho):

RISCH: He did not direct you to let it go?
COMEY: Not in his words, no.
RISCH: He did not order you to let it go?
COMEY: Again, those words are not an order.
RISCH: He said, I hope. Now, like me, you probably did hundreds of cases, maybe thousands of cases, charging people with criminal offenses and, of course, you have knowledge of the thousands of cases out there where people have been charged. Do you know of any case where a person has been charged for obstruction of justice or, for that matter, any other criminal offense, where they said or thought they hoped for an outcome?
COMEY: I don't know well enough to answer. The reason I keep saying his words is I took it as a direction.

Later in the testimony, Comey had the following exchange with Senator Angus King (I-Maine).

KING: I think in response to Mr. Risch, to Senator Risch, you said he said, "I hope you will hold back on that." But when you get a—when a President of the United States in the Oval Office says something like "I hope" or "I suggest" or "would you," do you take that as a directive?
COMEY: Yes. Yes, it rings in my ear as kind of, "Will no one rid me of this meddlesome priest?"
KING: I was just going to quote that. In 1170, December 29, Henry II said, "Who will rid me of this meddlesome priest?" And then, the next day he was killed, Thomas a Becket. That's exactly the same situation. We're thinking along the same lines.

❑   Based on your knowledge of the context in which the utterance 'I hope you can let this go' occurred, what kind of speech act do you think it was? Try to support your judgment using the tools from pragmatics discussed in 5A and 5B. Do you think your argument is strong enough to conclude that Trump tried to obstruct justice?

❑   In his testimony, Comey also said that this conversation occurred after a number of other conversations in which Trump had asked him if he wanted to keep his job. How might this information have affected how Comey might have interpreted this utterance?

Saying 'No'

In section 5B, we talked about two different perspectives on how people make sense of what people mean by what they say: pragmatics and conversation analysis. According to pragmatics, people figure out what other people mean based on analysing the immediate context of the utterance (who said it, to whom it was said, what was happening in the relationship between them or in the physical environment when it was said, and whether or not people are conforming to some very basic expectations about conversation). According to conversation analysis, people figure out what other people mean by looking at what was said before and making their utterances relevant within a particular *sequence* of utterances. Both of these perspectives, however, tend to ignore another very important aspect of the way people make sense of other people's utterances: the fact that sometimes utterances make sense because of our broader understanding of what certain kinds of people are supposed to say in certain kinds of situations.

In earlier sections (A4, B2, B4, D4), I talked about how *cultural models* – deep-seated, sometimes unconscious expectations about how the social world is organised and how certain kinds of people are supposed to act – can affect how people design and interpret written texts. In spoken discourse, we might talk about *cultural scripts*, deep-seated expectations about who should say what to whom, when, where and how (see A7, B7). In a way, the adjacency pairs that conversation analysts talk about are kinds of *cultural scripts*. We can think of them as 'mini-scripts'; for example, exchanges such as 'A: Thank you, B: You're welcome', and 'A: Would you like a piece of cake', 'B: Yes, I'd love one'. Not only do these scripts come with set phrases that signal to others what kind of utterance is being produced (such as an 'offer' or a 'request'), but they are also governed by the expectations about *preferred responses* (see 5B), so that certain responses, such as accepting an invitation or offer, are considered culturally more appropriate.

This whole idea of preferred responses and their relationship to cultural scripts is highly relevant to the speech act of *refusal*. Refusals are among the most difficult speech acts to deliver. It is never pleasant to disappoint someone; to turn down the offer of a job, for example, or to turn down someone who wants to date you but whom you don't fancy, or even to refuse to give someone a pen if they need one. In some cases, such as when an utterance is interpreted as an order, the hearer might find it almost impossible to refuse. Refusals are *dispreferred responses* to requests or invitations because they threaten the 'face' (see A6. B6) of the person who has made the request or issued the invitation, and they usually require an explanation as well as some other kind of speech act to soften the blow, such as an apology ('I'm sorry. I'm afraid I only have one pen, and I need it to take the exam.') or a compliment ('You're a really nice guy, but I already have a boyfriend').

One area of life where refusals are particularly important is in the area of sexual interaction. Of course, it is important whenever people engage in sexual activity that both parties have consented to it, and to force someone to have sex without their consent is a crime. But the way consent and refusal work can be extremely complicated and depends a great deal on the context, including the relationship between the parties (e.g. are they long-time partners or have they just met?), the conditions under which the sexual activity is taking place (e.g. are they drunk or sober?) and the nature of the sexual activity itself.

Experts like campus counsellors often advise people, particularly women, to 'just say no' when they wish to refuse sexual activity, but sometimes this is not so simple. One reason for this is that because of a deep-seated cultural script in some societies that says that women should display a reluctance to have sex (even when they want to), some men think that 'no' might mean 'yes' or 'maybe'. Another problem, pointed out by the feminist conversation analysts Celia Kitzinger and Hannah Frith (1999), is that refusals are particularly complex speech acts to produce since they are *dispreferred responses* and might hurt the feelings of the other party; in most other kinds of situations (such as refusing the offer of a piece of cake), refusals usually incorporate things like delays, hedges, apologies and accounts, and quite often people try to refuse *without* saying 'no'. Kitzinger and Frith argue that, in an ideal world, women should not have to say 'no' to be 'heard' as refusing sex. Of course, in such cases, it is always best to be as clear as possible, but Kitzinger and Frith do show us why sometimes it might be 'conversationally awkward' for a woman to say 'no' to sexual advances, even when she wants to.

The issues of what constitutes sexual consent, how people ought to communicate consent, and the kinds of utterances and actions that people might interpret as signalling consent are thorny ones. How can the tools of conversation analysis and pragmatics help us to sort out these issues? Specifically:

❑ What kinds of utterances are needed to signal consent? Is it possible to signal consent non-verbally?

❑ What other *felicity conditions* are necessary to make the utterances or non-verbal behaviours you discussed above successfully perform the speech act of consent?

❑ Is there something about the *sequencing* of certain utterances or behaviours, their function in adjacency pairs or the preference structure of these pairs that might affect how people might give or refuse consent or interpret or misinterpret the signals others?

❑ Look at the text below published by the University of Pittsburgh-Bradford. How does it compare to your own analysis? Can you think of any challenges you might have implementing this advice from the point of view of pragmatics or conversation analysis? How might you deal with these challenges?

Text C5.1: What is consent?

Pitt Bradford defines consent as an informed, affirmative decision made freely and actively by all parties to engage in mutually acceptable sexual activity. Consent is given by clear words or actions and may not be inferred from silence, passivity, or lack of resistance alone. Existence of a current or previous dating, marital, and/or sexual relationship is not sufficient to constitute consent to additional sexual activity. Consent to one type of sexual activity does not imply consent to other types of sexual activity.

Only "YES" means "YES". The absence of "NO" does not mean "YES"!

Someone who is unconscious, asleep, or otherwise mentally or physically incapacitated, whether due to alcohol, drugs, or some other condition, cannot give consent. Consent cannot be obtained by force, intimidation, threat, coercion, isolation, or confinement. Agreement obtained under such conditions does not constitute consent.

http://www.upb.pitt.edu/oaadi/

 Do more activities on the online website.

C6 ANALYSING CONVERSATIONAL STRATEGIES

Conversational strategies online

In this section, you will have a chance to apply some of the ideas about conversational strategies that were introduced in A6 and B6. The kinds of interactions I would like to explore here, however, are not face-to-face conversations but rather computer-mediated interactions, in particular, interactions using Facebook and WhatsApp.

As noted in A6, mediated interactions are different from face-to-face spoken conversations in a number of ways. For one thing, in much computer-mediated communication, people type their 'utterances' rather than speaking them. In addition, these interactions rarely involve the same kind of synchrony that face-to-face conversation does. Whereas face-to-face interactions occur in 'real time', giving us access to other people's utterances as they are forming them, most computer-mediated interactions are asynchronous, involving a 'time lag' between production and reception, whether it be the momentary lag between the time when one party types a message and the other person reads it, which we experience in instant messaging and texting, or the much longer time lags associated with email, blogs and social networking sites.

Perhaps the most important difference between face-to-face interaction and computer-mediated interaction is that many of the non-verbal and paralinguistic resources available in face-to-face communication are not available in text-based computer-mediated communication. This is significant because these are precisely the resources people often use as *contextualisation cues* to frame their conversational activities, and they can also play an important role in the face strategies of *involvement* and *independence*. Users of text-based communication tools, then, need to make use of different resources such as graphics, emoticons, orthography and punctuation to fulfil the functions that non-verbal and paralinguistic communication do in face-to-face encounters.

Face strategies on Facebook

Perhaps more than any other kind of computer-mediated communication, social networking sites are designed to give users tools to communicate about and manage their social relationships with others. Facebook is about 'face' precisely in the sense in which we defined it in unit A6: 'the negotiated public image mutually granted to each other by participants in a communicative event'. Users of Facebook are centrally concerned with constructing and maintaining their 'public images', with saving face and with 'giving face' to others.

It is not uncommon for people to have many Facebook 'friends' (hundreds or even thousands), and yet they do not enjoy the same kind of relationships with all of these 'friends': with some of them they are socially close and with others they are socially distant; some of them are their social equals, while others are in a hierarchical relationship with them. The problem with Facebook, however, is that it is biased towards a face system of **symmetrical solidarity** (in which the parties are both close and relatively equal in status). Nearly all of the resources it makes available, from the initial mechanism of 'friending', to photo sharing, to the exchange of virtual tokens such as 'likes' and 'reactions', are designed to *express involvement*. Some (see e.g. Kiesler, 1986; Landow, 1992) have even suggested that it is a fundamental characteristic of *all* computer-mediated communication that it flattens hierarchies and encourages self-disclosure, a phenomenon Joseph Walther (1996) calls 'hyperpersonal communication'.

For some users this is not a problem – the whole point of a social networking site for them is to help them get closer to those in their social network – and it certainly is not a problem for the company that runs Facebook, since the more people share with one another using involvement strategies, the more information about them is available to sell to advertisers. It does become a problem, however, when people who are accustomed to hierarchical or deference face systems in face-to-face communication have to negotiate their relationships in an environment that is biased towards involvement, as when students and professors or employees and employers become 'friends'.

These difficulties are especially salient in the ways people comment on other people's posts, since these comments constitute 'publicly performed conversations' that people who are not involved in them typically have access to. Therefore, the relationships people enact in these interactions are not just negotiated between the interactants but are also displayed to a larger audience.

The example in Figure C6.1 illustrates how one of my students strategically mixed independence and involvement strategies when 'tagging' me in a picture and commenting on it.

Figure C6.1 Excerpt from the author's Facebook newsfeed.

The first thing that should be noted regarding this example is that 'tagging' someone in a photo on Facebook is a clear example of *involvement*. Not only does it assume a relationship of solidarity, but it also makes the assumption that the person tagged does not mind advertising this relationship to other users. Consequently, it is also a threat to the 'negative face' of the person who has been tagged, potentially violating their desire for autonomy and privacy. There are also other instances of involvement in this example, such as the optimistic and complimentary message, the informal language and the use of emoticons (such as :) and :D) and unconventional spelling and punctuation (like 'ur', 'jokessssss', and the repetition of the exclamation point at the end of the message).

At the same time, there are also instances of independence strategies, most notably the use of the title 'Prof. Jones' to address me. What is interesting about this is that, like many university professors, I am on a 'first-name basis' with my students. In other words, this student uses an independence strategy on Facebook that she probably would *not* use in face-to-face interaction with me. One reason for this may be to compensate for the involvement strategies that otherwise dominate the message and to mitigate the potential threat to my negative face.

1   Analyse the posts and comments on your Facebook newsfeed or some other social network service you use. Does this service encourage the adoption of a particular face system among users? Do the people in your network (including yourself) use different mixtures of independence and involvement strategies when interacting with people with whom they have different kinds of relationships?

2   How do people who are socially distant or who are in hierarchal relationships manage face strategies using this service? Can you find examples of interactions that would have been managed differently had they taken place face-to-face?

Contextualisation cues in WhatsApp

As I have said above, text-based communication using applications like WhatsApp and Facebook Messenger differs from face-to-face conversation in that users do not have access to many of the resources normally used to issue contextualisation cues, such as body language, facial expressions and paralinguistic signals. As a result, they have, over the years, developed a multitude of other ways with which to frame and reframe their utterances, including emojis, screen names, status updates, unconventional spellings, creative use of punctuation and code-mixing (the mixing of words from different languages). A number of scholars (see for example Danet *et al.*, 1997; Herring, 2001) have shown how users of chat and messaging systems use such cues to signal 'what's going on' in online interaction.

Figure C6.2 is an example of how such resources can be used as *contextualisation cues* in a WhatsApp exchange between a woman named Elaine and her boyfriend, in which they discuss her Christmas present. Giving gifts is, in most cultures, a complex ritual that is itself a form of communication, and there are different conventions regarding how it should be done. In some cases, parties agree among themselves what gifts should be exchanged, or they explicitly inform others about what gifts they want (sometimes though services like Amazon 'Wish List'), but in other cases, parties are expected to surprise each other, and the choice of gift is meant to communicate how intimately one person knows the other. In any event, talking about gift giving can be awkward. In the conversation below, Elaine's boyfriend uses emojis to show his embarrassment (and 'panic') at not having chosen a gift for her, and his desperation when she doesn't tell him what she wants. These emojis don't mean that he really is as panicked or as desperate as the expressions on the faces of the emojis imply. Rather, he is using the emojis to *reframe* what might otherwise be a serious conversation into a kind of dramatic performance. As for Elaine, she uses her emojis in two ways. First, she uses a 'thinking emoji' to playfully tell him to think harder about what to get her, and, at the end of the conversation, and she uses a 'grimacing face' emoji to frame her request for him to save the receipts as slightly embarrassing (since the request implies that she does not trust him to choose a suitable gift).

Figure C6.2 WhatsApp conversation.

❑ Choose an utterance that you have sent to a friend via WhatsApp, Facebook, Messenger or some other messaging app.) and discuss how the message could be 'framed' differently by attaching to it one of the emojis from the range of choices in Figure C6.3.

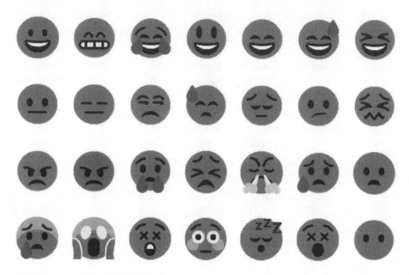

Figure C6.3 Emojis (from Twitter).

❑ Save a WhatsApp or Facebook Messenger conversation as a 'history file' and analyse it in terms of how things such as code choice, spelling, punctuation, capitalisation and emoticons are used to strategically frame and re-frame messages.

 Do more activities on the companion website.

C7   ANALYSING CONTEXTS

Analysing the communicative competence that members of a particular speech community bring to a particular speech event requires more than just the analysis of texts or transcripts (though one can often tell a lot from such an analysis). It requires actually *observing* people interacting in the speech event and talking to them about what they think they need to know in order to participate in it successfully. Often one must talk with multiple participants in order to find out what it is like for people playing different roles in the event.

The anthropologist Gregory Bateson and the psychiatrist Jurgen Ruesch (Ruesch and Bateson, 1968) say that there are at least four kinds of information an ethnographer should gather about a speech event: (1) members' generalisations (what participants think other people need to know and do to participate in the speech event); (2) individual experiences (the specific, concrete knowledge and experiences of individual people who have participated in the speech event in the past); (3) 'objective' observation (the observation of people participating in the speech event); and (4) the analyst's comparison of what he or she has observed and heard from participants with his or her own knowledge and behaviour in similar speech events in his or her own speech community. Sometimes these different kinds of information contradict one another: participants, for example, may attribute certain behaviour to other members of their speech community but say that they themselves do things differently, or they may say they behave in a particular way but can be observed behaving in an entirely different way. The important thing for the analyst is not to privilege any of these four kinds of information, but to take them together in order to get a full picture of what is going on from the point of view of the participants. It is important to remember that the ethnographer of speaking is less interested in what is 'objectively' occurring in a speech event as in what participants *think* is occurring and what they need to *know* to participate as legitimate members of their group.

Sample analysis: 'Don't bite my shit'

It would be impossible to conduct a full ethnographic analysis of a speech event in the space of this unit. What I can do, however, is discuss the meaning and significance of a particular utterance in the social and cultural context in which it occurs. The utterance, one that I heard frequently during my ethnographic study of urban skateboarders in Hong Kong (reported in Jones, 2008; 2011), is: 'Hey man, don't bite my shit'. I heard this utterance or some variation of it many times during my fieldwork, sometimes uttered in a playful manner and sometimes with deadly seriousness.

One way of trying to understand the meaning of this phrase might be to look it up in the dictionary. According to the *Urban Dictionary* (http://www.urbandictionary.com), a popular Internet dictionary of slang, *bite my shit* means:

> to steal originality or to get on someone's case, depending on context.

While this definition can give us some insights into the possible meaning of the phrase when used by the skateboarders I observed, we can't really tell which of the two definitions apply without, as the entry itself states, referring to the *context*. Just knowing the meaning of 'don't bite my shit' is not enough. What we really need to know is how it is *used*: who says it to whom, when, where and how and to what effect? In order to know this, it is necessary to understand something about the *cultural* context in which it occurs.

Skateboarding in Hong Kong, as in most places, takes place within the context of a speech situation called a 'skate session'. These sessions usually occur at skate parks but sometimes occur in other places such as on sidewalks, in parking lots and in city squares. Skaters regard the skating that goes on in parks and that which goes on in these other places to be two different *genres* of skating, one which is called 'park skating' and the other which is called 'street skating'. In Hong Kong, 'park skating' always occurs during the day when the skate parks are open, and 'street skating' almost always occurs at night, when fewer people are around to interfere with the activity. Skate sessions can last many hours and sometimes involve skaters moving from setting to setting. They may, for example, begin a session in the skate park in the afternoon and then move to the street after the skate park closes (*setting*).

Skaters generally participate in skate sessions in 'crews' or 'posses', groups of people who usually skate together and who often share a certain style of dressing or acting (for example 'punk' or 'hip-hop') and are usually of a similar level of skill (*participants*). People hardly ever skate alone. One reason for this is that among the main aims of a skating session is to let others witness one performing daring or difficult tricks (*ends*). This aim of making oneself a spectacle for others is reinforced by the fact that skaters often bring video cameras with them during skate sessions to film one another (*instrumentalities*).

At a skate park at any given time, there are likely to be multiple 'crews', and one of the core competencies for members of this community is understanding how to manage the use of space in order to avoid conflicts among crews. In street skating sessions, these conflicts can sometimes become intense if one crew claims the exclusive right to skate at a particular spot and tries to deny access to other crews. At skate parks, this does not happen since these parks are public property, and the right for all skaters to use them is policed by park attendants and security guards. Therefore, different crews must cooperate and carefully negotiate the use of space (*norms*).

Skate sessions normally consist of multiple 'speech events' including conversations, horseplay, games of 'SKATE' (a highly structured game in which skaters compete in performing tricks) and 'doing lines'. 'Doing lines' involves skaters taking turns executing sequences of 'tricks' (many of which have standard names such as 'ollie' and 'kickflip') upon various obstacles (such as rails, stairs and ramps). Skaters work to compose lines that showcase their skill and imagination. Often members of different crews will occupy different parts of the park and content themselves with different obstacles. Sometimes, however, people from different crews make use of the same obstacle, having to take turns with one another (*act sequence*). It is in the mechanism of turn-taking among members of different crews that the notion of 'biting someone's shit' becomes relevant.

'Biting someone's shit' in the context of the 'speech event' of 'doing lines' refers to the action of imitating or repeating the line executed by the previous person in the queue. The meaning of this action depends crucially on the relationship between the person who does it and the person whose line has been imitated. When it is done by a member of a different crew, it can be taken as a challenge or sign of disrespect – a transgression of the rules of etiquette associated with 'doing lines'. In this case, the utterance 'Hey man, don't bite my shit', can be interpreted as a warning or a threat. In cases where the person who 'bites one's shit' is a member of one's own crew, it can be seen as a matter of friendly competition or even a way of showing respect for one's crew member by emulating him. In this case, the utterance 'Hey man, don't bite my shit', might be uttered in a more playful *key* and interpreted as teasing. In the context of a different speech event, such as a game of 'SKATE', repeating the trick that the previous person has done is expected and so does not constitute 'biting someone's shit'.

The point that this example illustrates is that the meaning of an utterance such as 'don't bite my shit' cannot be interpreted with reference to only the definition in the *Urban Dictionary* or with reference to only one component of the SPEAKING model, but can only be understood as a matter of the *interaction* among multiple components: place, participants, goals, the expected sequence of acts, the tone in which the utterance is said, the various media involved in the communication (including things such as participants' dress, their skateboards and other things such as video cameras), norms about what constitutes 'showing respect' to others, and the genre – whether it is 'park skating' or 'street skating'. More importantly, successful use of and interpretation of this speech act incorporates a complex range of cultural knowledge regarding the values, identities and norms of conduct of this particular community of young (mostly male) skateboarders in Hong Kong.

❑ Choose a speech event in which people that you know normally participate but with which you are not entirely familiar. Interview the people involved with the aim of finding out what their expectations are about who should say what to whom, when, how and why. Use the components of the SPEAKING model as a guide for your questioning. Ask people both about the kinds of communicative competences most members of their speech community have and about their own personal experiences with this particular speech event.
❑ After that, see if you can find an occasion to observe people taking part in this speech event. Notice not just what is said, but also who says it, when and how. Fill out Table C7.1 with information from both your interviews and your observation.

Table C7.1 Analysing a speech event

Date and time of observation: Name of event:
Setting
Participants
Ends
Act sequence
Key
Instrumentalities
Norms
Genre

Refining your analysis

The greatest danger in using a model such as Hymes's SPEAKING model is that the analyst simply describes the expectations participants have regarding each of the components in a rather mechanical way, like filling out a checklist, without offering much in the way of analysis. While this can at least provide a general idea of how the speech event happens, it does not tell us very much about *why* it happens the way it does. The analyst cannot stop at just describing the various components, but also needs to ask: (1) *why* different components have particular expectations associated with them; (2) *how* the expectations associated with different components interact and affect one another; and (3) *why* certain components seem more important and other components less important to participants.

Below are some useful tips to help you avoid falling into the trap of mechanical description.

Be specific

It is important for the analyst to be as specific as possible in his or her description of the expectations people have about the different components. This sometimes involves asking probing questions or observing what people say or do carefully, paying close attention to detail.

Remember that all components are not equal

One of the most important things an analyst will want to notice is that participants may regard the expectations governing some components to be stricter than those governing others and that some behaviour might be regarded as more or less 'compulsory' while other behaviour might be regarded as 'optional'. It is also important to note how expectations regarding one component can affect the kinds of expectations participants have about other components. In other words, it is important to notice which kinds of behaviour tend to co-occur in speech events (e.g. the genre of a joke may tend to co-occur with a humorous or light-hearted key).

Compare and contrast

One way to really understand whether the communicative competencies you have uncovered through your analysis are really significant is to compare and contrast different speech events or the different experiences and perspectives of different participants engaged in the same speech event. One of the reasons Ruesch and Bateson recommend that analysts compare the speech event they are studying with one that is more familiar to them is to help them to better notice those aspects of the speech event that they might be a misunderstanding or taking for granted.

Explore transgressions

One good way to understand what people are expected to do in a particular situation is to find out what happens when they fail to do what they are expected to do. This is because, while appropriate behaviour usually passes unremarked upon, inappropriate behaviour is often an occasion for participants to explicitly discuss their otherwise tacit assumptions and expectations. Therefore, noticing or talking with participants about mistakes, transgressions, inappropriate behaviour or 'incompetence' can be a good way to clarify what they regard as appropriate and why.

Activity

1   Further refine the analysis you did in the last activity by doing the following:

❏   Talk to your participants about what you have written down for each component and ask them if they think it is accurate. See if they can help you to make your descriptions of the knowledge that members need about each component more specific.

❏   Try to determine what kind of knowledge is most important for successful participation in the speech event. Is knowledge about some components more important than knowledge about others?

❏   Try to determine what the relationships among components might be and how they affect one another.

❑   Compare and contrast this speech event with a similar speech event
    that you are also familiar with. How can you account for the similari-
    ties and differences?
❑   Ask your participants what would happen if any of the conventions
    associated with this speech event were violated. How would people
    react? What would need to be done to repair such a violation?

  Do more activities on the companion website.

DOING MEDIATED DISCOURSE ANALYSIS   C8

In this unit, you will explore how to apply the tools of mediated discourse analysis to
the analysis of social actions, social practices and *sites of engagement*. The three concepts that we will be working with are:

1   the notion of *affordances* and *constraints*: the idea that different kinds of cultural
    tools make certain kinds of actions and certain kinds of social identities associ-
    ated with those actions either more or less possible;
2   the notion of *social practices*: the idea that certain actions combined with other
    actions and with certain cultural tools come to be regarded as recognisable social
    practices and that discourse can play an important role in maintaining and pro-
    moting these social practices;
3   the notion of *sites of engagement*: the idea that actions take place at the *nexus* of
    cultural tools, social relationships and the experiences, knowledge and skill of
    individual social actors, and the way these three elements come together can help
    us to understand how a particular social action will be performed.

'Fifty ways to leave your lover'

In her book *The Breakup 2.0*, Ilana Gershon (2010) discusses how different kinds of media
affect the way people perform the action of 'breaking up' with a romantic partner and
the way they come to regard this action as a particular kind of *social practice*. Of course,
there are many ways this action could be performed. One might confront the person with
whom one wishes to break up face-to-face, either in public or in a private place, call him or
her on the telephone or send what is known as a 'Dear John Letter'. Technology has introduced a number of new cultural tools with which to perform this action: one could send
an email, for example; negotiate the break-up using instant messaging or mobile phone–
based text messaging; or post a message or change one's 'relationship status' on Facebook.

      Gershon interviewed a large number of people about their ideas about and experi-
ences of breaking up and found that people had very strong feelings about how the
medium used can affect the action of breaking up. In particular, they felt that people
who used the 'wrong' medium risked enacting the 'wrong' kind of social identity, that
is, being considered 'the wrong kind of person' by others.

C8

Activity

❏ Think about the *affordances* and *constraints* of the different kinds of media one might use to accomplish the action of breaking up. For example, breaking up face-to-face makes it easier for the person doing the breaking up to gauge the other person's reaction and adapt his or her message accordingly, but it can make it more difficult to end the conversation (and the relationship) quickly and easily. This medium also makes it easier for the person being 'broken up with' to respond and ask for reasons and clarification, but it may make it more difficult for him or her to hide any feelings of disappointment or sadness that might arise. Because of these affordances and constraints, people tend to think some media are 'better' for breaking up than other media and associate different media for breaking up with different 'kinds of people'.

❏ Fill in Table C8.1 based on your own beliefs and experiences about the things different media make harder or more difficult to do during the breaking-up process. Then *rank* the different media in terms of (1) how much you would prefer to use it if you are breaking up with someone; and (2) how much you would prefer it to be used if you are the one being broken up with. Note if there is a difference in your ranking for these two situations. How do you account for this difference? What does this tell you about the relationship between cultural tools and social identities?

❏ Compare your answers with those of someone else and discuss if and why you have different opinions about the kinds of people associated with different media for breaking up.

Table C8.1 Cultural tools for breaking up

Medium	Affordances and constraints	Rank	
		(1)	*(2)*
Face-to-face conversation			
Telephone conversation			
Letter or email			
WhatsApp			
Snapchat			
Facebook relationship status			

Of course, most of the time when people engage in a complex social practice such as breaking up with a lover, they use a combination of cultural tools, including a combination of media. They might begin breaking up with a text message, continue the negotiation of the break-up through a telephone conversation, and complete the process in a face-to-face meeting.

Think about how the social practice of breaking up is constructed in your social circle. What smaller actions are usually included in this practice (such as 'making an appointment to meet' or 'apologising for hurting the other person's feelings') and how are these usually combined? What sorts of cultural tools (such as objects, media, genres, social languages, gestures or facial expressions) are used, and how do these tools affect how the practice is accomplished?

'Buy with one click'

Both of the readings on mediated discourse analysis in section D8 deal with moments when people are making decisions about buying things. Scollon talks about all of the discourses that need to come together to make purchasing a cup of coffee possible, and Jones talks about how a slight change to the discourse on a package of microwave popcorn made him decide not to buy it, even though the contents of the box had not changed.

Moments when we decide to buy something are usually not sudden or impulsive; they occur at the intersection of multiple itineraries of discourse that might include conversations you have had with friends about your planned purchase, advertisements you have seen from different companies and online reviews you may have read. Nevertheless, the very moment of the purchase is often crucial because of the way the *different discourses and other cultural tools* (online shopping sites, credit cards, signs in shops announcing sales), the relationship you have with the person you are buying from and with other people involved in the purchase (such as your parents who might be providing the funds), and your own *history* of buying things and of planning to buy this particular item.

❑   Think about the last time you bought something and analyse the *site of engagement* at which the purchase occurred.
❑   Think about the different 'itineraries of discourse' that led up to that site of engagement.
❑   Analyse the way the interaction among (1) the *discourses in place*, (2) the *interaction order* and (3) your own *historical body* made the purchase possible and think about the ways in which this interaction may have affected your decision making.

 Do more activities on the companion website.

ANALYSING MULTIMODALITY   C9

In this section, you will practise applying some of the ideas introduced in units A9 and B9 to the analysis of multimodality in texts and face-to-face interactions. You will explore how the analysis of multimodality can help us not only to understand how texts and interactions are structured, but also how they promote certain ideologies and power relationships.

Multimodal discourse analysis is a complex and rapidly developing field, and it would be impossible to demonstrate all of the many tools and concepts analysts have developed for the analysis of things such as images, gestures, gaze and posture. Instead, I will introduce a few basic tools and key questions that can guide you in this kind of analysis and encourage you to refer to the sources in the list of further reading for information on other tools and procedures.

When analysing 'static' images in print or on the Internet, many analysts adapt Halliday's framework of the different functions of language (discussed in sections A4 and B9). Based on this framework, we might use the following set of questions to guide us in analysing images:

Ideational function

❏ Who/what are the main participants in the image?
❏ Is the image a narrative image, an analytical image or a classificatory image?
❏ What are the processes portrayed in the image and how are they portrayed?
❏ What are the primary vectors formed by actions, gestures, gaze and the positioning of the figures?
❏ If there are multiple vectors, how do they interact with one another?

Interpersonal function

❏ From what perspective are the figures in the image shown? How does this create a position for the viewer?
❏ Are the figures depicted close up or far away from the viewer?
❏ Are the figures looking at the viewer or away?
❏ What kind of relationship do they establish with the viewer through things such as gaze and gesture?
❏ Does the image seem realistic, and how does this affect how the viewer relates to the figures in the image?

Textual function

❏ What are the most prominent and least prominent elements in the image?
❏ What is in the centre of the image?
❏ What is the relationship between the background and the foreground?
❏ What is in the top section of the image and what is in the bottom section?
❏ What is on the left and what is on the right?
❏ How does the placement of elements in the image affect how the viewer's eyes are likely to move across it?
❏ Are there other modes combined with the image (such as text or arrows/lines)? How do these elements interact with the image?

Ideology

❏ How do the choices about what has been included in the image and what has been excluded portray a certain version of reality?
❏ Are the figures in the image portrayed in stereotypical or unexpected ways?
❏ Are some figures active and others passive? What is the significance of this?
❏ What do you think the image is trying to get you to think or do?

Snapchat

One of the most common ways people use images to communicate nowadays is through social media platforms such as Snapchat and Instagram. Although such images are often very different from those taken by professional photographers that we encounter in print publications and online, they are carefully constructed, with their creators usually paying a great deal of attention to the people and objects that are included in the images, the way these people and/or objects are arranged, the way other elements like written text are used to help give meaning to the elements that are represented, and the kind of inter-personal relationship the image constructs between the viewer and the photographer and/or the people or objects in the image. Furthermore, despite their status as informal and 'fun' forms of communication, images sent over social media platforms also serve to express or reinforce certain ideologies and relationships of power.

Consider the image below, which was posted on the Snapchat 'story' of a female university student in Saudi Arabia (Figure C9.1, from Albwardi, 2018).

Figure C9.1 Life is hard in translation class, from Albwardi.

Like many images shared on Snapchat, this image captures an 'ordinary' moment in the photographer's life by depicting everyday objects in her translation classroom: the surface of the desk, her notebook and her bag. In some respects, this image might be considered an analytical one, which uses the 'hard' surface of the desk to communicate the experience of being in translation class. It might also be considered a classificatory image that simply communicates the types of objects found on a students' desk in a university classroom. At the same time, there is a vector created by the diagonal line of the desk that runs from the lower left of the image to the upper right. The process communicated by this vector is the act of 'looking', the gaze of the photographer look-ing over her desk towards something or someone outside of the fame of the image, presumably the teacher. In this respect, the image tells the story of the photographer sitting in her translation class and taking a picture.

The way the elements are arranged in the image also contributes to the way it cre-ates meaning. The placement of the students' belongings on the left of the picture presents them as 'given' and reproduces the direction of readers' gazes as they move from left to right, reading the caption 'Life is hard in translation class', settling on the two small emojis at the end of the sentence. The sentence is placed at the bottom of the image, usually reserved for the 'real', and the upper section of the image, the 'ideal', is the unseen activity of the classroom that the photographer is gazing at. As in the WhatsApp conversation we analysed in C6, the emojis serve as contextualisation cues, communicating an ironic attitude towards the utterance.

The most important aspect of this image is the interpersonal meaning the photographer creates by holding the camera behind her desk, inviting the viewer to share the perspective of someone sitting in her translation class and surreptitiously taking a picture and uploading it onto Snapchat. In fact, the contrast between the message in the caption and the transgressive activity the photographer is engaged in is what creates the humour in this image and positions the viewer in a kind of conspiratorial relationship with the photographer.

Based on this analysis, we might conclude that this is an image about power and solidarity – the 'hard' power that teachers exert over students by prohibiting activities such as using mobile phones during lessons, the 'soft' power students exert by secretly breaking these rules and the solidarity students create with each other by sharing stories of such transgressions.

'Eyeliner on fleek'

Now consider the image below, also taken by a Saudi university student. Use the questions above to analyse how this photographer represents a certain kind of reality, creates a certain kind of relationship with the viewer, and promotes a certain ideology. Pay special attention to the way different modes (image, writing, font, emojis) are combined to create meaning (Figure C9.2).

Figure C9.2 Eyeliner on fleek, from Albwardi, 2018.

Fifteen seconds in a writing centre

Now we will turn to how you might go about analysing multimodality in face-to-face interaction, using as an example just 15 seconds of interaction in a university writing centre where students go to get advice about their written assignments from peer tutors. The fact that we will only be looking at a very small segment attests to the multimodal richness of most face-to-face interaction – quite a lot can occur in just 15 seconds. At the same time, this kind of microanalysis can also be risky if the analyst loses sight of the higher-level actions that the segment under analysis is part of. Thus, in a thorough multimodal analysis of interaction, the analyst always alternates his or her attention from the small details to the 'big picture', always asking how microelements such as gaze and posture shifts, gesture and intonation contours help participants to accomplish the higher-level actions they are engaged in.

This example also demonstrates one way of producing a multimodal transcription. The segment of interaction to be analysed is presented in 12 frames captured from a digital video of the tutoring session (see Figure C9.3). The frames were not captured at any regular time interval. Rather, a frame was captured each time a new meaningful lower-level action such as a gaze shift, a gesture or a 'tone unit' of speech was produced. As can be seen in the images, in many of the frames, multiple meaningful actions were performed across multiple modes simultaneously. In the type of transcription demonstrated here (adapted from Norris 2004), things such as head movements, the trajectory of gestures and the direction of gaze are marked with arrows, and the speech of participants is represented in text of varying sizes above their heads, the size and direction of the letters representing stress and intonation.

The analysis I will demonstrate here will focus on **intermodal relationships**, how actions taken with different modes of communication work together and affect one another. It will make use of two basic concepts: *sequentiality* – the idea that lower-level actions are arranged in meaningful sequences to form higher-level actions – and *simultaneity* – the idea that when actions are produced at the same time, they can affect how each should be interpreted. Related to these two concepts is the notion that all actions are mutually negotiated between participants in interaction. The actions that one person performs are always in some ways influenced or constrained by the actions that the other person performs.

As mentioned above, one aim of such an analysis is to identify the lower-level actions and understand how they combine to form higher-level actions. The ultimate aim, however, is to use such an analysis to understand how people use the many resources that are available to them to perform *social practices* and enact *social identities* in ways that promote and reinforce particular 'Discourses' or social relationships.

The two participants in this segment are the tutor (the woman seated on the right) and the client (the man seated on the left). The session begins with the tutor saying, 'so … ummm', and making two small **beat gestures** with her pen towards the client's essay lying on the table in time with the two syllables (frame a). *Beat gestures* are perhaps the most common kinds of gestures. We use them to keep time in interactions, often tracking the rhythm of our speech, and they are important in helping participants synchronise things such as turn-taking. They can also function to signal that a new higher-level action or a new 'frame' is being taken up, much like *discourse markers* (see B6). In this case, the two beats along with the utterance signal that a new part of the tutoring session is about to start.

C9

Figure C9.3 An interaction in a writing centre.

In frames b through f, the tutor asks, 'Is there anything in particular you think you want some more help with?'. This utterance is accompanied by a complex combination of actions that contribute to constructing the meaning of the utterance and the relationship between the participants. As she says the words 'anything in particular', the tutor points to the client's essay and inscribes a circle in the air with her pen. This is followed by a downward motion on the stressed syllable 'TIC'. Gestures like this, which involve pointing, are known as **deictic gestures**. The tutor follows this deictic gesture towards the essay with another one, pointing her pen towards the client when she says, 'YOU think'. Right after she utters the word 'think,' the client leans slightly forward and raises his hand to his chin, forming the **iconic gesture** of a person deep in thought. Iconic gestures are those that symbolise some kind of abstract idea or higher-level action in a rather conventionalised way. This gesture on the part of the client is a good example of the way listeners use modes such as gesture to contribute to conversations even when they do not make use of the resource of speech.

As the tutor says 'you want some more help with', she gazes at the client, signalling that she is preparing to end her turn. Gaze is an important resource for the management of turn-taking in conversation, with speakers often looking away when they are speaking and then turning their gaze back to their interlocutors when they are finished. When the tutor finishes her question, she leans back slightly and brushes the hair from her face, almost as if she is clearing interactional space for the client's response as he issues a hesitant 'ummmmm'.

As she is waiting for his response, the tutor tilts her head downwards and directs her gaze towards the essay, as if signalling that it is there that the client might find the answer to her questions (frame i). This is also a kind of deictic gesture, but she is using her head to point rather than her hand. The client answers this downward motion with an upward motion of his arm to touch his glasses, another iconic gesture signalling that he is 'searching' for something he would like help with. Then the client lowers his hand and asks, 'Do you know the meaning of this paragraph?' inscribing exactly the same kind of circle above his essay that the tutor had made just moments before (frame k).

The modes of gaze, head movement, posture, gesture and prosody in this short segment do not just help participants to frame their utterances and organise the interaction. These modes also work together to construct the higher-level action of 'having a tutorial' and to construct the relationship between the two participants as one of unequal power. The tutor demonstrates her power over the client in a number of small ways: through gaze (she gazes at him much more than he does at her), through her posture (she sits higher and straighter than he does) and through gestures (she frequently points at him and at his essay with her pen and her head). Furthermore, all of the client's gestures (the 'thinking' gesture, the 'searching' gesture and the imitation of the tutor's deictic circle) seem to be in response to the tutor's words or gestures, as if she is controlling him like a puppet. Another important mode the tutor uses to maintain control of the interaction, which we have not mentioned, is **object handling**. Not only does she hold a pen throughout the interaction (while the client is empty handed), but she also keeps her left hand placed on the edge of the client's essay during this entire segment as if she is prepared to take it away from him at any moment.

❑   Videotape a short interaction and divide a segment of the video into frames using an easy-to-use computer program such as iMovie (Mac) or Windows Movie Maker. Analyse how participants use the modes of gesture, gaze, posture, head movement and prosody along with the mode of spoken language to create meaning and manage the interaction. Pay attention to how lower-level actions are sequenced to form higher-level actions and how actions performed simultaneously affect one another's meaning.

 Do more activities on the companion website.

C10   ANALYSING CORPORA

What happened to Taylor Swift?

In order to illustrate the procedures for corpus-assisted discourse analysis explained in unit B10, in this section I will examine a corpus of song lyrics by the American pop star Taylor Swift. The reason I'm so interested in this celebrity is not that I think her music is so great, but that I think it provides a good example of what people in the music business call a 'brand pivot' and what people in the discourse analysis business might call a 'Discourse pivot', a movement from one Discourse to another. The word 'pivot' is often used in politics to describe when a politician changes the ideological content of their speeches and public statements to appeal to a different (usually a wider) audience. But politicians aren't the only ones that pivot. Pop stars do it too. By analysing the discursive characteristics of such pivots, we can understand something about how discourse is related to the social world and what kinds of discourse appeal to different kinds of audiences.

When she started to make a name for herself in the music industry in 2005, Taylor Swift projected the sweet, innocent persona of a country singer. Starting in 2012, however, she began changing her image, engaging in a number of high-profile feuds with other celebrities like Katy Perry, Kim Kardashian, Lorde and Demi Lovato and changing the kinds of things she sang about to appeal to a different market demographic. Many of her early fans accused her of 'going pop' or 'selling out', making her music more superficial and becoming 'self-absorbed'. This change in style was signalled by Taylor herself: in her 2017 single 'Look What You Made Me Do', she informed her fans that the 'old Taylor' is 'dead'.

In this analysis, I am going to use corpus tools to compare Taylor's pre-2012 music with her post-2012 music in terms of the kinds of words she uses and the ways she portrays herself.

Before you read further in this unit, I recommend that you download AntConc or some other software program for corpus analysis, and as you read, try to replicate the procedures described on a corpus of your own creation. You might, for example, create a similar corpus of lyrics from another singer such as Beyoncé or Rihanna and compare your findings with those generated from the corpora analysed here.

My corpus consists of the lyrics of 100 songs released by Taylor Swift from 2006 to 2017. Song lyrics are a good example of a type of text that might have to be 'cleaned' or otherwise altered before being suitable for inclusion in a corpus. For example, such texts often include things such as labels indicating 'chorus' or 'verse', which are not relevant to the analysis and should be removed. Sometimes repeated words or phrases are written in a kind of shorthand (e.g. I love you × 3). These need to be written out fully so that the texts reflect exactly what is sung. For my corpus, song titles and labels such as 'chorus' and 'verse' were deleted. Each song was saved in a separate text file, and then the songs released before 2012 and after 2012 were put into separate directories. Each of these corpora consisted of 50 songs. Table C10.1 shows the size of each of the

Table C10.1 Size of corpora and type token ratio

	No. of texts	No. of tokens	No. of types	Type token ratio
Pre-2012	50	39,831	2316	17.1
Post-2012	50	21,286	1668	12.7

corpora and the number of tokens (actual words) and types (specific words), as well as the 'type token ratio'.

The first thing we might notice is that the type token ratio for both of these corpora is rather low compared with the BNC written (45.53) and spoken (32.96) corpora. This is not surprising. Pop music generally involves quite a lot of repetition and a fairly narrow range of lexical items. As can be seen from the table, the type token ratio for the pre-2012 corpus is slightly higher than that of the post-2012 corpus, suggesting that Taylor Swift's earlier music exhibited more lexical complexity than her later music. Not only have her songs become 'simpler' and more repetitious, but they have also become shorter: the average length of her pre-2012 songs was 796.6 words, whereas the average length of the post-2012 songs was 425.7 words. One explanation for this is that shorter and simpler songs might better suit a more commercial market.

Table C10.2 shows the frequency of the most frequently occurring words in the two corpora along with their overall ranking, their numerical frequency and the percentage of the total tokens they represent. Note that the percentage of total tokens is important when you are comparing corpora of different sizes. Some programs will calculate this for you, but with AntConc, users must do this themselves.

The fact that *function words* like pronouns, conjunctions and articles are the most frequent words in these texts is not surprising; this is the case with most texts. The fact that the most frequent words in both of these corpora are 'I' and 'you' is also consistent with other corpus-based studies of popular music. Murphey (1992), for example, found a similar degree of frequency for these pronouns in a corpus of English pop songs from the late 1980s. This, of course, makes sense, given that pop songs usually involve a singer (or singer *persona*) singing to another person, usually a lover. What is interesting here is that the items 'you' and 'I' are reversed in the two corpora, with 'you' being the most frequent word in the pre-2012 corpus and 'I' being the most frequent word in the post-2012 corpus. Although the differences in the percentages of the two

Table C10.2 Top five words

Pre-2012				Post-2012			
Word	Rank	Freq.	% of tokens	Word	Rank	Freq.	% of tokens
you	1	2226	5.6	I	1	1169	5.5
I	2	2154	5.4	you	2	1101	5.1
the	3	1182	2.9	the	3	509	2.4
and	4	1160	2.9	and	4	433	2.2
It	5	863	2.1	it	5	398	2.03

words are not high, this lends some support to the suggestion that Taylor's music has become more self-absorbed – more about her.

Word frequency lists can often suggest suitable candidates for concordance searches and collocation analyses. In this case, I have decided to look more closely at the word 'I' in the pre and post-2012 corpora to find out not just how much but also *how* Taylor talked about herself in these periods. Figure C10.1 shows a comparison of the words that most frequently *followed* the word 'I' in the two corpora. The way I generated this was by choosing 'collocates' in the AntConc menu and adjusting the Window Span to from 0L to 3R. This will presumably tell me what verbs are associated with 'I' (what Taylor portrayed herself as doing), as well how she described herself (Table C10.3).

Table C10.3 Right collocates of 'I'

Pre-2012	Post-2012
'm	I
you	you
was	'm
don't	it
know	know

There are a few observations that we can make about this list of collocates right off the bat. The first is that in the pre-2012 corpus, the auxiliary verbs 'am' ('m) and 'was' are in the top three right collocates of I, suggesting that in her earlier songs, Taylor spent less time talking about what she did and more time talking about what she *was like* or what someone else had *done to her*. Another interesting observation is the presence of the word 'don't' in the pre-2012 corpus, suggesting that not only did she not frequently put herself in the role of agent (*doing* things), but also that she frequently talked about what she *didn't* do. It is also important to note the unusual fact that in the post-2012 corpus, the most frequent collocate of 'I' was 'I', and that both 'you' and 'know' were frequent collocates of 'I' in both corpora, but from this list alone we can't tell if they were used in the same way.

In order to make sense of lists like this, it is usually necessary to look at the collocates in question in the context in which they occurred, using the concordance tool. For example, if we generate a concordance for I *am* (I'm) in the pre-2012 corpus (Figure C10.1), we find that in many cases, Taylor uses this construction to talk not about what she is but what she is *not* ('I'm no one special', 'I'm not a princess', 'I'm not so sure', 'I'm not the one').

The concordance of I *am* (I'm) in the post-2012 corpus reveals a much more active and confident Taylor (with phrases like 'I'm telling you', 'I'm gonna dance', and 'I'm the one'). A particular focus on the item 'not' (Figure C10.2) shows that it collocates with 'I'm' much less frequently in the post-2012 corpus, and, when it does, it is often used to portray Taylor in a positive light or put her in an agentive position (more 'in charge' of the situation) (in phrases such as 'I'm not a bad girl', 'I'm not dancing with you', 'I'm not even going to try').

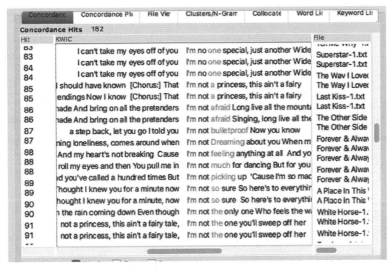

Figure C10.1 Partial concordance list for 'I'm' in pre-2012 corpus.

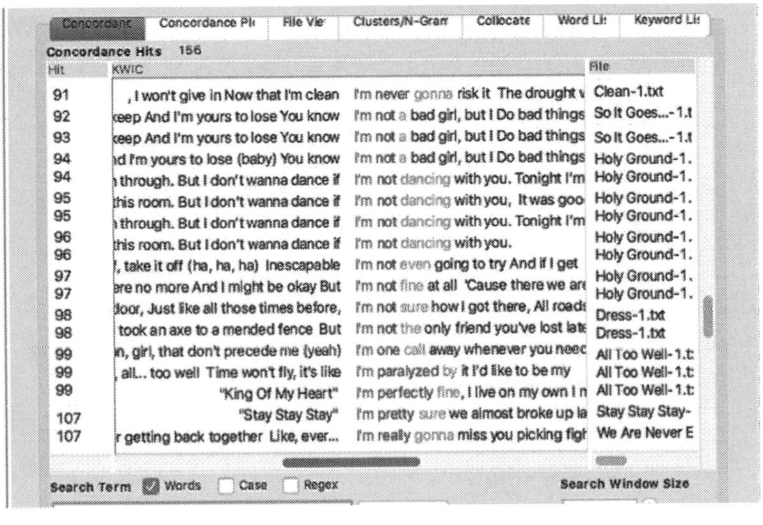

Figure C10.2 Partial concordance list for 'I'm' in post-2012 corpus.

Similar differences can be found in other words common to the pre and post-2012 lists. In the pre-2012 corpus, for example, the word 'know' is most often used to talk about what Taylor *doesn't* know (in phrases such as 'I didn't know it at fifteen', and 'I don't know how it gets better'), whereas in the post-2012 corpus, the word 'know' is most often used to talk about what she *does* know (in phrases such as 'I know exactly where it leads', and 'I know what you heard about me'). Similarly, in the pre-2012 collocates of 'I' with 'you', the most common word linking these items is 'love' (as in 'I love you'), whereas in the post-2012 corpus, love only appears twice; much more common constructions are 'I want you' and 'I wish you …'). The odd case of the frequent collocation of 'I' with 'I' in the post-2012 corpus is the result of Taylor frequently repeating the word (in phrases such as 'I, I, I like it' and 'I, I, I shake it off').

From this initial analysis, we can hypothesise that the Taylor of the post-2012 corpus is more agentive, confident, practical and self-absorbed, whereas the Taylor of the pre-2012 corpus is more modest, self-deprecating, romantic and unsure of herself. Of course, this is only a hypothesis, one that needs to be tested through a close discourse analysis of the actual texts.

One final method I will demonstrate for interrogating the differences between the two corpora is keyword analysis. *Keyness* refers to the degree to which a particular word appears more frequently in one corpus *compared* to another corpus. When doing keyword analyses, analysts usually compare a small, specialised corpus (such as a corpus of newspaper articles about Muslims) with a larger, more general corpus (such as a more general corpus of newspaper articles or the British National Corpus of Written Language).

In our case, our main question already has to do with comparing one corpus to another, and so it makes sense to use the post-2012 corpus as the reference corpus for the pre-2012 corpus and vice versa. In this way, what *keyness* will represent is not the degree to which Taylor uses certain words compared to other singers, but the difference between the words used by the 'old Taylor' and the 'new Taylor'.

The two lists (see Table C10.4) give some hints as to the kinds of things Taylor was preoccupied with in her pre and post-2012 music. The keyness of the word 'she' in the pre-2012 corpus, for example, reflects the frequency with which Taylor was singing about 'the other woman' who had stolen her lover in this period (in phrases such as 'she's never gonna love you like I want to'). Words like 'rains', 'grows' and 'smile' also reflect the generally more romantic orientation of her earlier period, whereas words like 'ooh' and 'shake' reflect the generally more hedonistic, 'pop' style of her later music.

Table C10.4 'Keywords' in the pre- and post-2012 corpora

Pre-2012 corpus	Post-2012 corpus
she	ooh
la	shake
rains	we
grow	new
smile	it

❏ Use the analysis described above as the starting point for a closer examination of Taylor Swift's lyrics (available at https://www.azlyrics.com/t/taylorswift.html), using some of the principles of text analysis discussed in section B4. You might, for example, focus on things such as *transitivity, indexicality* and *intertextuality*. Does your close reading of the texts confirm and build upon any of the findings of the corpus analysis?

❏ Conduct a similar analysis using the same procedures on your own corpus of pop songs.

 Do more activities on the companion website.

NOTES

1 https://www.facebook.com/asociacionequinac.org/posts/1480068602042371
2 https://www.facebook.com/asociacionequinac.org/photos/a.573101472739093.1073741828.
   565154453533795/1481375795244985/?type=3&theater
3 https://www.facebook.com/asociacionequinac.org/posts/1485542178161680
4 https://pacma.es/muere-una-cria-de-delfin-en-almeria-por-el-acoso-de-los-banistas/
5 https://www.facebook.com/asociacionequinac.org/posts/1486027154779849

Section D
EXTENSION
READINGS IN DISCOURSE ANALYSIS

THREE PERSPECTIVES ON DISCOURSE

In this section you will read three excerpts from important figures in the field of discourse analysis, each illustrating one of the three perspectives on discourse that we discussed in section B1. The first is from the famous 1952 essay by the linguist Zellig Harris in which he coined the term 'discourse analysis'. In it he outlines the limitations of traditional approaches to language and explains why we need a method to examine language beyond the level of the clause.

The second is an excerpt from the PhD dissertation of H.G. Widdowson in which he questions some of the assumptions made by Harris and argues that the analysis of discourse must go beyond just looking at how texts are put together to exploring how people use language to perform social actions. In making this argument he acknowledges his debt to the American sociolinguist William Labov (see section D2), who advanced the idea that 'the object of linguistics must ultimately be the instrument of communication used by the speech community, and if we are not talking about *that* language there is something trivial in our proceedings' (1972a: 187).

The last excerpt comes from the American discourse analyst and educationalist James Paul Gee. In this excerpt he defines discourse even more broadly as the way we build social identities and social activities by combining language with 'other stuff'.

As you read these three excerpts, try to consider how these different scholars are responding to or building upon what the others have said. Think about how their respective approaches to discourse differ from one another and also ways in which they might be reconciled.

A. Discourse analysis

Zellig Harris **Zellig Harris** (reprinted from *Language 28*(1) (1952): 1–30)

The problem

One can approach discourse analysis from two types of problem, which turn out to be related. The first is the problem of continuing descriptive linguistics beyond the limits of a single sentence at a time. The other is the question of correlating 'culture' and language (i.e. non-linguistic and linguistic behavior).

The first problem arises because descriptive linguistics generally stops at sentence boundaries. This is not due to any prior decision. The techniques of linguistics were constructed to study any stretch of speech, of whatever length. But in every language it turns out that almost all the results lie within a relatively short stretch, which we may call a sentence. That is, when we can state a restriction on the occurrence of element A in respect to the occurrence of element B, it will almost always be the case that A and B are regarded as occurring within the same sentence. Of English adjectives, for instance, we can say that they occur before a noun or after certain verbs (in the same sentence): the dark clouds, the future seems bright; only rarely can we state restrictions across sentence boundaries, e.g. that if the main verb of one sentence has a given tense-suffix, the main verb of the next sentence will have a particular other tense-suffix. We cannot say that if one sentence has the form NV, the next sentence will have the form N. We can only say that most sentences are NV, some are N, and so on; and that these structures occur in various sequences.

In this way descriptive linguistics, which sets out to describe the occurrence of elements in any stretch of speech, ends up by describing it primarily in respect to other elements of the same sentence. This limitation has not seemed too serious, because it has not precluded the writing of adequate grammars: the grammar states the sentence structure; the speaker makes up a particular sentence in keeping with this structure, and supplies the particular sequence of sentences.

The other problem, that of the connection between behavior (or social situation) and language, has always been considered beyond the scope of linguistics proper. Descriptive linguistics has not dealt with the meanings of morphemes; and though one might try to get around that by speaking not of meanings, but of the social and interpersonal situation in which speech occurs, descriptive linguistics has had no equipment for taking the social situation into account: it has only been able to state the occurrence of one linguistic element in respect to the occurrence of others. Culture-and-language studies have therefore been carried on without benefit of the recent distributional investigations of linguistics. For example, they list the meanings expressed in the language by surveying the vocabulary stock; or they draw conclusions from the fact that in a particular language a particular set of meanings is expressed by the same morpheme; or they discuss the nuances of meaning and usage of one word in comparison with others (e.g. in stylistics). Culture-and-language studies have also noted such points as that phrases are to be taken in their total meaning rather than as the sum of the meanings of their component morphemes, e.g. that 'How are you?' is a greeting rather than a question about health—an example that illustrates the correlation of speech with social situation. Similarly, personality characteristics in speech have been studied by correlating an individual's recurrent speech features with recurrent features of his behavior and feeling.

Distribution within discourse

Distributional or combinatorial analysis within one discourse at a time turns out to be relevant to both of these problems. On the one hand, it carries us past the sentence limitation of descriptive linguistics. Although we cannot state the distribution of sentences (or, in general, any inter-sentence relation) when we are given an arbitrary conglomeration of sentences in a language, we can get quite definite results about certain relations across sentence boundaries when we consider just the sentences of a particular connected discourse—that is, the sentences spoken or written in succession by one or more persons in a single situation. This restriction to connected discourse does not detract from the usefulness of the analysis, since all language occurrences are internally connected. Language does not occur in stray words or sentences, but in connected discourse—from a one-word utterance to a ten-volume work, from a monolog to a Union Square argument. Arbitrary conglomerations of sentences are indeed of no interest except as a check on grammatical description; and it is not surprising that we cannot find interdependence among the sentences of such an aggregate. The successive sentences of a connected discourse, however, offer fertile soil for the methods of descriptive linguistics, since these methods study the relative distribution of elements within a connected stretch of speech.

On the other hand, distributional analysis within one discourse at a time yields information about certain correlations of language with other behavior. The reason is that each connected discourse occurs within a particular situation, whether of a person speaking, or of a conversation, or of someone sitting down occasionally over a period of months to write a particular kind of book in a particular literary or scientific tradition. To be sure, this concurrence between situation and discourse does not mean that discourses occurring in similar situations must necessarily have certain formal characteristics in common, while discourses occurring in different situations must have certain formal differences. The concurrence between situation and discourse only makes it understandable, or possible, that such formal correlations should exist. It remains to be shown as a matter of empirical fact that such formal correlations do indeed exist, that the discourses of a particular person, social group, style, or subject-matter exhibit not only particular meanings (in their selection of morphemes) but also characteristic formal features. The particular selection of morphemes cannot be considered here. But the formal features of the discourses can be studied by distributional methods within the text; and the fact of their correlation with a particular type of situation gives a meaning-status to the occurrence of these formal features.

The nature of the method

We have raised two problems: that of the distributional relations among sentences, and that of the correlation between language and social situation. We have proposed that information relevant to both of these problems can be obtained by a formal analysis of one stretch of discourse at a time. What KIND of analysis would be applicable here? To decide this, we consider what is permitted by the material.

Since the material is simply a string of linguistic forms arranged in successive sentences, any formal analysis is limited to locating linguistic elements within these sentences—that is, to stating the occurrence of elements. We cannot set up any method for investigating the nature or composition of these elements, or their correlations with non-linguistic features, unless we bring in new information from outside.

Furthermore, there are no particular elements, say but or I or communism, which have a prior importance, such as would cause us to be interested in the mere fact of their presence or absence in our text. Any analysis which aimed to find out whether certain particular words, selected by the investigator, occur in the text or not, would be an investigation of the CONTENT of the text and would be ultimately based on the MEANINGS of the words selected. If we do not depend upon meaning in our investigation, then the only morphemes or classes which we can deal with separately are those which have grammatically stated peculiarities of distribution.

Since, then, we are not in general interested in any particular element selected in advance, our interest in those elements that do occur cannot be merely in the tautologic statement THAT they occur, but in the empirical statement of HOW they occur: which ones occur next to which others, or in the same environment as which others, and so on—that is, in the relative occurrence of these elements with respect to each other. In this sense, our method is comparable to that which is used, in the case of a whole language, in compiling a grammar (which states the distributional relations among elements), rather than in compiling a dictionary (which lists all the elements that are found in the language, no matter where).

Finally, since our material is a closed string of sentences, our statement about the distribution of each element can only be valid within the limits of this succession of sentences, whether it be a paragraph or a book. We will see, we can sometimes use information about the distribution of an element outside our material; but this can be only an external aid, brought in after the distribution of the element within the discourse has been completely stated.

Issues to consider

❏   For Harris, one of the aims of discourse analysis is to *describe* texts in the same way linguists describe sentences, by explaining the occurrences of elements in relation to the occurrence of other elements. What might be the advantages of trying to discover the 'rules' that govern the ways texts are put together in the same way we can talk about the 'rules' that govern the way sentences are put together? What could such knowledge be used for? Do you think the logic that governs the way we look at sentence-level grammar can be extended to longer stretches of text or conversation?

❏   Harris suggests that by studying the formal distribution of elements in texts used in different social situations, we will be able to discover correlations between certain kinds of structures and certain kinds of social behaviour. Can you think of some examples of text structures that nearly always occur in connections with certain kinds of social practices? What are some of the limitations of this approach?

B. An applied linguistic approach to discourse analysis

Henry G. Widdowson (reprinted from his unpublished doctoral dissertation 1973)

Henry G.
Widdowson

(Harris's) aim is simply to establish formal patterns without reference to meaning. But Harris nevertheless believes that his analysis has some bearing on how discourse is understood as communication. At first sight it would appear that his aim is to contribute to studies of contextualized language in both of the senses distinguished at the beginning of this chapter. In a prolegomenon to his actual analysis he makes the comment:

> One can approach discourse analysis from two types of problem, which turn out to be related. The first is the problem of continuing descriptive linguistics beyond the limits of a single sentence at a time. The other is the question of correlating "culture" and language (i.e. nonlinguistic and linguistic behavior).
>
> (Harris 1952/1964: 356)

It turns out, however, that what Harris has in mind in the second of these problems is something very like the Hallidayan notion of register. He appears to believe that the kind of distributional analysis of morpheme sequences that he proposes will provide a basis for correlating the formal properties of different pieces of language with the social situations in which they occur.

*****

Since Harris has taken a considerable number of steps in the description of discourse, the question naturally arises as to how he has managed to do this without considering speech events and social contexts at all, even though, as we have seen, he acknowledges that his description should bear upon the problem of how language is understood in social situations.

The answer to this question is, of course, that whereas Harris conceives of discourse as contextualized language data in one of the senses we have distinguished, Labov thinks of it as contextualized language data in the other sense. Harris looks for patterns of linguistic elements which link sentences together into a larger formal structure, and Labov looks at the way linguistic elements are used to perform communicative acts, and this kind of enquiry takes him outside the actual linguistic properties of the text not, as with Harris, to the linguistic properties of the code but to the extra-linguistic factors of the social situation. Labov's emphasis, therefore, is on the performance of social actions rather than on the incidence of linguistic forms

*****

It seems clear, then, that we are confronted here with two quite different kinds of enquiry both contending for the same name. A terminological distinction seems to be called for. The kind of investigation carried out by Harris into the formal structure of a piece of language might be called text analysis. Its purpose is to discover the patterning of linguistic elements beyond the limit of the sentence, and what it is that provides a text with its cohesion. Thus what Harris calls 'discourse analysis' will be referred to as 'text analysis'. One is to some degree justified in thus taking liberties with Harris's terminology by the fact that Harris himself appears to use the terms 'text' and 'discourse' interchangeably, as for example, in the following quotation:

> The formal features of the discourses can be studied by distributional methods within the text.
>
> (Harris 1952/1964: 357)

We may now use the term discourse analysis to refer to the kind of investigation proposed by Labov into the way linguistic elements are put to communicative use in the performing of social actions. Its purpose is to discover what sentences count as utterances and what it is that provides a discourse with its coherence as a piece of communication.

Issues to consider
❑   Widdowson contrasts Harris's view of discourse, which focuses on linguistic patterns and tries to correlate them to different social situations with that of Labov, who focuses on how language is used to perform particular communicative acts.

What arguments could be made for and against these two contrasting views? Is there any way they could be fruitfully combined or are they mutually exclusive?

❑ Widdowson associates the perspective of Harris (discourse as language beyond the clause) more with the study of *cohesion* and the perspective of Labov (discourse as language in use) more with the study of the *coherence* of discourse 'as a piece of communication'. How can you explain this distinction based on the discussion of cohesion and coherence in section B2?

C. Discourses

James Paul Gee (reprinted from *Introduction to Discourse Analysis* (2010): 28–29)

James
Paul Gee

People build identities and activities not just through language, but by using language together with other "stuff" that isn't language. If you want to get recognized as a street-gang member of a certain sort you have to speak in the "right" way, but you also have to act and dress in the "right" way, as well. You also have to engage (or, at least, behave as if you are engaging) in characteristic ways of thinking, acting, interacting, valuing, feeling, and believing. You also have to use or be able to use various sorts of symbols (e.g., graffiti), tools (e.g., a weapon), and objects (e.g., street corners) in the "right" places and at the "right" times. You can't just "talk the talk", you have to "walk the walk" as well.

The same is true of doing/being a corporate lawyer, Marine sergeant, radical feminist, or a regular at the local bar. One and the same person might talk, act, and interact in such a way as to get recognised as a "street gang member" in one context and, in another context, talk, act, and interact in quite different ways so as to get recognised as a "gifted student". And, indeed, these two identities, and their concomitant ways of talking, acting, and interacting, may well conflict with each other in some circumstances (where different people expect different identities from the person), as well as in the person's own mind.

I use the term "Discourse", with a capital "D", for ways of combining and integrating language, actions, interactions, ways of thinking, believing, valuing, and using various symbols, tools, and objects to enact a particular sort of socially recognisable identity. Thinking about the different Discourses a piece of language is part of is another tool for engaging in discourse analysis.

*****

A Discourse is a characteristic way of saying, doing, and being. When you speak or write anything, you use the resources of English to project yourself as a certain kind of person, a different kind in different circumstances. You also project yourself as engaged in a certain practice or activity. If I have no idea who you are and what you are doing, then I cannot make sense of what you have said, written, or done.

You project a different identity at a formal dinner party than you do at the family dinner table. And, though these are both dinner, they are nonetheless different practices or activities (different "games"). The fact that people have differential access to different identities and practices, connected to different sorts of status and social goods, is a root source of inequality in society. Intervening in such matters can be a contribution to social justice. Since different identities and activities are enacted in and through language, the study of language is integrally connected to matters of equity and justice.

Issues to consider

☐ 'Discourses' are larger systems for making meaning and enacting social identities in which language plays a part, along with other things such as dress, behaviour, attitude, etc. You can list the languages that you speak (such as English, Japanese and Korean). Can you list some 'Discourses' that you 'speak'?

☐ Gee says that sometimes the way we 'talk, act and interact' in order to 'do/be' one kind of person might conflict with the way we 'talk, act and interact' in order to 'do/be' another kind of person, and that sometimes this causes problems in regard to things such as social equity and justice. Can you think of any examples of this?

D2 THREE PERSPECTIVES ON TEXTURE

In this section we have included excerpts from three texts which address the problem of *texture*. The first is from *Cohesion in English* by M.A.K. Halliday and Ruqaiya Hasan. In this excerpt the authors explain their basic idea of cohesion and the different kinds of devices that create cohesion in texts. The second is from the book *Language in the Inner City: Studies in the Black English Vernacular* by William Labov (1972b). Labov is a famous sociolinguist who, apart from analysing how people from different places and belonging to different groups talk differently, analysed the structure of the stories people told him in sociolinguistic interviews. You will recall that Widdowson (see section D1) contrasted Labov's approach to discourse analysis to the more form focused approach of Harris, saying that the purposes of Labov's analysis is to understand 'the way linguistic elements are put to communicative use in the performing of social actions' and 'to discover what sentences count as utterances and what it is that provides a discourse with its coherence as a piece of communication.' In the third excerpt, Scollon and his colleagues discuss the different devices people use to create links between texts and other texts (intertextuality) and how these links establish particular kinds of *relationships* between different kinds of people and different kinds of points of view.

A. The concept of cohesion

Michael Halliday and Ruqaiya Hasan (reprinted from *Cohesion in English*, 1976, London: Longman, pp 1–9)

Michael Halliday and Ruqaiya Hasan

1.1.1 Text

The word TEXT is used in linguistics to refer to any passage, spoken or written, of whatever length, that ... (forms) a unified whole. We know, as a general rule, whether any specimen of our own language constitutes a TEXT or not. This does not mean there can never be any uncertainty. The distinction between a text and a collection of unrelated sentences is in the last resort a matter of degree, and there may always be instances about which we are uncertain—a point that is probably familiar to most teachers from reading their students' compositions. But this does not invalidate the general observation that we are sensitive to the distinction between what is text and what is not …

A text may be spoken or written, prose or verse, dialogue or monologue. It may be anything from a single proverb to a whole play, from a momentary cry for help to an all-day discussion on a committee. A text is a unit of language in use. It is not a grammatical unit, like a clause or a sentence; and it is not defined by its size. A text is sometimes envisaged to be some kind of super-sentence, a grammatical unit that is larger than a sentence but is related to a sentence in the same way that a sentence is related to a clause, a clause to a group and so on: by CONSTITUENCY, the composition of larger units out of smaller ones. But this is misleading. A text is not something that is like a sentence, only bigger; it is something that differs from a sentence in kind.

A text is best regarded as a SEMANTIC unit: a unit not of form but of meaning. Thus it is related to a clause or sentence not by size but by REALIZATION, the coding of one symbolic system in another. A text does not CONSIST OF sentences; it is REALIZED BY, or encoded in, sentences. If we understand it in this way, we shall not expect to find the same kind of STRUCTURAL integration among the parts of a text as we find among the parts of a sentence or clause. The unity of a text is a unity of a different kind.

1.1.2 Texture

The concept of TEXTURE is entirely appropriate to express the property of 'being a text'. A text has texture, and this is what distinguishes it from something that is not a text. It derives this texture from the fact that it functions as a unity with respect to its environment.

What we are investigating in this book are the resources that English has for creating texture. If a passage of English containing more than one sentence is perceived as a text, there will be certain linguistic features present in that passage which can be identified as contributing to its total unity and giving it texture.

Let us start with a simple and trivial example. Suppose we find the following instructions in the cookery book:

[1:1] Wash and core six cooking apples. Put them into a fireproof dish.

It is clear that them in the second sentence refers back to (is ANAPHORIC to) the six cooking apples in the first sentence. This ANAPHORIC function of them gives cohesion to the two sentences, so that we interpret them as a whole; the two sentences together constitute a text. Or rather, they form part of the same text; there may be more of it to follow.

The texture is provided by the cohesive RELATION that exists between *them* and *six cooking apples*. It is important to make this point, because we shall be constantly focusing attention on the items, such as them, which typically refer back to something that has gone before; but the cohesion is effected not by the presence of the referring item alone but by the presence of both the referring item and the item that it refers to. …

What is the MEANING of the cohesive relation between them and six cooking apples? The meaning is that they refer to the same thing. The two items are identical in reference, or COREFERENTIAL. The cohesive agency in this instance, that which provides the texture, is the coreferentiality of *them* and *six cooking apples*. The signal, or the expression, of this coreferentiality is the presence of the potentially anaphoric item *them* in the second sentence together with a potential target item *six cooking apples* in the first.

Identity of reference is not the only meaning relation that contributes to texture; there are others besides. Nor is the use of a pronoun the only way of expressing identity of reference. We could have had:

[1:3] Wash and core six cooking apples. Put the apples into a fireproof dish.

Here the item functioning cohesively is the apples, which works by repetition of the word apples accompanied by the as an anaphoric signal. One of the functions of the definite article is to signal identity of reference with something that has gone before. (Since this has sometimes been said to be its only function, we should perhaps point out that it has others as well, which are not cohesive at all; for example none of the instances in (a) or (b) has an anaphoric sense:

[1:4] a. None but the brave deserve the fair.

b. The pain in my head cannot stifle the pain in my heart.)

1.1.3 Ties

We need a term to refer to a single instance of cohesion, a term for one occurrence of a pair of cohesively related items. This we shall call a TIE. The relation between them and six cooking apples in example [1:1] constitutes a tie.

We can characterize any segment of a text' in terms of the number and kinds of ties which it displays. In [1:1] there is just one tie, of the particular kind which we shall be calling REFERENCE. In [1:3], there are actually two ties, of which one is of the 'reference' kind, and consists in the anaphoric relation of *the* to *six cooking apples*, while the other is of a different kind and consists in the REPETITION of the word apples, a repetition which would still have a cohesive effect even if the two were not referring to the same apples.

The concept of a tie makes it possible to analyse a text in terms of its cohesive properties, and give a systematic account of its patterns of texture. Various types of question can be investigated in this way, for example concerning the difference between speech and writing, the relationship between cohesion and the organization of written texts into sentences and paragraphs, and the possible differences among different genres and different authors in the numbers and kinds of tie they typically employ.

The different kinds of cohesive tie are: reference, substitution, ellipsis, conjunction, and lexical cohesion.

1.1.4 Cohesion

The concept of cohesion is a semantic one; it refers to relations of meaning that exist within the text, and that define it as a text.

Cohesion occurs where the INTERPRETATION of some element in the discourse is dependent on that of another. The one PRESUPPOSES the other, in the sense that it cannot be effectively decoded except by recourse to it. When this happens, a relation of cohesion is set up, and the two elements, the presupposing and the presupposed, are thereby at least potentially integrated into a text.

This is another way of approaching the notion of a tie. To return to example [1:1], the word *them* presupposes for its interpretation something other than itself. This requirement is met by the *six cooking apples* in the preceding sentence. The presupposition, and the fact that it is resolved, provide cohesion between the two sentences, and in so doing create text.

As another example, consider the old piece of schoolboy humour:

[1:5] Time flies.

—You can't; they fly too quickly.

The first sentence gives no indication of not being a complete text; in fact it usually is, and the humour lies in the misinterpretation that is required if the presupposition from the second sentence is to be satisfied. Here, incidentally the cohesion is expressed in no less than three ties: the elliptical form *you can't*, the reference item *they* and the lexical repetition *fly*.

Cohesion is part of the system of a language. The potential for cohesion lies in the systematic resources of reference, ellipsis and so on that are built into the language itself. The actualization of cohesion in any given instance, however, depends not merely on the selection of some option from within these resources, but also on the presence of some other element which resolves the presupposition that this sets up. It is obvious that the selection of the word *apples* has no cohesive force by itself; a cohesive relation is set up only if the same word, or a word related to it such *fruit*, has occurred previously. It is less obvious, but equally true, that the word them has no cohesive force either unless there is some explicit referent for it within reach. In both instances, the cohesion lies in the relation that is set up between the two...

Cohesion is expressed partly through the grammar and partly through the vocabulary. We can refer therefore to GRAMMATICAL COHESION and LEXICAL COHESION. In example [1:3], one of the ties was grammatical (reference, expressed by *the*), the other lexical (repetition, expressed by *apples*). The distinction between grammatical and lexical is really only one of degree, and we need not make too much of it here. It is important to stress, however, that when we talk of cohesion as being 'grammatical or lexical', we do not imply that it is a purely formal relation, in which meaning is not involved. Cohesion is a semantic relation. But, like all components of the semantic system, it is realized through the lexicogrammatical system; and it is at this point that the distinction can be drawn. Some forms of cohesion are realized through the grammar and others through the vocabulary.

Issues to consider

☐   Halliday and Hasan emphasize a number of times in this excerpt that *cohesion* is a *semantic* concept rather than just a formal property of texts. What do they mean by this and what does it reveal about their perspective on discourse?

❑ Halliday and Hasan say that 'A text does not CONSIST OF sentences; it is REALISED BY, or encoded in, sentences'. What exactly is meant by this distinction? How can it be related to the contrasting views of Harris and Widdowson (and Labov) that we saw in the last section?

B. The transformation of experience in narrative syntax

William Labov (reprinted from *Language in the inner city: Studies in Black English* Vernacular, 1972. Philadelphia: University of Pennsylvania Press, pp. 259–366)

The overall structure of narrative

Some narratives ... contain only narrative clauses; they are complete in the sense that they have a beginning, a middle, and an end. But there are other elements of narrative structure found in more fully developed types. Briefly, a fully-formed narrative may show the following:

1   Abstract.
2   Orientation.
3   Complicating action.
4   Evaluation.
5   Result or resolution.
6   Coda.

Of course there are complex chainings and embeddings of these elements, but here we are dealing with the simpler forms. Complicating action has been characterized in section 1, and the *result* may be regarded for the moment as the termination of that series of events. We will consider briefly the nature and function of the abstract, orientation, [and] coda.

1   The *Abstract* It is not uncommon for narrators to begin with one or two clauses summarizing the whole story.

11   (Were you ever in a situation where you thought you were in serious danger of being killed?)

    a   I talked a man out of—Old Doc Simon I talked him out of pulling the trigger.

When this story is heard, it can be seen that the abstract does encapsulate the point of the story. In 12 there is a sequence of two such abstracts:

12   (Were you ever in a situation where you were in serious danger of being killed?)

    a   My brother put a knife in my head. (How'd that happen?)
    b   Like kids, you get into a fight
    c   and I twisted his arm up behind him.
    d   This was just a few days after my father died ...

Here the speaker gives one abstract and follows it with another after the interviewer's question. Then without further prompting, he begins the narrative proper.

The narrative might just as well have begun with the free clause d; b and c in this sense are not absolutely required, since they cover the same ground as the narrative as a whole. Larry's narrative (2) is the third of a series of three, and there is no question just before the narrative itself, but there is well-formed abstract:

2   a   An' then, three weeks ago I had a fight with this other dude outside.
    b   He got mad 'cause I wouldn't give him a cigarette.
    c   Ain't that a bitch?

Larry does not give the abstract in *place* of the story; he has no intention of stopping there, but goes on to give the full account.

What then is the function of the abstract? It is not an advertisement or a warning: the narrator does not wait for the listener to say, "I've heard about that," or "Don't tell me that now." If the abstract covers the same ground as the story, what does it add? We will consider this problem further in discussing the evaluation section below.

2. Orientation

At the outset, it is necessary to identify in some way the time, place, persons, and their activity or the situation. This can be done in the course of the first several narrative clauses, but more commonly there is an orientation section composed of free clauses. In Boot's narrative (1), clause a sets the time *(Sunday)*; clause b the persons (we), the situation (nothin' to do) and further specification of the time (after we came from church); the first narrative clause follows. In Larry's narrative (2), some information is already available in the abstract (the time-*three weeks ago*; the place-*outside of school)*; and the persons—this other dude *and* Larry). The orientation section then begins with a detailed picture of the situation- Larry *sittin'* on the corner, high.

Many of John L.'s narratives begin with an elaborate portrait of the main character- in this case, clauses *a-i* are all devoted to the baddest *girl in* the neighborhood, and the first narrative clause brings John L. and the girl face to face in the schoolyard.

The orientation section has some interesting syntactic properties; it is quite common to find a great many past progressive clauses in the orientation section—sketching the kind of thing that was going on before the first event of the narrative occurred or during the entire episode. But the most interesting thing about orientation is its *placement*. It is theoretically possible for all free orientation clauses to be placed at the beginning of the narrative, but in practice, we find much of this material is placed at strategic points later on, for reasons to be examined below.

3   *The* Coda There are also free clauses to be found at the ends of narratives; for example, John L.'s narrative ends:

    cc That was one of the most important.

This clause forms the coda. It is one of the many options open to the narrator for signalling that the narrative is finished. We find many similar forms.

13   And that was that.
14   And that—that was it, you know.

Codas may also contain general observations or show the effects of the events on the narrator. At the end of one fight narrative, we have

15   I was given the rest of the day off. And ever since then I haven't seen the guy

    'cause I quit,
    I quit, you know. No more problems.

Some codas which strike us as particularly skillful are strangely disconnected from the main narrative. One New Jersey woman told a story about how, as a little girl, she thought she was drowning, until a man came along and stood her on her feet—the water was only four feet deep.

16   And you know that man who picked me out of the water? He's a detective in Union City. And I see him every now and again.

These codas (15–16) have the property of bridging the gap between the moment of time at the end of the narrative proper and the present. They bring the narrator and the listener back to the point at which they entered the narrative. There are many ways of doing this: in 16 the other main actor is brought up to the present: in 15, the narrator. But there is a more general function of codas which subsumes both the examples of 15–16 and the simpler forms of 13–14. Codas close off the sequence of complicating actions and indicate that none of the events that followed were important to the narrative. A chain of actions may be thought of as successive answers to the question "Then what happened?"; "And then what happened?" After a coda such as That *was* that, the question "Then what happened?" is properly answered, "Nothing; I just told you what happened." It is even more obvious after the more complex codas of 15 and 16; the time reference of the discourse has been reshifted to the present, so that "what happened then?" can only be interpreted as a question about the present; the answer is "Nothing; here I am." Thus the "disjunctive" codas of 15 and 16 forestall further questions about the narrative itself: the narrative events are pushed away and sealed off.

Issues to consider

❑   The two excerpts presented so far approach the problem of *texture* from two very different perspectives, one focusing on how the clauses are *connected grammatically* through devices like conjunction and reference, and the other focusing on how clauses are *ordered sequentially*. Both approaches, however, take the 'clause' as the building block of the text. Why do you think this is?

❑   In the excerpt from Widdowson in A4, he contrasted the approach of Harris to that of Labov, saying that: 'Harris looks for patterns of linguistic elements which link sentences together into a larger formal structure, and Labov looks at the way linguistic elements are used to perform communicative acts, and this kind of enquiry takes him outside the actual linguistic properties … to the extra-linguistic factors of the social situation.' How does Labov's approach to texture in the excerpt above depend on 'extra-linguistic factors' and 'the social situation'?

❑ The stories Labov analysed were accounts of fights and near-death experiences. Do other kinds of stories have different conventional formats, or do they conform to the structure Labov has laid out? Consider fairy tales, jokes, confessions, Snapchat stories.

C. Voice appropriation and discourse representation

Ron Scollon et al. (reprinted from Scollon, R., Tsang W.K., Li, D. Yung, V. and Jones, R. (2021998) Voice appropriation and discourse representation in a student writing task. *Linguistics and Education* 9 (3): 227–250)

Ron Scollon et al.

Types of discourse representation

Given that all texts are intertextual and that they contain a variety of voices which link up to other voices outside of themselves, it remains to ask how these multiple, conflicting, contesting and polyphonic voices are actually represented linguistically, and how do we know?

Studies of quotation and citation have focused primarily on coming to understand the linguistic means and the semantic functions accomplished by embedding one stretch of text within another. Notable among such studies for our purposes are Halliday (1985), Caldas-Coulthard (1993), and Fairclough (1992, 1995). Halliday's concern is primarily with *projection* which is the process by which a clause represents other language rather than experience. If one writes, *He said, 'That's ridiculous'* the text within quotation marks is set off from the reporting clause 'He said' as belonging to two different classes of utterance. The reporting clause is what is being said in this utterance, the reported clause is being *projected* as being uttered text, not as utterance in itself. Caldas-Coulthard's (1993) concern is with social practices by which participants in discursive events are positioned. She prefers to use the term 'speech representation', especially since her main interest is in journalistic narratives in which women are positioned as holding less significant social statuses than men through being represented discursively as having lesser voice.

Kamberelis and Scott (1992), in their attempt to elucidate principles of critical language awareness in literacy classes for children, provide a typology of discourse representation incorporating 'appropriation, transformation and resistance' which includes such practices as 'direct quotation', 'adoption' (when a writer's voice completely merges with another's), stylization (in which the writer 'tries on' the discourse or style of another while still retaining some degree of objectivity towards it), parody, hidden polemic and idealization. These categories, while providing useful insights, in our view more accurately represent what might be called 'stances' that writers take up towards the voices they appropriate, operating on a level rather far from the text. In order to discover how writers represent these voices linguistically requires a set of text-based categories.

We prefer Fairclough's (1992) formulation of 'discourse representation' because of the perspective he takes, looking at how the polyvocality of utterance is accomplished in discursive acts. His concern, like ours, is with linking the concrete features in texts with various kinds of discursive practices and locating the means by which discursive participants are positioned in relationship to historical, cultural and social practices.

Fairclough identifies two broad classes of discourse representation: cases in which the boundary between voices is marked and cases in which the boundary is not marked. Within those two classes he then further identifies a number of means by which this representation takes place.

Boundaries Marked

There are three main ways in which the boundaries between voices can be marked: direct discourse (quotation), indirect discourse (quotation), and the use of scare quotes. In direct discourse there is a reporting clause (He said), a verb of saying (said), a reported clause (That's ridiculous), and boundary punctuation (, '…'):

He said, 'That's ridiculous!'

Indirect discourse has a reporting clause (He said), a verb of saying (said), a reported clause (xxx ridiculous), but has a changed subject/verb ('That's' becomes 'it was') and there is no boundary punctuation:

He said that it was ridiculous.

'Scare' quotes give emphasis, call attention, or focus on particular words or phrases, though the text thus represented is polyvocal according to Fairclough in that it is both use and projection or appropriation. The material placed within scare quotes is both being referenced as in another voice and it is being used by the utterer:

I don't care if you do think it is 'ridiculous', it's what I'm going to do.

No Boundaries Marked

Fairclough (1992) identifies four ways in which discourse is represented as appropriated into another text: presupposition, negation, metadiscourse and irony. Other voices may be presupposed, often in nominalized form. In the following case, the use of the word 'ridicule' implies dialogically that this utterance is responding to a stated or implied claim that the utterer's ideas or claims are ridiculous:

In spite of your *ridicule*, I'm going to do it.
Negation similarly presupposes polyvocality as in:

My idea is not ridiculous.

Metadiscourse in Fairclough's formulation of discourse representation is a rather complex category for which we will give only a few examples. What is important in his argument is that metalinguistic or metadiscursive utterances, by being about the utterance itself, introduce polyvocality. There is the voice speaking on the one hand and the voice speaking about that utterance as well. Thus hedges in many cases are polyvocalic:

That idea is *sort of* ridiculous.

Saying an idea is 'sort of ridiculous simultaneously says that it is ridiculous and disclaims that statement.

Text may also be marked as belonging to another text or utterance with phrases such as 'as Fairclough might put it', 'in scientific terms', and 'metaphorically speaking':

That idea might be called ridiculous.

Paraphrase may also be used to appropriate another voice into one's utterance. The other has said one's ideas are 'ridiculous' and one might answer that they are not 'absurd'.

As absurd as you think this idea is, I'm doing it anyway.

Finally, irony embeds other voices while calling those voices into question. It should be clear that this category is much like the use of scare quotes noted above except that the boundary is not explicitly marked:

I'm going to go ahead with this ridiculous idea of mine.

Interdiscursivity

We have discussed the polyvocality of these texts so far from the point of view of intertextuality. That is, as texts or voices embedded within other utterances. Fairclough (1992) distinguishes between this level of appropriation for which he uses the word intertextuality from a broader kind of appropriation in which it is forms, styles, genres, registers, vocabulary sets, and other broad discourse types which are being appropriated, not just words, phrases and sentences. That is to say, the concept of *interdiscursivity* covers the appropriation of discursive frames as well as the texts themselves.

It is somewhat more difficult to trace interdiscursivity and its sources in people's writing as it depends not on establishing a specific prior text but prior 'conventions'— packages of wordings, formats, styles and the like. Although it is often not hard to spot conventions of, for example, 'medical' talk in the language of doctors or 'academic style' in the talk of linguists, the problem is working out *apriori* systems (potentials) from which interdiscursive borrowings are made...

Issues to consider

❑   The different ways of representing other people's words that Scollon and his colleagues talk about usually imply a certain attitude towards those words. Which kinds of discourse representation are most effective when you want to align yourself to someone else's words? Which kind is most effective when you want to distance yourself?

❑   You probably borrow other people's words quite a lot when you write essays and other school assignments. When you do this, you have to make choices about how to represent these words (e.g. 'Should I use a direct quotation or a paraphrase, or should I just mention the idea in passing and add a citation?'). What principles do you use to govern your choices in these situations?

❑ Scollon and his colleagues say: 'Although it is often not hard to spot conventions of, for example, "medical" talk in the language of doctors or "academic style" in the talk of linguists, the problem is working out *apriori* systems (potentials) from which interdiscursive borrowings are made'. Gee (see D1) would refer to these 'systems' of communication such as 'medical talk' as 'Discourses'. Why is identifying 'Discourses' a 'problem', and how would you go about trying to do it?

❑ Look at the question above and identify all of the different kinds of discourse representation you can find.

GENRES, DISCOURSE COMMUNITIES AND CREATIVITY

The two excerpts below are from two important figures in the field of genre analysis. In the first, John Swales, clarifies the concept of 'discourse community' by providing six 'defining characteristics' having to do with people's relationships to one another and to the texts that they use together. In the second, Vijay Bhatia talks about generic hybridity and creativity.

A. A conceptualisation of discourse community

John Swales

John Swales (reprinted from J. Swales, *Genre Analysis*, Cambridge: Cambridge University Press, 1990, pp. 24–27)

I would now like to propose six defining characteristics that will be necessary and sufficient for identifying a group of individuals as a discourse community.

1. A discourse community has a broadly agreed set of common public goals

These public goals may be formally inscribed in documents (as is often the case with associations and clubs), or they may be more tacit. The goals are *public*, because spies may join speech and discourse communities for hidden purposes of subversion, while more ordinary people may join organizations with private hopes of commercial or romantic advancement. In some instances, but not in many, the goals may be high level or abstract. In a Senate or Parliament there may well exist overtly adversarial groups of members, but these adversaries may broadly share some common objective as striving for improved government. In the much more typical non-adversarial discourse communities, reduction in the broad level of agreement may fall to a point where communication breaks down and the discourse community splits. It is commonality of goal, not shared object of study that is criterial, even if the former often subsumes the latter. But not always. The fact that the shared object of study is, say, the Vatican, does not imply that students of the Vatican in history departments, the

Kremlin, dioceses, birth control agencies and liberation theology seminaries form a discourse community.

2. A discourse community has mechanisms of intercommunication among its members

The participatory mechanisms will vary according to the community: meetings, telecommunications, correspondence, newsletters, conversations and so forth. This criterion is quite stringent because it produces a negative answer to the case of 'The Cafe Owner Problem' (Najjar, personal communication). In generalized form, the problem goes as follows: individuals A, B, C and so on occupy the same professional roles in life. They interact (in speech and writing) with the same clienteles; they originate, receive and respond to the same kind of messages for the same purposes; they have an approximately similar range of genre skills. And yet, as cafe owners working long hours in their own establishments, and not being members of the Local Chamber of Commerce, A, B and C never interact with one another. Do they form a discourse community? We can notice first that 'The Cafe Owner Problem' is not quite like those situations where A, B and C operate as 'point'. A, B and C may be lighthouse keepers on their lonely rocks, or missionaries in their separate jungles, or neglected consular officials in their rotting outposts. In all these cases, although A, B and C may never interact, they all have lines of communication back to base, and presumably acquired discourse community membership as a key element in their initial training. Bizzell (1987) argues that the cafe owner kind of social group will be a discourse community because 'its members may share the social-class based or ethnically-based discursive practices of people who are likely to become cafe owners in their neighborhood' (1987: 5). However, even if this sharing of discursive practice occurs, it does not resolve the logical problem of assigning membership of a community to individuals who neither admit nor recognize that such a community exists.

3. A discourse community uses its participatory mechanisms primarily to provide information and feedback

Thus, membership implies uptake of the informational opportunities. Individuals might pay an annual subscription to the *Acoustical Society of America* but if they never open any of its communications they cannot be said to belong to the discourse community, even though they are formally members of the society. The secondary purposes of the information exchange will vary according to the common goals: to improve performance in a football squad or in an orchestra, to make money in a brokerage house, to grow better roses in a gardening club, or to dent the research front in an academic department.

4. A discourse community utilizes and hence possesses one or more genres in the communicative furtherance of its aims

A discourse community has developed and continues to develop discoursal expectations. These may involve appropriacy of topics, the form, function and positioning of discoursal elements, and the roles texts play in the operation of the discourse community. In so far as 'genres are how things get done, when language is used to accomplish them' (Martin, 1985: 250), these discoursal expectations are created by the *genres* that articulate the operations of the discourse community. One of the purposes of this criterion is to question discourse community status for new or newly-emergent groupings. Such groupings need, as it were, to settle down and work out their communicative proceedings and practices before they can be recognized as discourse communities. If a new grouping 'borrows' genres from other discourse communities, such borrowings have to be assimilated.

5. In addition to owning genres, a discourse community has acquired some specific lexis

This specialization may involve using lexical items known to the wider speech communities in special and technical ways, as in information technology discourse communities, or using highly technical terminology as in medical communities. Most commonly, however, the inbuilt dynamic towards an increasingly shared and specialized terminology is realized through the development of community-specific abbreviations and acronyms. The use of these (ESL, EAP, WAC, NCTE, TOEFL, etc.) is, of course, driven by the requirements for efficient communication exchange between "experts." It is hard to conceive, at least in the contemporary, English-speaking world, of a group of well-established members of a discourse community communicating among themselves on topics relevant to the goals of the community and not using lexical items puzzling to outsiders. It is hard to imagine attending perchance the convention of some group of which one is an outsider and understanding every word, if it were to happen—as might occur in the inaugural meeting of some quite new grouping—then that grouping would not yet constitute a discourse community.

6. A discourse community has a threshold level of members with a suitable degree of relevant content and discoursal expertise

Discourse communities have changing memberships; individuals enter as apprentices and leave by death or in other less involuntary ways. However, survival of the community depends on a reasonable ratio between novices and experts.

Issues to consider

❏   The second criterion for a discourse community discussed by Swales is that members must have a means of intercommunication among members. He then, however, gives an example of people in the same profession (cafe owners) who do not necessarily have a means of communicating with one another. Do you think this group constitutes a discourse community? Why or why not? Can you think of other groups that have a similar ambiguous status based on this criterion or other criteria listed by Swales?

❏   What groups do you belong to that you think can be considered discourse communities? What genres are associated with these communities and how do you learn to use them? Swales says the newly formed groups take time to 'settle down' and establish themselves as discourse communities. Can you think of any groups that are in the process of becoming discourse communities but have not yet attained full status?

B. The power and politics of genre

Vijay K. Bhatia (reprinted from *Critical Genre Analysis: Investigating interdiscursive performance in professional practice*, London: Taylor & Francis, 2016, pp. 39–44)

Vijay K. Bhatia

Appropriation of semiotic resources and generic hybridity

... As mentioned earlier, interdiscursivity encourages innovative attempts to create various forms of hybrid and relatively novel constructs by appropriating or exploiting established conventions or resources associated with other genres and practices. I would now like to take specific instances of interdiscursivity from a variety of professional contexts not only to illustrate that it operates at all levels – generic, professional practice and professional culture – but also to claim that it allows a rigorous and comprehensive analysis of genres in and as professional practice. Let me first begin with one of the most dominant forms of professional discourse that is very much part of our daily life, namely advertising, to see how this gives rise to different interdiscursively created hybrid forms.

The primary and most dominant form of promotional discourse is what is commonly known as advertising discourse, which of course has a number of exponents. Variations, in terms of forms ('hard sell' and 'soft sell'), medium (radio, TV or print), range of products (cars, cosmetics and computers) and the strategies employed partly capture the enormous potential that promotional discourse displays in a culture of consumerism...[The genre of the advertisement] can be further distinguished in terms of what we might view as sub-genres by reference to contextual factors such as the medium employed, the product or service being promoted or the audience that is targeted. Depending on these factors, one may find a more distinctive and subtle use of promotional appeals and lexico-grammatical resources.

We also find a category of genres that are essentially informative and traditionally nonpromotional in intent, but are being increasingly influenced and even colonised by promotional concerns. The main communicative purpose they serve is still informative, but they can sometimes be mixed or hybrid in appearance. Fairclough (1995) discusses several interesting instances of academic course descriptions and job advertisements, which, he rightly claims, are becoming increasingly promotional. Similarly, Bhatia (1995, 1997) points out two interesting developments in the case of academic introductions (i.e., book introduction, preface and foreword). First, he finds the traditional distinctions, although very subtle in nature, between these closely related genres disappearing in practice, so that it is very difficult to establish each one as having a separate generic integrity of its own. Second, and perhaps more interestingly, from our point of view..., most of these forms of academic introductions are becoming increasingly promotional in practice, so that sometimes it becomes rather difficult not to take notice of such promotional elements in these essentially informative genres, particularly in the case of book introductions.

Another interesting case in point here is that of review as a genre, which is meant to be essentially a balanced evaluation, incorporating a reasonable description of the book, which may focus on positive as well as negative aspects of the book in question. However, in the case of reviews of food and restaurants, software, new cars and a number of other similar products, one may find a number of them predominantly promotional in character, focusing mainly on positive description and evaluation. Leaflets on services from corporations, banking as well as financial, medical and health institutions, travel industries and government departments are primarily informative, but some mixture of promotional or persuasive overtones cannot be ruled out in most cases. Similarly, brochures and reports, whether they report on the company services, financial matters, investment appreciation or travel opportunities, are essentially mixed genres, incorporating informative as well as promotional elements. In most of these instances of genre-mixing, one may notice that most of these contributing genres are somewhat compatible with each other, in that they do not show any conflict in communicative purposes. A closer look at these instances will indicate that it often is the case that informative functions are more likely to be colonised by promotional functions rather than any other. The most popular promotional strategy in advertising has been *to describe and evaluate a product or service in a positive manner*, which may be seen as the information-giving function of language. These two functions of language (i.e., informational and promotional) are therefore unlikely to create tension, even if they may not be entirely complementary to each other. A number of such instances of mixed genres are getting established and are being given innovative names, such as *infomercial, infotainment* or *advertorial*. Although it may appear that this kind of genre-mixing is more common in genres that are less likely to create functional tension, it will be somewhat premature to assume that this will always be the case. It is possible to view this subtle colonisation of genres in terms of appropriation and mixing of genres, depending upon the nature and degree of invasion one may find in individual members of promotional colony. One of the main reasons for this kind of colonisation is that advertisers are constantly making creative attempts to innovate rhetorical strategies to disguise advertising messages as editorial content, which is particularly true of the growing online exploitation of new media, such as websites, blogs, FaceTime, Twitter, LinkedIn and even search engines such as Google and Yahoo, oftentimes leading to what is viewed as 'native advertising', in which the advertising content aligns with the digital site's established conventions, especially in terms of style and tone, invariably meeting the expectations of its typical audience. Such strategies tend to make native advertising content almost indistinguishable from genuine digital content. Although there are no specific rules or guidelines as to how native advertising content is distinguished from genuine digital content, it is sometimes specified as 'sponsored feature', 'sponsored Report' or occasionally, even 'review'. However, just like any advertisement, most native advertising is paid content, the key aspect of which is that the promotional message is deceptively designed with implication that it comes from an unbiased source. The US Federal Trade Commission (FTC) in their survey of online publishers found that 73 per cent of them allowed *native advertising*, the digital descendant of the newspaper 'advertorial' and television 'infomercials', claiming that advertisers have moved beyond their conventional advertising to a more seamless and inconspicuous attempts to disguise their advertising content as genuine digital content. FTC chairwoman Edith Ramirez argues that by presenting ads that resemble editorial content, an advertiser risks implying, deceptively, that the information comes from a non-biased source (http://www.scmp.com/business/companies/article/1373616/ online-ads-must-not-masquerade-editorial-content-us-consumer).

Interdiscursivity in advertising campaigns

In more recent years, especially after the invasion of new media in all forms of professional and social contexts, promotional documents have become increasingly multimodal as well as interdiscursive, where, instead of an advertisement, corporations these days resort to advertising campaigns that consist of a number of different, though strategically differentiated range of advertisements for the same product or service, keeping in mind variation in the composition of audiences, their interests, their preferences, their cultural differences and most of all the variety of new and creative media available. Let me now take up another example of what is commonly known as the 'advertising campaign', which consists of a coordinated series of linked advertisements through several types of media with a single interdiscursively rich theme. It often focuses on a common theme for a particular brand, product or service, and is directed at specific sections of society. Such advertising campaigns are often more successful than individual advertisements and have a much longer shelf life. They integrate a variety of marketing strategies and media to suit the goals of a particular product or service. The integration of several advertising efforts into a single campaign provides a number of additional benefits to companies, including a single interdiscursively crafted voice, which brings with it efficiency of message proliferation and savings in costs. Besides these advantages, campaigns also make it possible for advertisers to use a variety of new social media, such as Facebook, Twitter, LinkedIn, Google, YouTube, etc., which reaches audiences in quicker and more successive bursts of promotion. An excellent example is the Apple's *Get-A-Mac* campaign which was created in 2006, with each ad in the campaign featuring popular actor Justin Long playing 'Mac' and John Hodgman playing 'PC'. The two actors are personifications of the two computers (i.e., Mac and PC) and echo some resemblances of their founders. Mac is presented as a young casually dressed Steve Jobs, and PC is more formally dressed like Bill Gates.

Mac looks young, friendly, casual, approachable and somewhat overconfident with his hands in his pant pockets, whereas PC appears more formal, sober, less approachable and somewhat diffident. The main theme of the campaign consists of the message that PCs are full of trouble, in that they are difficult to use and are unstable and vulnerable to viruses. Macs, in comparison, are user-friendly, stable and immune to viruses. The theme of the product is based on what in conventional advertising has been known as 'product differentiation', which is considered a key concept in persuasive advertising. Advertisers often analyse all the background information, and available 'evidence' in an attempt to discover what makes a particular product different from that of competitors. A good illustration of this strategy we find in an old story, which goes somewhat like the following:

In the good old days, there were two shops selling sausages in the same street in London. Initially both were doing well, but as days went by, the competition became tough and the promotional activities intense. Suddenly, one fine morning the shop on the right side of the road put up a poster claiming, "We sell the best sausages in London". The next morning, the shop on the left side, in an attempt to outsmart his competitor came up with the claim "We sell the best sausages in England". The next day, the first one came up with the claim, "Our sausages are the best in the world". The second one responded by saying, "We sell sausages to the Queen", to which the first one responded the following day by displaying a huge poster saying, "God save the Queen!"

The Apple's *Get-A-Mac* campaign uses this strategy of 'product differentiation' in 19 advertisements in the form of vignettes in its first year with the same theme. The campaign continued for a few years with a total 66 advertisements, each of which consisted of a brief vignette highlighting a typical advantage of Mac over PC, such as ease of use, immunity to viruses, automatic updating of programmes, Internet connectivity, ease of restarting, smooth running, etc. Advertising campaigns such as this one offer a rich resource for the analysis of intertextual and interdiscursive appropriation of various forms of semiotic resources. The campaign is also rich in interdiscursivity in the sense that it makes use of other social media, such as Facebook, Twitter, Google, LinkedIn and YouTube, where we can see interesting patterns of large-scale appropriation of semiotic resources. However, here I will not be going into a more comprehensive analysis; instead, I would like to move onto yet another aspect of interdiscursivity that results from the management of participation mechanism.

Issues to consider

- [ ] To illustrate the way 'informational' genres are being 'colonised' by 'promotional' genres, Bhatia gives the example of book introductions, which are often used not just to talk about what is in the book, but also to 'sell' the book to customers. Look at the book that you are reading. Where can you find examples of where promotional discourse has 'colonised' the academic discourse of the book?
- [ ] Bhatia talks about new genres of 'infomercials' and 'advertorials' which became popular on television and in print media starting in the 1980s. Can you think of any new media genres (for example, different kinds of YouTube videos) in which promotional intentions are 'dressed up' in a genre that seems to have the purpose of informing you. What strategies do authors of these genres use to disguise their promotional intentions or to make them 'fit in' to a genre which is not explicitly designed for promotion?
- [ ] Bhatia talks about how Apple's *Get-A-Mac* advertising campaign contains a rich range of examples of interdiscursivity. Have a look at some of these commercials on-line (one place you can find them is: http://www.adweek.com/creativity/apples-get-mac-complete-campaign-130552/) and see you if you can find some of these examples. Is there another advertising campaign that you know of that also makes use of the kind of interdiscursivity Bhatia discusses?

D4 IDEOLOGIES IN DISCOURSE

The excerpts presented in this section discuss some of the basic conceptual and analytical tools you can use to do critical discourse analysis. The first is from James Paul Gee's book *Social Linguistics and Literacies*. In this excerpt Gee also takes up the topics of 'social languages' (see section A4, B4) and intertextuality, or, as he calls it, *heteroglossia*, in his analysis of a label on an aspirin bottle. He also discusses 'cultural models' (see section A2, B2 and A4) and their relationship to power and ideology. In the second excerpt, from his book *The Sociolinguistics of Globalization*, Jan Blommaert talks about the concept of indexicality by analysing a French language sign outside of a Japanese shop, and introduces the term 'orders of indexicality' which is discussed in section B4.

A. Ideology, social languages and cultural models

James Paul Gee (reprinted from *Social Linguistics and Literacies*, London: Taylor and Francis, 1996, pp. 69–79)

James
Paul Gee

Heteroglossia

It is important to extend our discussion of social languages by pointing out that they are very often 'impure'. That is, when we speak or write, we very often mix together different social languages. This is a practice that the Russian literary theorist Mikhail Bakhtin (1981, 1986) called heteroglossia (multiple voices) ... To see a clear example of such heteroglossia, and its ties to sociopolitical realities, consider the following warning(s) taken from a bottle of aspirin.

> Warnings: **Children and teenagers should not use this medication for chicken pox or flu symptoms before a doctor is consulted about Reye Syndrome, a rare but serious illness reported to be associated with aspirin.** Keep this and all drugs out of the reach of children. In case of accidental overdose, seek professional assistance or contact a poison control center immediately. As with any drug, if you are pregnant or nursing a baby, seek the advice of a health professional before using this product. IT IS ESPECIALLY IMPORTANT NOT TO USE ASPIRIN DURING THE LAST 3 MONTHS OF PREGNANCY UNLESS SPECIFICALLY DIRECTED TO DO SO BY A DOCTOR BECAUSE IT MAY CAUSE PROBLEMS IN THE UNBORN CHILD OR COMPLICATIONS DURING DELIVERY. See carton for arthritis use and Important Notice.

This text starts with a sentence of very careful and very specific information indeed: the initial sentence talks (in bold) about 'children *and* teenagers'; it specially says '*this* medication'; gives us an exclusive list of two relevant diseases, 'chicken pox *or* flu'; mentions a specific syndrome, Reye Syndrome, and explicitly tells us that it is 'rare *but* serious'. Then, all of a sudden, with the second sentence we enter a quite different sort of language, marked both by the phrasing and by the disappearance of the bold print. Now, the text talks not about aspirin specifically, as in the first sentence, but about 'this and *all* drugs' (second sentence) and '*any* drug' (fourth sentence). We are told to keep 'this and all drugs' out of the reach of 'children', but what now has happened to the teenagers? We get three different references to the medical profession, none of them as direct and specific as 'doctor' (which was used in the first sentence): 'professional assistance', 'poison control center', and 'health professional'. We are told to seek help in case of 'accidental overdose', making us wonder what should happen if the overdose was not accidental. The language of this middle part of the text speaks out of a (seemingly not all that dangerous) world where institutional systems (companies, professionals, centers) take care of people who only through ignorance (which these systems can cure) get themselves into trouble. Then, all of a sudden, again, we make a transition back to the social language of the opening of the text, but this time it is shouted at us in bold capitals. We are confronted with the phrase 'especially important'. We return to quite specific language: we again get 'aspirin', rather than 'all drugs' or 'any drug', time is handled quite specifically ('last 3 months'), we no longer 'seek assistance or advice' from 'professionals', rather we once again consult with our 'doctor' and do not take the aspirin 'unless specifically directed'. This is, once again, a dangerous world in which we had better do what (and only what) the doctor says. This dire warning about pregnancy, however, does make us wonder why a rather general and gentle warning about pregnancy and nursing is embedded in the more moderate language of the middle of the text. The text ends with small print, which appears to tell us to look on the carton for an 'Important Notice' (weren't these 'warnings' the important notice?).

So, in this text we have at least two rather different social languages (voices) intermingled, juxtaposed rather uncomfortably side by side. Why? At one time, the aspirin bottle had only the middle text (sentences 2, 3, and 4) on it as a 'warning' (singular). Various medical, social, cultural, and political changes, including conflicts between and among governmental institutions, medical workers, consumers, and drug companies, have led to the intrusion of the more direct and sharper voice that begins and ends the 'warnings'. Thus, we see, the different social languages in this text are sedimented there by social, political, and cultural happenings unfolding in history. In fact, even what looks like a uniform social language—for example, the moderate middle of this text—is very often a compendium of different social languages with different historical, social, cultural, and political sources, and looks to us now to be uniform only because the workings of multiple social languages have been forgotten and effaced.

Similarity in the 'eye of the beholder'

One of the key ways humans think about the world is through seeking out similarities (Hofstadter and the fluid Analogies Research Group 1995; Holyoak and Thagard 1995). We try to understand something new in terms of how it resembles something old. We attempt to see the new thing as a type, thus, like other things of the same or similar type. And very often a great deal hangs on these judgments: for example, is spanking a child a type of discipline or a type of child abuse? When we answer this question we claim either that spanking a child is more similar to paradigmatic instances of discipline or to paradigmatic instances of child abuse.

Judgments like whether spanking is discipline or child abuse are still 'open' and widely discussed in the culture thanks to on-going social changes. However, any language is full of such similarity judgments that have been made long ago in the history of the language—in another time and another place—and which are now taken for granted and rarely reflected upon by current speakers of the language.

Let me take another example that is relevant to those of us interested in language and learning. Consider a sentence like 'The teacher taught the students French' (see also Birch 1989: pp. 25–29; Halliday 1976). This sentence has the same grammar as (the language treats it the same as) sentences like 'John handed Mary the gun', 'John gave Mary the gun', 'John sent Mary the gun', and many more. This type of sentence seems to mean (if we consider prototypical cases like 'give', 'hand', and 'send') that an agent transfers something to someone.

And so we are led to think of teaching French as transferring something (French) from one person (the teacher) to someone else (the student), though this transfer is a mental one, rather than a physical one. This suggestion (about the meaning of teaching languages), which we pick up from our grammar, happens to fit with one of the most pervasive ways of thinking, (what I will later call a master myth) embedded in our language and in culture. We tend to think of meaning as something speakers or writers take out of their heads (its original container), package, like a gift, into a package or container (i.e., words and sentences) and convey (transfer) to hearers, who unpackage it and place its contents (i.e., 'meaning') into their heads (its final container).

This container/conveyor metaphor (Lakoff and Johnson 1980; Reddy 1979) is, as we will see below, a fallacious view of meaning. It gives rise to idioms like 'I catch your meaning', 'I can't grasp what you are saying', 'I've got it', 'Let me put the matter in plain terms', 'I can't put this into words', and a great many more. So, it is easy for us to accept the suggestion of our grammar and see teaching languages as a form of mental transference of neatly wrapped little packages (drills, grammar lessons, vocabulary lists) along a conveyor belt from teacher to student.

At a more subtle level, the fact that 'The teacher teaches the students French' has the same grammar as 'The teacher teaches the students history (physics, linguistics, algebra)' suggests that teaching a language (like French) is a comparable activity to teaching a disciplinary content like physics (Halliday 1976). Our schools, with their classrooms, curricula, discrete class hours (five times a week for an hour we learn French), encourage us further to think that, since all these teachers are standing in the same sort of space, playing the same sort of role in the system, they could be or even must be doing the same (sort of) thing.

We note, as well, that the driving teacher spends too much time in a car and the coach spends too much time on the field to be respected as *teachers*. Note, too, that we don't say things like 'The coach teaches football'—football cannot be taught, one can only help someone master it in a group with other apprentices. Our mental model of teaching makes us compare 'teaching French' to 'teaching history' and not to 'coaching football' or 'training someone to drive', despite the fact that it may well be that learning a language is a lot more like learning to drive a car or play football than it is like learning history or physics.

What we see here, then, is that language encapsulates a great many frozen theories (generalizations about what is similar to what)—we have just witnessed frozen theories of communication and language acquisition. We do not have to accept the theories our various social languages offer us. Though we can hardly reflect on them all, we can reflect on some of them and come to see things in new ways.

Meaning

Having established the context of social languages, we can turn directly to meaning. Meaning is one of the most debated terms in linguistics, philosophy, literary theory, and the social sciences. To start our discussion of meaning, let us pick a word and ask what it means. Say we ask: 'What does the word *sofa* mean?'

Imagine that my friend Susan and I go into my living room, where I have a small white, rather broken down seat big enough for more than one person, and a larger and nicer one. I point to the larger, nicer one and say, 'That sofa has a stain on it.' Susan sees nothing exceptional about what I have said, assumes we both mean the same thing by the word 'sofa', and points to the smaller object, saying, 'Well, that sofa has a lot more stains on it.' I say, 'That's not a sofa, it's a settee.' Now Susan realizes that she and I do not, in fact, mean the same thing by the word 'sofa'.

Why? The reason is that I am making a distinction between two words, 'sofa' and 'settee', where something is either the one or the other, and not both, while Susan does not make such a distinction, either because she does not have the word 'settee' or because she uses it in the same way as she uses 'sofa'. When I use the word 'sofa', I mean it to exclude the word 'settee' as applicable; when I use the word 'settee', I mean it to exclude the word 'sofa'. Susan, of course, does not exactly know the *basis* on which I make the distinction between 'sofa' and 'settee' (how and why I distinguish 'sofa' and 'settee'), a matter to which we will turn in the next section.

Now someone else, Kris, comes in, having overheard our conversation, and says, 'That's not a settee, nor a sofa, it's a divan.' I and Susan now realize that when Kris uses the word 'divan', she distinguishes among the words 'sofa', 'settee', and 'divan'.

Now, assume that I say 'Well they are both couches,' and we all agree on this. This shows that my use of the word 'couch' does not exclude 'sofa' or 'settee' as (also possibly) applicable, nor do these words exclude 'couch', though they exclude each other. And for Susan and Kris the use of the word 'couch' does not exclude their other words (which are different than mine), nor do their other words exclude 'couch' (though their other words exclude each other). Thus, by default almost, we mean (pretty much) the same thing by 'couch'.

What is emerging here is that what we mean by a word depends on which other words we have available to us and which other words our use of the word (e.g., 'sofa') is meant to exclude or not exclude as possibly also applying (e.g., 'sofa' excludes 'settee', but not 'couch'). It also depends on which words are 'available' to me in a given situation. For example, I may sometimes use the word 'love seat', which I consider a type of settee, but in the above situation with Susan and Kris I may have not viewed this as a possible choice, perhaps because I am reluctant to use the term in front of close friends who might think it too 'fancy'. This is to say that I am currently using a social language in which 'love seat' is not available.

The sorts of factors we have seen thus far in our discussion of 'sofa' reflect one central principle involved in meaning, a principle I will call the *exclusion principle*. Susan, Kris, and I all have the word 'sofa', but it means different things to each of us because each of has a different set of related words. The exclusion principle says that the meaning of a word is (in part—there are other principles) a matter of what other words my use of a given word in a given situation is intended to exclude or not exclude as also possibly applicable (though not actually used in this case). Meaning is always (in part) a matter of intended exclusions and exclusions (contrasts and lack of contrasts) within the assumed semantic field.

*****

Cultural models as the basis of meaning choices and guesses

So far I have left out one crucial principle of meaning. This is the principle that determines what I have called the basis of the distinctions we make (e.g., 'sofa' versus 'settee', with 'couch' applicable to both). Why do we mean the way we do?

To get at what constitutes the basis of our choices and assumptions in the use of words, let us consider what the word 'bachelor' means (Fillmore 1975; Quinn and Holland 1987). All of us think we know what the word means. Dictionaries say it means 'an unmarried man' *(Webster Handy College Dictionary,* 1972), because it seems clear that in most contexts in which the word is used it excludes as applicable words like 'woman', 'girl', 'boy', and 'married': Let me ask you, then, is the Pope a bachelor? Is a thrice-divorced man a bachelor? Is a young man who has been in an irreversible coma since childhood a bachelor? What about a eunuch? A committed gay man? An elderly senile gentleman who has never been married? The answer to all these questions is either 'no' or 'I'm not sure' (as I have discovered by asking a variety of people). Why? After all, all these people are unmarried men.

The reason why the answer to these questions is 'no', despite the fact that they all involve cases of clearly unmarried males, is that in using the word 'bachelor' we are making exclusions we are unaware of and are assuming that the contexts in which we use the word are clear and transparent when they are not. Context has the nasty habit of almost always seeming clear, transparent, and unproblematic, when it hardly ever actually is.

Our meaningful distinctions (our choices and guesses) are made on the basis of certain beliefs and values. This basis is a type of theory ..., in the case of many words a social theory. The theories that form the basis of such choices and assumptions have a particular character. They involve (usually unconscious) assumptions about models of simplified worlds. Such models are sometimes called cultural models, folk theories, scenes, schemas, or frames. I will call them *cultural models*.

I think of cultural models as something like movies or videotapes in the mind. We all have a vast store of these tapes, each of which depicts prototypical (what we take to be 'normal') events in a simplified world. We conventionally take these simplified worlds to be the 'real' world, or act as if they were. We make our choices and guesses about meaning in relation to these worlds.

These cultural models are emblematic visions of an idealized, 'normal', 'typical' reality, in much the way that, say, a Bogart movie is emblematic of the world of the 'tough guy' or an early Woody Allen movie of the 'sensitive, but klutzy male'. They are also variable, differing across different cultural groups, including different cultural groups in a society speaking the same language. They change with time and other changes in the society, but we are usually quite unaware we are using them and of their full implications.

These cultural models are, then, pictures of simplified worlds in which prototypical events unfold. The most commonly used cultural model for the word 'bachelor' is (or used to be) something like the following (Fillmore 1975): Men marry women at a certain age; marriages last for life; and in such a world, a bachelor is a man who stays unmarried beyond the usual age, thereby becoming eminently marriageable. We know that this simplified world is not always true, but it is the one against which we use the word 'bachelor', that is, make choices about what other words are excluded as applicable or not, and make assumptions about what the relevant context is in a given case of using a word. Thus, the Pope is not a bachelor because he just isn't in this simplified world, being someone who has vowed not to marry at any age. Nor are gay men, since they have chosen not to marry women.

Such cultural models involve us in exclusions that are not at first obvious and which we are often quite unaware of making. In the case of 'bachelor' we are actually excluding words like 'gay' and 'priest' as applying to ('normal') unmarried men, and in doing so, we are assuming that men come in two ('normal') types: ones who get married early and ones who get married late. This assumption *marginalizes* people who do not want to get married or do not want to marry members of the opposite sex. It is part of the function of such cultural models to set up what count as central, typical cases, and what count as marginal, non-typical cases.

There is even a more subtle exclusion being made via this cultural model. If men become 'eminently marriageable' when they stay unmarried beyond the usual age, then this can only be because we have assumed that after that age there is a shortage of 'desirable' men and a surplus of women who want them, women who, thus, are not 'eminently marriageable', or, at least, not as 'eminently marriageable' as the men. Hence, we get the most common cultural model associated with 'spinster'. So we see that our usual use of 'bachelor' involves also an exclusion of the phrase 'eminently marriageable' as applicable to 'older' women, and the assumption that the reverse of 'bachelor', namely 'spinster', *is* applicable.

Such hidden exclusions are … ideological. They involve social theories (remember, cultural models are a type of theory), quite tacit ones involving beliefs about the distribution of goods—prestige, power, desirability, centrality in society. Furthermore, the fact that we are usually unaware of using these cultural models and of their full implications means that the assumptions they embody are the distribution of social goods appear to us natural, obvious, just the ways things are, inevitable, even appropriate. And this is so despite the fact that cultural models vary across both different cultures and different social groups.

Issues to consider

❑ The mixing of 'social languages' that Gee observes on the bottle of aspirin is also a kind of intertextuality, sometimes called *interdiscursivity*. This kind of intertextuality occurs when larger aspects of discourse such as speech styles, social languages, genres and even ideologies are borrowed from others. What do you think the reason for and effect of mixing social languages were in this text? Can you think of other texts that mix broader aspects of discourse (such as social languages or genres) in order to strategically advance a particular ideology or to present the authors or the readers as certain kinds of people?

❑ Gee says that our choices of and assumptions about the meanings of words are often determined by 'cultural models', which are idealized versions of 'normal, typical reality'. Cultural models often involve ideas about certain 'types' of people, such as 'bachelors' and how they are supposed to act. Consider the cultural models surrounding some kind of important event or activity in your society (such as studying in university or getting married). What sorts of cultural models does your society associate with these events or activities? What kinds of people do the cultural models include, and what kinds of people do they marginalize or exclude?

B. Orders of indexicality

Jan Blommaert (reprinted from *The Sociolinguistics of Globalization*, Cambridge: Cambridge University Press, 2010, pp. 29–39)

Nina's derrière

A few years ago I was visiting an up-market department store in Central Tokyo, and in the very exclusive and expensive food section of that store I noticed a chocolate shop which bore the name Nina's Derrière. The stylized lettering and the choice of French betray an aspiration to considerable chic, and the prices of the chocolate on sale materialized that aspiration. But the name of the shop was, let us say, a rather unhappy choice, and I hoped that not too many Japanese customers would know enough French to understand the meaning of the name. I confess that I myself found the thought of offering someone a chocolate obtained from Nina's bum intensely entertaining.

It was also useful in bringing an important point home to me. This was not French. At least: while the origins of 'derrière' are clearly French, and while its use in the shop's name drew on indexicals of French chic, the word did not function as a linguistic sign. Linguistically it was only French in a minimal sense, as a word whose origins lie in the stock vocabulary of the language we conventionally call French. Its Frenchness was semiotic rather than linguistic: important was not its linguistic function as a denotational sign, but the emblematic function it had in signalling a complex of associative meanings, the things I captured under the term French chic. This is why the chocolate shop was still in business in spite of its dramatically inappropriate name: the sign did not function linguistically in the context of a Tokyo department store – linguistic knowledge of French being a very rare commodity in Tokyo – but it functioned, and functioned well, emblematically. The sign suddenly becomes a linguistic sign only when someone like me, who has linguistic competence in French, sees it and reads it as an instance of (linguistic) French. Prior to that the sign is not 'French' but 'Frenchness'. At least, as long as the sign remains in its particular environment. When it is 'exported', so to speak, to the environment that someone like me brings along, it changes.

*****

Orders of indexicality

Indexicality, even though largely operating at the implicit level of linguistic/semiotic structuring, is not unstructured but ordered. It is ordered in two ways, and these forms of indexical order account for 'normativity' in semiosis. The first kind of order is what Silverstein (2003) called 'indexical order': the fact that indexical meanings occur in patterns offering perceptions of similarity and stability that can be perceived as 'types' of semiotic practise with predictable (presupposable/entailing) directions. 'Register' is a case in point: clustered and patterned language forms that index specific social personae and roles can be invoked to organize interactional practices (e.g. turns at talk, narrative), and have a prima facie stability that can sometimes be used for typifying or stereotyping (e.g. 'posh' accents – see Rampton 2003). Speaking or writing through such registers involves insertion in recognizable (normative) repertoires of 'voices': one then speaks as a man, a lawyer, a middle-aged European, an asylum seeker and so forth, and if done appropriately, one will be perceived as speaking as such. Thus, indexical order is the metapragmatic organizing principle behind what is widely understood as the 'pragmatics' of language.

Such forms of indexical order sometimes have long and complex histories of becoming (Silverstein 2003 and Agha 2003 offer excellent illustrations). These histories are often connected to the histories of becoming of nation states and to their cultural and sociolinguistic paraphernalia – the notion of a 'standard language' and its derivative, a particular 'national' ethnolinguistic identity ... Yet, they also display a significant degree of variability and change, they can erupt and fade under pressure of macro-developments such as capitalist consumer fashions ... Indexical order of this sort is a positive force, it produces social categories, recognizable semiotic emblems for groups and individuals, a more or less coherent semiotic habitat.

It does so, however, within the confines of a stratified general repertoire in which particular indexical orders relate to others in relations of mutual valuation – higher/lower, better/worse. This is where we meet another kind of order to indexicalities, one that operates on a higher plane of social structuring: an order in the general systems of meaningful semiosis valid in groups at any given time. This kind of ordering results in what I call orders of indexicality – a term obviously inspired by Foucault's 'order of discourse'. Recall that Foucault was interested in the general rules for the production of discourses: their positive emergence as well as their erasure and exclusion. He started from the hypothesis that in every society the production of discourse is at once controlled, selected, organized and redistributed by a certain number of procedures whose role is to ward off its powers and dangers, to gain mastery over its chance events, to evade its ponderous, formidable materiality. (Foucault 1984 :109)

If we now paraphrase Foucault's hypothesis we see that ordered indexicalities operate within large stratified complexes in which some forms of semiosis are systemically perceived as valuable, others as less valuable and some are not taken into account at all, while all are subject to rules of access and regulations as to circulation. That means that such systemic patterns of indexicality are also systemic patterns of authority, of control and evaluation, and hence of inclusion and exclusion by real or perceived others. This also means that every register is susceptible to a politics of access. And it also means that there is an economy of exchange, in which the values attached by some to one form of semiosis may not be granted by others: the English spoken by a middle-class person in Nairobi may not be (and is unlikely to be) perceived as a middle-class attribute in London or New York.

'Order of indexicality' is a sensitizing concept that should index ('point a finger to') important aspects of power and inequality in the field of semiosis. If forms of semiosis are socially and culturally valued, these valuation processes should display traces of power and authority, of struggles in which there were winners as well as losers, and in which, in general, the group of winners is smaller than the group of losers. The concept invites different questions – sociolinguistic questions on indexicality – and should open empirical analyses of indexicality to higher-level considerations about relations within sociolinguistic repertoires, the (non-)exchangeability of particular linguistic or semiotic resources across places, situations and groups, and so forth. It invites, in sum, different questions of authority, access and power in this field.

Issues to consider

❑ Blommaert says that 'orders of indexicality' are systems that govern how we value different forms of semiosis and who has access to them. What is the relationship between this concept and the concept of cultural models that Gee introduced in the first excerpt of this section?

❑ In sections A4 and B4 we discussed how authors used different 'social languages' in order to create certain relationships with readers. One point that Blommaert makes is that the ability to use social languages is subject to what he calls a 'politics of access'. In other words, not everyone has access to some social languages, and social languages have different meanings or effects when used by different people. Can you think of some examples of social languages that are restricted to particular groups or people or of social languages that change their indexical meaning when used by different people?

TWO PERSPECTIVES ON CONVERSATION   D5

The two readings in this section represent two different perspectives on conversation. The first, by John Austin, is a basic outline of the principles of speech act theory. In particular, Austin makes an argument about why a perspective which focuses only on the propositional content of utterances cannot adequately explain how people actually use language. The second excerpt is from a classic article by conversation analyst Emanuel Schegloff. The focus of the article is conversational closings, but Schegloff uses this topic to illustrate one of the basic principles of adjacency pairs, the principle of *conditional relevance*.

A. How to do things with words

John L. Austin (reprinted from *How to Do Things with Words*, Oxford: Oxford University Press, 1976, 1990, pp. 359–371)

John L. Austin

What I shall have to say here is neither difficult nor contentious; the only merit I should like to claim for it is that of being true, at least in parts. The phenomenon to be discussed is very widespread and obvious, and it cannot fail to have been already noticed, at least here and there, by others. Yet I have not found attention paid to it specifically.

It was for too long the assumption of philosophers that the business of a 'statement' can only be to 'describe' some state of affairs, or to 'state some fact', which it must do either truly or falsely. Grammarians, indeed, have regularly pointed out that not all 'sentences' are (used in making) statements: there are, traditionally, besides (grammarians') statements, also questions and exclamations, and sentences expressing commands or wishes or concessions. And doubtless philosophers have not intended to deny this, despite some loose use of 'sentence' for 'statement'. Doubtless, too, both grammarians and philosophers have been aware that it is by no means easy to distinguish even questions, commands, and so on from statements by means of the few and jejune grammatical marks available, such as word order, mood, and the like: though perhaps it has not been usual to dwell on the difficulties which this fact obviously raises. For how do we decide which is which? What are the limits and definitions of each?

But now in recent years, many things which would once have been accepted without question as 'statements' by both philosophers and grammarians have been scrutinized with new care . . . It has come to be commonly held that many utterances which look like statements are either not intended at all, or only intended in part, to record or impart straightforward information about the facts: for example, 'ethical propositions' are perhaps intended, solely or partly, to evince emotion or to prescribe conduct or to influence it in special ways . . . We very often also use utterances in ways beyond the scope at least of traditional grammar. It has come to be seen that many specially perplexing words embedded in apparently descriptive statements do not serve to indicate some specially odd additional feature in the reality reported, but to indicate (not to report) the circumstances in which the statement is made or reservations to which it is subject or the way in which it is to be taken and the like. To overlook these possibilities in the way once common is called the 'descriptive' fallacy; but perhaps this is not a good name, as 'descriptive' itself is special. Not all true or false statements are descriptions, and for this reason I prefer to use the word 'Constative' . . . Utterances can be found ... such that:

A. they do not 'describe' or 'report' or constate anything at all, are not 'true or false'; and

B. the uttering of the sentence is, or is a part of, the doing of an action, which again would not normally be described as, or as 'just', saying something.

Examples:

(a)   'I do (sc. take this woman to be my lawful wedded wife)' – as uttered in the course of the marriage ceremony.
(b)   'I name this ship the Queen Elizabeth' – as uttered when smashing the bottle against the stern.
(c)   'I give and bequeath my watch to my brother' – as occurring in a will.
(d)   'I bet you sixpence it will rain tomorrow.'

In these examples it seems clear that to utter the sentence (in, of course, the appropriate circumstances) is not to describe my doing of what I should be said in so uttering to be doing or to state that I am doing it: it is to do it. None of the utterances cited is either true or false: I assert this as obvious and do not argue it.

It needs argument no more than that 'damn' is not true or false: it may be that the utterance 'serves to inform you' – but that is quite different. To name the ship is to say (in the appropriate circumstances) the words 'I name, etc.'. When I say, before the registrar or altar, 'I do', I am not reporting on a marriage: I am indulging in it.

What are we to call a sentence or an utterance of this type? I propose to call it a performative sentence or a performative utterance, or, for short, 'a performative'. The term 'performative' will be used in a variety of cognate ways and constructions, much as the term 'imperative' is. The name is derived, of course, from 'perform', the usual verb with the noun 'action': it indicates that the issuing of the utterance is the performing of an action – it is not normally thought of as just saying something. Are we then to say things like this:

'To marry is to say a few words', or

'Betting is simply saying something'?

Such a doctrine sounds odd or even flippant at first, but with sufficient safeguards it may become not odd at all.

*****

The uttering of the words is, indeed, usually a, or even the, leading incident in the performance of the act (of betting or what not), the performance of which is also the object of the utterance, but it is far from being usually, even if it is ever, the sole thing necessary if the act is to be deemed to have been performed. Speaking generally, it is always necessary that the circumstances in which the words are uttered should be in some way, or ways, appropriate, and it is very commonly necessary that either the speaker himself or other persons should also perform certain other actions, whether 'physical' or 'mental' actions or even acts of uttering further words. Thus, for naming the ship, it is essential that I should be the person appointed to name her; for (Christian) marrying, it is essential that I should not be already married with a wife living, sane and undivorced, and so on; for a bet to have been made, it is generally necessary for the offer of the bet to have been accepted by a taker (who must have done something, such as to say 'Done'); and it is hardly a gift if I say, 'I give it you' but never hand it over . . .

But we may, in objecting, have something totally different, and this time quite mistaken, in mind, especially when we think of some of the more awe-inspiring performatives such as 'I promise to ...'. Surely the words must be spoken 'seriously' and so as to be taken 'seriously'? This is, though vague, true enough in general – it is an important commonplace in discussing the purport of any utterance whatsoever. I must not be joking, for example, nor writing a poem . . .

Well we shall next consider what we actually do say about the utterance concerned when one or another of its normal concomitants is absent. In no case do we say that the utterance was false but rather that the utterance – or rather the act, e.g., the promise – was void, or given in bad faith, or not implemented, or the like. In the particular case of promising, as with many other performatives, it is appropriate that the person uttering the promise should have a certain intention, viz. here to keep his word: and perhaps of all concomitants this looks the most suitable to be that which 'I promise' does describe or record. Do we not actually, when such intention is absent, speak of a 'false' promise? Yet so to speak is not to say that the utterance 'I promise that ...' is false, in the sense that though he states that he does he doesn't, or that though he describes he misdescribes – misreports. For he does promise: the promise here is not even void, though it is given in bad faith. His utterance is perhaps misleading, probably deceitful and doubtless wrong, but it is not a lie or a misstatement. At most we might make out a case for saying that it implies or insinuates a falsehood or a misstatement (to the effect that he does intend to do something): but that is a very different matter. Moreover, we do not speak of a false bet or a false christening; and that we do speak of a false promise need commit us no more than the fact that we speak of a false move. 'False' is not necessarily used of statements only.

*****

Besides the uttering of the words of so-called performative, a good many other things have as a general rule to be right and to go right if we are to be said to have happily brought off our action. What these are we may hope to discover by looking at and classifying types of case in which something goes wrong and the act – marrying, betting, bequeathing, christening, or what not – is therefore at least to some extent a failure: the utterance is then, we may say, not indeed false but in general unhappy. And for this reason we call the doctrine of the things that can be and go wrong on the occasion of such utterances, the doctrine of the infelicities.

Suppose we try first to state schematically – and I do not wish to claim any sort of finality for this scheme – some at least of the things which are necessary for the smooth or 'happy' functioning of a performative (or at least of a highly developed explicit performative, such as we have hitherto been alone concerned with), and then give examples of infelicities and their effects …

> A.1 There must exist an accepted conventional procedure having a certain conventional effect, that procedure to include the uttering of certain words by certain persons in certain circumstances, and further,
>
> A.2 the particular persons and circumstances in a given case must be appropriate for the invocation of the particular procedure invoked.
>
> B.1 The procedure must be executed by all participants both correctly and
>
> B.2 completely.
>
> C.1 Where, as often, the procedure is designed for use by persons having certain thoughts or feelings, or for the inauguration of certain consequential conduct on the part of any participant, then a person participating in and so invoking the procedure must in fact have those thoughts or feelings, and the participants must intend so to conduct themselves, and further
>
> C.2 must actually so conduct themselves subsequently.

Now if we sin against any one (or more) of these six rules, our performative utterance will be (in one way or another) unhappy.

Issues to consider

❏ Some of the felicity conditions for speech acts are external, that is, they can be determined through observation. Things such as the time, place and people involved are examples. But some are internal, having to do with the intentions, thoughts, feelings and even 'sanity' of the person issuing the speech act or the person to whom it is being issued. What complications does this introduce for the successful interpretation of speech acts?

❏ The feminist critic Judith Butler (1990/2006) says that when a doctor announces the gender of a newborn baby (e.g. 'It's a girl!'), he or she is issuing a performative. It is by naming the child's gender that gender is assigned. Do you agree with this interpretation? What conditions do you think must be met for such a speech act to be felicitous?

Emanuel A. Schegloff and Harvey Sacks

B. Opening up closings

Emanuel A. Schegloff and Harvey Sacks (reprinted from *Semiotica 7*, 1973: 289–327)

It seems useful to begin by formulating the problem of closing technically in terms of the more fundamental order of organization, that of turns. Two basic features of conversation are proposed to be: (1) at least, and no more than, one party speaks at a time in a single conversation; and (2) speaker change recurs.

The achievement of these features singly, and especially the achievement of their cooccurrence, is accomplished by co-conversationalists through the use of a 'machinery' for ordering speaker turns sequentially in conversation. The turn-taking machinery includes as one component a set of procedures for organizing the selection of 'next speakers', and, as another, a set of procedures for locating the occasions on which transition to a next speaker may or should occur. The turn-taking machinery operates utterance by utterance. That is to say, it is within any current utterance that possible next speaker selection is accomplished, and upon possible completion of any current utterance that such selection takes effect and transition to a next speaker becomes relevant. We shall speak of this as the 'transition relevance' of possible utterance completion ... Whereas these basic features ... deal with a conversation's ongoing orderliness, they make no provision for the closing of conversation. A machinery that includes the transition relevance of possible utterance completion recurrently for any utterance in the conversation generates an indefinitely extendable string of turns to talk. Then, an initial problem concerning closings may be formulated: HOW TO ORGANIZE THE SIMULTANEOUS ARRIVAL OF THE CO-CONVERSATIONALISTS AT A POINT WHERE ONE SPEAKER'S COMPLETION WILL NOT OCCASION ANOTHER SPEAKER'S TALK, AND THAT WILL NOT BE HEARD AS SOME SPEAKER'S SILENCE. The last qualification is necessary to differentiate closings from other places in conversation where one speaker's completion is not followed by a possible next speaker's talk, but where, given the continuing relevance of the basic features and the turn-taking machinery, what is heard is not termination but attributable silence, a pause in the last speaker's utterance, etc. It should suggest why simply to stop talking is not a solution to the closing problem: any first prospective speaker to do so would be hearable as 'being silent' in terms of the turn-taking machinery, rather than as having suspended its relevance ...

How is the transition relevance of possible utterance completion lifted? A proximate solution involves the use of a 'terminal exchange' composed of conventional parts, e.g., an exchange of 'good-byes' ... We note first that the terminal exchange is a case of a class of utterance sequences which we have been studying for some years, namely, the utterance pair, or, as we shall refer to it, the adjacency pair ... Briefly, adjacency pairs consist of sequences which properly have the following features: (1) two utterance length, (2) adjacent positioning of component utterances, (3) different speakers producing each utterance. The component utterances of such sequences have an achieved relatedness beyond that which may otherwise obtain between adjacent utterances. That relatedness is partially the product of the operation of a typology in the speakers' production of the sequences. The typology operates in two ways: it partitions utterance types into 'first pair parts' (i.e., first parts of pairs) and second pair parts; and it affiliates a first pair part and a second pair part to form a 'pair type'. 'Question-answer', 'greeting-greeting', 'offer-acceptance/refusal' are instances of pair types. Adjacency pair sequences, then, exhibit the further features (4) relative ordering of parts (i.e. first pair parts precede second pair parts) and (5) discriminative relations (i.e., the pair type of which a first pair part is a member is relevant to the selection among second pair parts) ...

In the case of that type of organization which we are calling 'overall structural organization', it may be noted that at least initial sequences (e.g., greeting exchanges), and ending sequences (i.e., terminal exchanges) employ adjacency pair formats. It is the recurrent, institutionalized use of adjacency pairs for such types of organization problems that suggests that these problems have, in part, a common character, and that adjacency pair organization ... is specially fitted to the solution of problems of that character.

But it may be wondered why are two utterances required for either opening or closing? ... What two utterances produced by different speakers can do that one utterance cannot do is: by an adjacently positioned second, a speaker can show that he understood what a prior aimed at, and that he is willing to go along with that. Also, by virtue of the occurrence of an adjacently produced second, the doer of a first can see that what he intended was indeed understood, and that it was or was not accepted.

We are then proposing: If WHERE transition relevance is to be lifted is a systematic problem, an adjacency pair solution can work because: by providing that transition relevance is to be lifted after the second pair part's occurrence, the occurrence of the second pair part can then reveal an appreciation of, and agreement to, the intention of closing NOW which a first part of a terminal exchange reveals its speaker to propose. Given the institutionalization of that solution, a range of ways of assuring that it be employed have been developed, which make drastic difference between one party saying "good-bye" and not leaving a slot for the other to reply, and one party saying "good-bye" and leaving a slot for the other to reply.

The former becomes a distinct sort of activity, expressing anger, brusqueness, and the like, and available to such a use by contrast with the latter. It is this consequentiality of alternatives that is the hallmark of an institutionalized solution ...

In referring to the components of terminal exchanges, we have so far employed "good-bye" as an exclusive instance. But, it plainly is not exclusively used. Such other components as "ok", "see you", "thank you", "you're welcome", and the like are also used. Since the latter items are used in other ways as well, the mere fact of their use does not mark them as unequivocal parts of terminal exchanges. The adjacency pair is one kind of 'local', i.e., utterance, organization. It does NOT appear that FIRST parts of terminal exchanges are placed by reference to that order of organization. While they, of course, occur after some utterance, they are not placed by reference to a location that might be formulated as 'next' after some 'last' utterance or class of utterances. Rather, their placement seems to be organized by reference to a properly initiated closing SECTION.

The [relevant] aspect of overall conversational organization concerns the organization of topic talk . . . If we may refer to what gets talked about in a conversation as 'mentionables', then we can note that there are considerations relevant for conversationalists in ordering and distributing their talk about mentionables in a single conversation. There is, for example, a position in a single conversation for 'first topic'. We intend to mark by this term not the simple serial fact that some topic gets talked about temporally prior to others, for some temporally prior topics such as, for example, ones prefaced by "First, I just want to say ...", or topics that are minor developments by the receiver of the conversational opening of "how are you" inquiries, are not heard or treated as 'first topic' is to accord it to a certain special status in the conversation. Thus, for example, to make a topic 'first topic' may provide for its analyzability (by coparticipants) as 'the reason for' the conversation, that being, furthermore, a preservable and reportable feature of the conversation. In addition, making a topic 'first topic' may accord it a special importance on the part of its initiator. These features of 'first topics' may pose a problem for conversationalists who may not wish to have special importance accorded some 'mentionable', and who may not want it preserved as 'the reason for the conversation'. It is by reference to such problems affiliated with the use of first topic position that we may appreciate such exchanges at the beginnings of conversations in which news IS later reported, as:

A: What's up.
B: Not much. What's up with you?
A: Nothing.

Conversationalists, then, can have mentionables they do not want to put in first topic position, and there are ways of talking past first topic position without putting them in.

A further feature of the organization of topic talk seems to involve 'fitting' as a preferred procedure. That is, it appears that a preferred way of getting mentionables mentioned is to employ the resources of the local organization of utterances in the course of the conversation. That involves holding off the mention of a mentionable until it can 'occur naturally', that is, until it can be fitted to another conversationalist's prior utterance …

There is, however, no guarantee that the course of the conversation will provide the occasion for any particular mentionable to 'come up naturally'.

This being the case, it would appear that an important virtue for a closing structure designed for this kind of topical structure would involve the provision for placement of hitherto unmentioned mentionables. The terminal exchange by itself makes no such provision. By exploiting the close organization resource of adjacency pairs, it provides for an immediate (i.e., next turn) closing of the conversation. That this close-ordering technique for terminating not exclude the possibility of inserting unmentioned mentionables can be achieved by placement restrictions on the first part of terminal exchanges, for example, by requiring 'advance note' or some form of foreshadowing.

Issues to consider
❏ Sacks and Schegloff say that adjacency pairs always play a part in the beginning and ending of conversations. Why is this necessary? Can you think of any situations in which this is not the case? What kind of effect is produced? Do people perform openings and closing differently in situations other than face-to-face communication (e.g. text messaging or telephone conversations)?
❏ According to Sacks and Schegloff, closing sequences are designed the way they are in order to help participants manage topics in conversations (i.e to make sure neither of the parties wishes to introduce a new topic). What role do adjacency sequences that occur at the beginnings of conversations have in helping people to manage topics? Which person – the initiator of the conversation or the responder – is usually the person who introduces the topic in face-to-face communication? Is this the same in other kinds of interaction such as instant messaging?

D6

D6 POLITENESS AND FRAMING IN INTERACTION

In the following two excerpts the authors illustrate the principles of *politeness* and *framing*, the two most important discursive resources we use to strategically manage 'who we are being' and 'what we are doing' in conversations. The first excerpt is from the classic book by Penelope Brown and Stephen Levinson *Politeness: Some Universals in Language Usage* in which the authors put forth what they regard as universal rules for managing face in conversation. In this excerpt they give a definition of 'face' and talk about the two kinds of 'face wants' people have. The second excerpt is from a famous article by Deborah Tannen and her collaborator Cynthia Wallat in which the authors give a clear and accessible definition of *interactive frames* and the theoretical basis for this concept. Using the example of a paediatrician examining a child, they illustrate how interactive frames and frame shifts operate to signal the different things the doctor is doing throughout the examination.

A. Face

Penelope Brown and Stephen Levinson

Penelope Brown and Stephen Levinson (reprinted from Brown, P. and Levinson, S.C. (1987). *Politeness: Some Universals in Language Usage (pp. 61–63).* Cambridge: Cambridge University Press.)

Face. Our notion of 'face' is derived from that of Goffman (1967) and from the English folk term, which ties face up with notions of being embarrassed or humiliated, or 'losing face'. Thus face is something that is emotionally invested, and that can be lost, maintained, or enhanced, and must be constantly attended to in interaction. In general, people cooperate (and assume each other's cooperation) in maintaining face in interaction, such cooperation being based on the mutual vulnerability of face. That is, normally everyone's face depends on everyone else's being maintained, and since people can be expected to defend their faces if threatened, and in defending their own to threaten others' faces, it is in general in every participant's best interest to maintain each others' face, that is to act in ways that assure the other participants that the agent is heedful of the assumptions concerning face given under (i) above. (Just what this heedfulness consists in is the subject of this paper.)

Furthermore, while the content of face will differ in different cultures (what the exact limits are to personal territories, and what the publicly relevant content of personality consists in), we are assuming that the mutual knowledge of members' public self-image or face, and the social necessity to orient oneself to it in interaction, are universal.

Face as wants. It would have been possible to treat the respect for face as norms or values subscribed to by members of a society (as perhaps most anthropologists would assume). Instead, we treat the aspects of face as basic wants, which every member knows every other member desires, and which in general it is in the interests of every member to partially satisfy. In other words, we take in Weberian terms the more strongly rational *zweckrational* model of individual action, because the *wert-rational* model (which would treat face respect as an unquestionable value or norm) fails to account for the fact that face respect is not an unequivocal right. In particular, a mere bow to face acts like a diplomatic declaration of good intentions; it is not in general required that an actor fully satisfy another's face wants. Secondly, face can be, and routinely is, ignored, not just in cases of social breakdown (affrontery) but also in cases of urgent cooperation, or in the interests of efficiency.

Therefore, the components of face may be restated as follows. We define:

> **negative face:** the want of every 'competent adult member' that his actions be unimpeded by others.
>
> **positive face:** the want of every member that his wants be desirable to at least some others.

Negative face, with its derivative politeness of non-imposition, is familiar as the formal politeness that the notion 'politeness' immediately conjures up. But positive face, and its derivative forms of positive politeness, are less obvious. The reduction of a person's public self-image or personality to a want that one's wants be desirable to at least some others can be justified in this way. The most salient aspect of a person's personality in interaction is what that personality requires of other interactants—in particular, it includes the desire to be ratified, understood, approved of, liked or admired. The next step is to represent this desire as the want to have one's goals thought of as desirable. In the special sense of 'wanting' that we develop, we can then arrive at positive face as here defined. To give this some intuitive flesh, consider an example. Mrs B is a fervent gardener. Much of her time and effort are expended on her roses. She is proud of her roses, and she likes others to admire them. She is gratified when visitors say 'What lovely roses; I wish ours looked like that! How do you do it?', implying that they want just what she has wanted and achieved.

Issues to consider
❑ Brown and Levinson characterize the desire to be 'liked' as 'positive face' and the desires for autonomy as 'negative face'. How do these terms correspond to the independence and involvement strategies I discussed in B5?
❑ Brown and Levinson talk about some instances where face is routinely ignored. Can you think of some concrete examples? Why is face ignored in these situations and what are the consequences?

B. Interactive frames and knowledge schemas in interaction

Deborah Tannen and Cynthia Wallat (reprinted from *Social Psychology Quarterly* 50(2), 1987: 205–216)

Deborah Tannen and Cynthia Wallat

Interactive frames
The interactive notion of frame refers to a definition of what is going on in interaction, without which no utterance (or movement or gesture) could be interpreted. To use Bateson's classic example, a monkey needs to know whether a bite from another monkey is intended within the frame of play or the frame of fighting. People are continually

confronted with the same interpretative task. In order to comprehend any utterance, a listener (and a speaker) must know within which frame it is intended: for example, is this joking? Is it fighting? Something intended as a joke but interpreted as an insult (it could of course be both) can trigger a fight.

Goffman (1974) sketched the theoretical foundations of frame analysis in the work of William James, Alfred Schutz and Harold Garfinkel to investigate the socially constructed nature of reality. Building on their work, as well as that of linguistic philosophers John Austin and Ludwig Wittgenstein, Goffman developed a complex system of terms and concepts to illustrate how people use multiple frameworks to make sense of events even as they construct those events. Exploring in more detail the linguistic basis of such frameworks, Goffman (1981) introduced the term "footing" to describe how, at the same time that participants frame events, they negotiate the interpersonal relationships, or "alignments," that constitute those events.

The interactive notion of frame, then, refers to a sense of what activity is being engaged in, how speakers mean what they say. As Ortega y Gas'set (1959: 3), a student of Heidegger, puts it, "Before understanding any concrete statement, it is necessary to perceive clearly 'what it is all about' in this statement and 'what game is being played.'" Since this sense is gleaned from the way participants behave in interaction, frames emerge in and are constituted by verbal and nonverbal interaction.

*****

One author (Tannen) was talking to a friend on the telephone, when he suddenly yelled, "YOU STOP THAT!" She knew from the way he uttered this command that it was addressed to a dog and not her. She remarked on the fact that when he addressed the dog, he spoke in something approximating a southern accent. The friend explained that this was because the dog had learned to respond to commands in that accent, and, to give another example, he illustrated the way he plays with the dog: "I say, 'GO GIT THAT BALL!'" Hearing this, the dog began running about the room looking for something to fetch. The dog recognized the frame "play" in the tone of the command; he could not, however, understand the words that identified an outer frame, "*referring* to playing with the dog," and mistook the reference for a literal invitation to play.

This example illustrates, as well, that people (and dogs) identify frames in interaction by association with linguistic and paralinguistic cues – the way words are uttered – in addition to what they say. That is, the way the speaker uttered "You stop that!" was associated with the frame "disciplining a pet" rather than "chatting with a friend." Tannen drew on her familiarity with the use of linguistic cues to signal frames when she identified her friend's interjection "You stop that!" as addressed to a dog, not her. But she also drew on the knowledge that her friend was taking care of someone's dog. This was part of her knowledge schema about her friend. Had her schema included the information that he had a small child and was allergic to dogs, she might have interpreted the same linguistic cues as signaling the related frame, "disciplining a misbehaving child." Furthermore, her expectations about how any speaker might express orders or emotions, i.e. frame such expressions, were brought to bear in this instance in conjunction with her expectations about how this particular friend is likely to speak to her, to a dog and to a child; that is, a schema for this friend's personal style. Thus frames and schemas interacted in her comprehension of the specific utterance.

Interactive frames in the pediatric examination
Linguistic registers

A key element in framing is the use of identifiable linguistic registers. Register, as Ferguson (1985) defines it, is simply "variation conditioned by use," conventionalized lexical, syntactic and prosodic choices deemed appropriate for the setting and audience . . . In addressing the child, the pediatrician uses "motherese": a teasing register characterized by exaggerated shifts in pitch, marked prosody (long pauses followed by bursts of vocalization), and drawn out vowel sounds, accompanied by smiling.

For example, while examining Jody's ears with an ophthalmoscope (ear light), the pediatrician pretends to be looking for various creatures, and Jody responds with delighted laughter:

> *Doctor:* Let me look in your ear. Do you have a monkey in your ear?
> *Child:* [laughing] No::::.
> *Doctor:* No:::? ... Let's see .... I .. see ..... a birdie!
> *Child:* [[laughing] No:::.
> *Doctor:* [smiling] No.

In stark contrast to this intonationally exaggerated register, the pediatrician uses a markedly flat intonation to give a running account of the findings of her examination, addressed to no present party, but designed for the benefit of pediatric residents who might later view the video-tape in the teaching facility. We call this "reporting register." For example, looking in Jody's throat, the doctor says, with only slight stumbling:

> Doctor: Her canals are are fine, they're open, um her tympanic membrane was thin, and light.

Finally, in addressing the mother, the pediatrician uses conventional conversational register, as for example:

> Doctor: As you know, the important thing is that she does have difficulty with the use of her muscles.

Register shifting

Throughout the examination the doctor moves among these registers. Sometimes she shifts from one to another in very short spaces of time, as in the following example in which she moves smoothly from teasing the child while examining her throat, to reporting her findings, to explaining to the mother what she is looking for and how this relates to the mother's expressed concern with the child's breathing at night.

> [Teasing register]
> *Doctor:* Let's see. Can you open up like this, Jody. Look.
>   [[Doctor opens her own mouth]
> *Child:* Aaaaaaaaaaaaaah.
> *Doctor:* [Good. That's good.
> *Child:* Aaaaaaaaaaaah

[Reporting register]
Doctor: /Seeing/ for the palate, she has a high arched palate →
Child: [Aaaaaaaaaaaaaaaaaaaaaaaaaah
Doctor: but there's no cleft,
          [maneuvers to grasp child's jaw]

[Conversational register]
          … what we'd want to look for is to see how she … moves her palate. . . .
          Which may be some of the difficulty with breathing that we're talk-
          ing *about.*

The pediatrician's shifts from one register to another are sometimes abrupt (for example, when she turns to the child and begins teasing) and sometimes gradual (for example, her reporting register in "high arched palate" begins to fade into conversational
register with "but there's no cleft," and come to rest firmly in conversational register
with "what we'd want to look for …"). In the following example, she shifts from entertaining Jody to reporting findings and back to managing Jody in a teasing tone:

[Teasing register]
Doctor: That's my light.
Child: /This goes up there./
Doctor: It goes up there. That's right.

[Reporting register]
          Now while we're examining her head we're feeling for lymph nodes in
          her neck … or for any masses … okay … also you palpate the midline
          for thyroid, for goiter … if there's any.

[Teasing register]
          Now let us look in your mouth. Okay? With my light. Can you open up
          real big? … Oh, bigger. . . . Oh bigger. . . . Bigger.

Frame shifting

Although register shifting is one way of accomplishing frame shifts, it is not the only
way. Frames are more complex than register. Whereas each audience is associated with
an identifiable register, the pediatrician shifts footings with each audience. In other
words, she not only talks differently to the mother, the child and the future video audience, but she also deals with each of these audiences in different ways, depending upon
the frame in which she is operating.

The three most important frames in this interaction are the social encounter, examination of the child and a related outer frame of its videotaping, and consultation with
the mother. Each of the three frames entails addressing each of the three audiences in
different ways. For example, the social encounter requires that the doctor entertain the
child, establish rapport with the mother and ignore the video camera and crew. The
examination frame requires that she ignore the mother, make sure the video crew is
ready and then ignore them, examine the child, and explain what she is doing for the
future video audience of pediatric residents.

The consultation frame requires that she talk to the mother and ignore the crew and the child—or, rather, keep the child "on hold," to use Goffman's term, while she answers the mother's questions. These frames are balanced nonverbally as well as verbally. Thus the pediatrician keeps one arm outstretched to rest her hand on the child while she turns away to talk to the mother, palpably keeping the child "on hold."

Juggling frames

Often these frames must be served simultaneously, such as when the pediatrician entertains the child and examines her at the same time, as seen in the example where she looks in her ear and teases Jody that she is looking for a monkey. The pediatrician's reporting register reveals what she was actually looking at (Jody's ear canals and tympanic membrane). But balancing frames is an extra cognitive burden, as seen when the doctor accidentally mixes the vocabulary of her diagnostic report into her teasing while examining Jody's stomach:

> [Teasing register]
> *Doctor:* Okay. All right. Now let me /?/ let me see what I can find in there. Is there peanut butter and jelly?
> Wait a minute.
> *Child:* No
> *Doctor:* No peanut butter and jelly in there?
> *Child:* No.
> [Conversational register]
> *Doctor:* Bend your legs up a little bit. . . . That's right.
> [Teasing register]
> Okay? Okay. Any peanut butter and jelly in here?
> *Child:* No
> *Doctor:* No.
> No. There's nothing in there. Is your spleen palpable over there?
> *Child:* No.

The pediatrician says the last line, "Is your spleen palpable over there?" in the same teasing register she was using for peanut butter and jelly, and Jody responds with the same delighted giggling "No" with which she responded to the teasing questions about peanut butter and jelly. The power of the paralinguistic cues with which the doctor signals the frame "teasing" is greater than that of the words spoken, which in this case leak out of the examination frame into the teasing register.

In other words, for the pediatrician, each interactive frame, that is, each identifiable activity that she is engaged in within the interaction, entails her establishing a distinct footing with respect to the other participants.

The interactive production of frames

Our analysis focuses on the pediatrician's speech because our goal is to show that the mismatch of schemas triggers the frame switches which make this interaction burdensome for her. Similar analyses could be performed for any participant in any interaction. Furthermore, all participants in any interaction collaborate in the negotiation of all frames operative within that interaction. Thus, the mother and child collaborate in the negotiation of frames which are seen in the pediatrician's speech and behavior.

For example, consider the examination frame as evidence in the pediatrician's running report of her procedures and findings for the benefit of the video audience.

Although the mother interrupts with questions at many points in the examination, she does not do so when the pediatrician is reporting her findings in what we have called reporting register. Her silence contributes to the maintenance of this frame. Furthermore, on the three of seventeen occasions of reporting register when the mother does offer a contribution, she does so in keeping with the physician's style: Her utterances have a comparable clipped style.

The homonymy of behaviors

Activities which appear the same on the surface can have very different meanings and consequences for the participants if they are understood as associated with different frames. For example, the pediatrician examines various parts of the child's body in accordance with what she describes at the start as a "standard pediatric evaluation." At times she asks the mother for information relevant to the child's condition, still adhering to the sequence of foci of attention prescribed by the pediatric evaluation. At one point, the mother asks about a skin condition behind the child's right ear, causing the doctor to examine that part of Jody's body. What on the surface appears to be the same activity—examining the child—is really very different. In the first case the doctor is adhering to a preset sequence of procedures in the examination, and in the second she is interrupting that sequence to focus on something else, following which she will have to recover her place in the standard sequence.

Conflicting frames

Each frame entails ways of behaving that potentially conflict with the demands of other frames. For example, consulting with the mother entails not only interrupting the examination sequence but also taking extra time to answer her questions, and this means that the child will get more restless and more difficult to manage as the examination proceeds. Reporting findings to the video audience may upset the mother, necessitating more explanation in the consultation frame. Perhaps that is the reason the pediatrician frequently explains to the mother what she is doing and finding and why.

Another example will illustrate that the demands associated with the consultation frame can conflict with those of the examination frame, and that these frames and associated demands are seen in linguistic evidence, in this case by contrasting the pediatrician's discourse to the mother in the examination setting with her report to the staff of the Child Development Center about the same problem. Having recently learned that Jody has an arteriovenous malformation in her brain, the mother asks the doctor during the examination how dangerous this condition is. The doctor responds in a way that balances the demands of several frames:

> *Mother:* I often worry about the danger involved too.→
> *Doctor:* Yes.
>
> Cause she's well I mean like right now, ... uh ... in her present condition. →

Doctor: mhm
Mother: I've often wondered about how dangerous they they are to her right now.
Doctor: We:ll … um … the only danger would be from bleeding. … From them. If there was any rupture, or anything like that. Which CAN happen … um …| that would be the danger.
Mother: mhm
Doctor: … For that. But they're . . . . . . mm . . . not going to be something that will get worse as time goes on.
Mother: Oh I see.
Doctor: But they're just there. Okay?

The mother's question invoked the consultation frame, requiring the doctor to give the mother the information based on her medical knowledge, plus take into account the effect on the mother of the information that the child's life IS in danger. However, the considerable time that would normally be required for such a task is limited because of the conflicting demands of the examination frame: the child is "on hold" for the exam to proceed. (Notice that it is the admirable sensitivity of this doctor that makes her aware of the needs of both frames. According to this mother, many doctors have informed her in matter-of-fact tones of potentially devastating information about her child's condition, without showing any sign of awareness that such information will have emotional impact on the parent. In our terms, such doctors acknowledge only one frame—examination—in order to avoid the demands of conflicting frames—consultation and social encounter. Observing the burden on this pediatrician, who successfully balances the demands of multiple frames, makes it easy to understand why others might avoid this.)

The pediatrician blunts the effect of the information she imparts by using circumlocutions and repetitions; pausing and hesitating; and minimizing the significant danger of the arteriovenous malformation by using the word "only" ("only danger"), by using the conditional tense ("that would be the danger"), and by stressing what sounds positive, that they're not going to get worse. She further creates a reassuring effect by smiling, nodding and using a soothing tone of voice.

In reviewing the video-tape with us several years after the taping, the pediatrician was surprised to see that she had expressed the prognosis in this way—and furthermore that the mother seemed to be reassured by what was in fact distressing information. The reason she did so, we suggest, is that she was responding to the immediate and conflicting demands of the two frames she was operating in: consulting with the mother in the context of the examination.

Evidence that this doctor indeed felt great concern for the seriousness of the child's condition is seen in her report to the staff regarding the same issue:

Doctor: …uh: I'm not sure how much counseling has been done, . . . with these parents, … around ,,, the issue … of the a-v malformation. Mother asked me questions, . . . about the operability, inoperability of it, … n·m … which I was not able to answer. She was told it was inoperable, and I had to say well yes some of them are and some of them aren't. … And I think that this is a … a … an important point. Because I don't know whether … the possibility of sudden death, intracranial hemorrhage, if any of this has ever been discussed with these parents.

Here the pediatrician speaks faster, with fluency and without hesitation or circumlocution. Her tone of voice conveys a sense of urgency and grave concern. Whereas the construction used with the mother, "only danger," seemed to minimize the danger, the listing construction used with the staff ("sudden death, intracranial hemorrhage"), which actually refers to a single possible event, gives the impression that even more dangers are present than those listed.

Thus the demands on the pediatrician associated with consultation with the mother; those associated with examining the child and reporting her findings to the video audience; and those associated with managing the interaction as a social encounter are potentially in conflict and result in competing demands on the doctor's cognitive and social capacities.

Issues to consider

❑ The different frames the doctor uses with the young patient and with her mother also involve different face strategies of independence and involvement. What do you think the relationship between framing strategies and face strategies is? How do they work together in interactions? How does this relate to Goffman's concept of 'footing'?

❑ The way we interpret frames depends crucially on our 'knowledge schema' for different situations. How do the knowledge schema the participants in the interaction described have about medical consultations affect how they produce and interpret contextualisation cues? Can you think of a situation in which you or someone you know approached a situation with an incomplete or faulty knowledge schema? What were the consequences?

❑ At one point in this interaction the doctor mixes a formal medical register ('Is your spleen palpable over there?') with a 'teasing frame,' and the child reacts as if this is part of the game. The authors use this as an example of how non-verbal contextualisation cues can sometimes be so powerful as to override the actual content of an utterance. Why do you think this is? Can you think of any examples of this from your own experience?

❑ Sometimes we have to manage the demands of two or more frames at one time. In this interaction, for example, the doctor has to manage communicating medical information to both the mother and the students watching the video and, at the same time, manage her young patient. In what way are the demands of these three different frames incompatible? What kinds of miscommunication can potentially arise from such situations?

D7 THE ETHNOGRAPHY OF COMMUNICATION

The first of the two readings that follow comes from a classic volume on the ethnography of communication: *Directions in Sociolinguistics*, edited by John Gumperz and Dell Hymes. In the first excerpt, Hymes lays out the distinction among speech situations, speech events and speech acts. In the second excerpt, Piia Varis introduces the idea of 'digital ethnography', and explores the extent to which the ideas of Hymes and other ethnographers of communication can be adapted to study online cultures and online communication.

A. Speech situations, speech events and speech acts

Dell Hymes (reprinted from *Directions in Sociolinguistics,* John J. Gumperz and Dell Hymes (eds), Oxford: Basil Blackwell, 1986, pp. 52–65)

Dell Hymes

Speech situation

Within a community one readily detects many situations associated with (or marked by the absence of) speech. Such contexts of situation will often be naturally described as ceremonies, fights, hunts, meals, lovemaking, and the like. It would not be profitable to convert such situations en masse into parts of a sociolinguistic description by the simple expedient of relabeling them in terms of speech. (Notice that the distinctions made with regard to speech community are not identical with the concepts of a general communicative approach, which must note the differential range of communication by speech, film, art object, music.) Such situations may enter as contexts into the statement of rules of speaking as aspects of setting (or of genre). In contrast to speech events, they are not in themselves governed by such rules, or one set of such rules throughout. A hunt, e.g., may comprise both verbal and nonverbal events, and the verbal events may be of more than one type.

In a sociolinguistic description, then, it is necessary to deal with activities which are in some recognizable way bounded or integral. From the standpoint of general social description they may be registered as ceremonies, fishing trips, and the like; from particular standpoints they may be regarded as political, esthetic, etc., situations, which serve as contexts for the manifestation of political, esthetic, etc., activity. From the sociolinguistic standpoint they may be regarded as speech situations.

Speech event

The term speech event will be restricted to activities, or aspects of activities, that are directly governed by rules or norms for the use of speech. An event may consist of a single speech act, but will often comprise several. Just as an occurrence of a noun may at the same time be the whole of a noun phrase and the whole of a sentence (e.g., "Fire!"), so a speech act may be the whole of a speech event, and of a speech situation (say, a rite consisting of a single prayer, itself a single invocation). More often, however, one will find a difference in magnitude: a party (speech situation), a conversation during the party (speech event), a joke within the conversation (speech act). It is of speech events and speech acts that one writes formal rules for their occurrence and characteristics.

Notice that the same type of speech act may recur in different types of speech event, and the same type of speech event in different contexts of situation. Thus, a joke (speech act) may be embedded in a private conversation, a lecture, a formal introduction. A private conversation may occur in the context of a party, a memorial service, a pause in changing sides in a tennis match.

Speech act

The speech act is the minimal term of the set just discussed, as the remarks on speech events have indicated. It represents a level distinct from the sentence, and not identifiable with any single portion of other levels of grammar, nor with segments of any particular size defined in terms of other levels of grammar. That an utterance has the status of a command may depend upon a conventional formula ("I hereby order you to leave this building"), intonation ("Go!" vs. "Go?"), position in a conversational exchange ["Hello" as initiating greeting or as response (perhaps used when answering the telephone)], or the social relationship obtaining between the two parties (as when an utterance that is in the form of a polite question is in effect a command when made by a superior to a subordinate). The level of speech acts mediates immediately between the usual levels of grammar and the rest of a speech event or situation in that it implicates both linguistic form and social norms.

To some extent speech acts may be analyzable by extensions of syntactic and semantic structure. It seems certain, however, that much, if not most, of the knowledge that speakers share as to the status of utterances as acts is immediate and abstract, depending upon an autonomous system of signals from both the various levels of grammar and social settings. To attempt to depict speech acts entirely by postulating an additional segment of underlying grammatical structure (e.g., "I hereby X you to ...") is cumbersome and counterintuitive. (Consider the case in which "Do you think I might have that last bit of tea?" is to be taken as a command.)

An autonomous level of speech acts is in fact implicated by that logic of linguistic levels according to which the ambiguity of "the shooting of the blacks was terrible" and the commonality of "topping Erv is almost impossible" and "it's almost impossible to top Erv" together requires a further level of structure at which the former has two different structures, the latter one. The relation between sentence forms and their status as speech acts is of the same kind. A sentence interrogative in form may be now a request, now a command, now a statement; a request may be manifested by a sentence that is now interrogative, now declarative, now imperative in form.

Discourse may be viewed in terms of acts both syntagmatically and paradigmatically; i.e., both as a sequence of speech acts and in terms of classes of speech acts among which choice has been made at given points.

Issues to consider

❑   The distinction between speech events and speech situations is potentially ambiguous. Hymes says that what distinguishes speech events from speech situations is that speech situations are not governed by one set of rules throughout. What distinguishes a speech event from a speech situation, then, is very much dependent on the distinctions that members of a speech community themselves make regarding things such as setting and genre. What are some ways an analyst can go about determining the boundaries of a speech event?

❑   Hymes's understanding of *speech acts* differs somewhat from the formulation we are familiar with from Austin (see section B5). Rather than understanding speech acts in relation to 'felicity conditions', Hymes suggests that we interpret speech acts in terms of the speech events in which they are embedded, just as we interpret speech events in terms of the broader speech situations in which they are embedded. What differences does this reveal between the way the ethnography of communication and other approaches to spoken discourse, such as pragmatics and conversation analysis, understand communication?

B. Digital ethnography

Piia Varis (reprinted from *The Routledge Handbook of Language and Digital Communication*, A. Georgakopoulou and T. Spilioti, eds. London: Routledge, pp. 55–68)

Ethnographic research on online practices and communications, and on offline practices shaped by digitalisation, has become increasingly popular in the recent years with the growing influence and presence of the internet in people's everyday lives. This research takes a myriad of forms, appearing within different disciplines and under several different labels such as 'digital ethnography', 'virtual ethnography', 'cyberethnography', 'discourse-centred online ethnography', 'internet ethnography', 'ethnography on the internet', 'ethnography of virtual spaces', 'ethnographic research on the internet', 'internet-related ethnography' and 'netnography'.

The common denominator for these studies is that they all include some kind of online data, and they all employ (a particular version or understanding of) ethnography in the research process. This is basically where the commonalities end; so diverse is the field – if such a field can even clearly be identified – of ethnographic research on digital culture and practices. This is not least because of the various types of data and environments covered in research on digital communication – social network sites, blogs, forums, gaming environments, websites, dating sites, wikis etc. – but also due to seemingly different understandings of what exactly 'ethnography' is, ranging from limiting it to specific techniques or data collection methods (mainly observation and interviews) to seeing it as an approach rather than a set of techniques. This chapter builds on this latter understanding of ethnography; that is, ethnography is not reduced to the employment of certain techniques, but seen as an approach to studying (digital) culture with specific epistemological claims (see e.g. Blommaert & Dong 2009).

*****

In … early research (on digital media), as Androutsopoulos (2008) points out, "The data were often randomly collected and detached from their discursive and social contexts, and generalisations were organised around media-related distinctions such as language of emails, newsgroups, etc.". The focus was thus on reified end products, texts and pieces of language, rather than production and uptake of discourse as socially meaningful, context-specific activity.

Broadly, then, the difference between the earlier and later research is a difference between the study of 'things' and the study of contextualised 'actions' – or the study of texts, and cultural practices. This largely corresponds with the two phases in social research on technologically mediated communication identified by Hine (2000: 7): the first one was characterised by experimental research, and the latter one by "(…) growing application of naturalistic approaches to online phenomena and the subsequent claiming of the Internet as a cultural context", with ethnographic research increasingly applied. Indeed, Hine (ibid.: 8) suggests that "(…) our knowledge of the Internet as a cultural context is intrinsically tied up with the application of ethnography."

Digital ethnography as an approach of course builds on 'pre-digital' ethnography. Ethnography, with its roots in anthropology, takes as its object of interest the very lived reality of people, of which it aims to produce detailed and situated accounts – in the words of Geertz (1973), 'thick descriptions'. As such, ethnography is the approach of choice against generalisation and narrow assumptions regarding the universality of digital experience in general (Coleman 2010), or, in terms of language use, against the kinds of sweeping statements on for instance 'the language of emails' produced in the first wave of research on technologically mediated communication. Seen in the perspective of long-term developments on the study of technologically mediated communication, research under the umbrella 'digital ethnography' has deepened our understanding of locally specific digital practices. Using the internet, and using language and other semiotic means in doing so, are locally situated experiences and entail locally specific practices, platforms and semiotisations, and ethnography has precisely the means of capturing this, taking the task of understanding informants' life-worlds and their situated practices and lived local realities. To this end, ethnographic fieldwork is essentially a learning process where research is guided by experience gathered in the field; it is a mode of discovery and learning (Blommaert & Dong 2009: Velghe 2011) – as Dell Hymes (1996: 13) put it,

> It [ethnography] is continuous with ordinary life. Much of what we seek to find out in ethnography is knowledge that others already have. Our ability to learn ethnographically is an extension of what every human being must do, that is, learn the meanings, norms, patterns of a way of life.

While ethnography assumes such a holistic position, the approach, digital and otherwise, is often reduced to specific methodologies and procedures (fieldwork with participant observation and interviews in many cases as the methods). As Blommaert and Dong (2009) point out, however, ethnography is not only a complex of fieldwork techniques. It has its origins in anthropology, and "These anthropological roots provide a specific direction to ethnography, one that situates language deeply and inextricably in social life and offers a particular and distinct ontology and epistemology to ethnography" (ibid.). From an ethnographic perspective, studying language means studying society and larger-scale sociocultural processes, and making a distinction between the linguistic and the non-linguistic is seen as a fundamentally artificial one.

Digitalisation has offered scholars of language and communication, also ethnographers, with opportunities to easily collect, store and sort (e.g. by 'tagging' contents in electronic databases) 'logs' of interaction, i.e. "characters, words, utterances, messages, exchanges, threads, archives, etc." (Herring 2004; see also Androutsopoulos 2008). While online environments provide opportunities for easy collection of huge amounts of data, from an ethnographic perspective this becomes problematic if the material is taken out of its context – a 'log' of communication only serves as ethnographic data if it is understood in its context. This is where more recent, ethnographically informed research on digital communications dramatically differs from the early studies on technologically mediated communication and their de-contextual analyses. Ethnographically speaking, context is an interactional achievement, and contexts should be investigated rather than assumed (e.g. Blommaert 2007). This is perhaps particularly important in today's complex world of globalisation, translocal communication environments and complex online-offline dynamics, where pre-digital presuppositions regarding contexts and communicators are often invalid.

Issues to consider
- ❑ Based on the observation made by Varis, how might a digital ethnography of a particular community differ from a more traditional ethnography?
- ❑ How do you think digital media affect our understanding of context?

DISCOURSE AND ACTION   D8

In this section you will read an excerpt from *Mediated Discourse: The Nexus of Practice*, the book in which Ron Scollon first articulated his theory of mediated discourse analysis, and an excerpt from an essay by Rodney Jones. Both of these excerpts have to do with rather ordinary actions: buying a cup of coffee and choosing a package of microwave popcorn from the shelf of a supermarket. The point that both Scollon and Jones make in these excerpts is not just that we need to pay attention to these small actions in order to understand how discourse actually influences our everyday lives, but also that the only way to understand 'big issues' like climate change, food safety, and the effects of globalization is to focus on the everyday actions we take and how they contribute to these issues. As you read, notice how Scollon and Jones distinguish their method from other approaches to discourse analysis. At the same time, take note of the similarities this method has with other methods discussed in this book and how it incorporates principles and tools from those methods.

Discourse and action: A cup of coffee

Ron Scollon (reprinted from *Mediated Discourse: The Nexus of Practice*. London: Routledge 2001, pp. 1–8)   **Ron Scollon**

One morning recently in San Diego, California I had a cup of coffee at the international chain coffee shop, Starbucks®. After a short time in the queue I ordered a tall latte and another drink for my friend. I paid for the drinks and then waited a few minutes while the drinks were made and then delivered to me. We took the drinks and sat down to drink them and have a conversation. As linguists and perhaps only linguists do, in and among the other topics of conversation we talked about what was printed on the cup.

Mediated discourse analysis is a framework for looking at such actions with two questions in mind: What is the action going on here? and How does Discourse figure into these actions? In a sense there is nothing very new or different about mediated discourse analysis in that it is a remedial position that seeks to develop a theoretical remedy for discourse analysis that operates without reference to social actions on the one hand and social analysis that operates without reference to discourse on the other. Virtually all of the theoretical elements have been proposed and developed in the work of others. In this, mediated discourse analysis takes the position that social action and Discourse are inextricably linked on the one hand (Chouliaraki and Fairclough 1999) but that on the other hand these links are sometimes not at all direct or obvious, and therefore in need of more careful theorization.

In having this cup of coffee I could say there is just a single action—having a cup of coffee as is implied in the common invitation, 'Let's go have a cup of coffee.' Or I could say there is a very complex and nested set of actions—queuing, ordering, purchasing, receiving the order, selecting a table, drinking coffee, conversing, busing our trash and the rest. Likewise, I could say there is just one discourse here—a conversation among friends. Or I could say there are many complex Discourses with rampant intertextualities and interdiscursivities—international neo-capitalist marketing of coffee, service encounter talk, linguistic conference talk, family talk and the rest. Mediated discourse analysis is a position which seeks to keep all of this complexity alive in our analyses without presupposing which actions and which Discourses are the relevant ones in any particular case under study.

As a way to at least temporarily narrow the scope of my analysis here, I want to focus on the coffee cup. It can be called the primary mediational means by which the coffee has been produced as something transferable, delivered to me, and ultimately consumed. Without the cup there is no <having a cup of coffee> in the literal sense. Throughout all the other actions which take place, the cup figures as the material line that holds this all together. From the point of view of an analysis of mediated action (Wertsch 1998), then, we would want to consider the cup—a paper one in this case—absolutely central to both the narrowly viewed actions of delivery or drinking and to the more broadly viewed actions of consumer purchasing/marketing or of <having a cup of coffee> as a conversational genre.

If we come to this social interaction from the point of view of discourse analysis, and if we set aside for the moment all of the complexities of service encounter talk and of casual conversation between friends, we still find that the cup itself (with its protective sleeve) is an impressive semiotic complex of at least seven different Discourses (Gee 2010).

> Commercial branding: There is a world-wide recognizable logo which appears twice on the cup and once on the cardboard protective sleeve.

> Legal: The logo is marked as a registered property (®) and the text on the sleeve is marked as copyrighted (©). A patent number is also given. In addition, there is a warning that the contents are 'extremely hot' which derives from a famous lawsuit against another international chain where a customer had held a paper cup of their coffee between his legs while driving and been uncomfortably scorched.

> E-commerce: A website is given where the consumer can learn more, though it does not indicate what we might learn about.

> Consumer correctness: An extended text tells us that the company cares for those who grow its coffee and gives a telephone number where the consumer can call to make a donation to CARE on behalf of plantation workers in Indonesia.

Environmental correctness: We are told that the sleeve is made of 60% recycled fiber and that it uses less material than would a second paper cup. The color scheme is in natural cardboard brown with green lettering which are widely associated with environmental friendliness.

Service information: There is a roster of possibilities ('Decaf', 'Shots', 'Syrup', 'Milk', 'Custom', and 'Drink') printed and superimposed is the handwritten 'L' (for 'latte').

Manufacturing information: Under the cup around the inside rim is the information about the cup itself, its size, and product labeling and number.

On the one hand we have a fairly clear and mundane social action—having a cup of coffee in a coffee shop—and a semiotic complex of Discourses which are also, at least now at the beginning of this century, rather mundane. We have an array of analytical positions from which we can analyze this action from seeing it as participating in a bit of micro-social interaction to seeing it as participating in the world-wide consumer practices of neo-capitalism. At the same time we have an array of analytical positions from which we can analyze the Discourses represented in these texts printed on this coffee cup. The problem that mediated discourse analysis is trying to engage is how we are to work out a way to understand the relationships among the actions—drinking the cup of coffee—and the Discourses. Ethnographic observation leads us to believe that, on the whole except for the odd linguist, the coffee is drunk without much attention being focused on this impressive discursive array on the cup. Correspondingly, the literature has many analyses of such Discourses in public places from the products of the news industry through to the broader popular culture industry which make scant reference at all to the actual social situations in which these Discourses are engaged in social action. Mediated discourse analysis is an attempt to theorize a way in which we can link the Discourse of commercial branding, for example, with the practice of drinking a cup of coffee in conversation without giving either undue weight to the action without reference to the Discourse or to the Discourse without reference to the actions within which it is appropriated.

A few central concepts

A mediated discourse analysis gives central importance to five concepts:

❏ Mediated action
❏ Site of engagement
❏ Mediational means
❏ Practice
❏ Nexus of practice

Mediated action: The unit of analysis of a mediated discourse analysis is the mediated action (not the Discourse or text or genre). That is, the focus is on social actors as they are acting because these are the moments in social life when the Discourses in which we are interested are instantiated in the social world as social action, not simply as material objects. We use the phrase 'mediated action' to highlight the unresolvable dialectic between action and the material means which mediate all social action (Wertsch 1998). That is, we take the position that action is materially grounded in persons and objects and that it is unproductive to work with purely abstracted conceptual systems of representation. Participation in the world-wide consumer society requires at some point the transfer of coins and cups, speaking and drinking. Conversely stated, this transfer of coins and cups and speaking and drinking inevitably entail participating in the consumer society. There is no action without participating in such Discourses; no such Discourses without concrete, material actions.

A site of engagement: A mediated action occurs in a social space which I have elsewhere called a 'site of engagement' (Scollon 1998, 1999). This is the real-time window that is opened through an intersection of social practices and mediational means (cultural tools) that make that action the focal point of attention of the relevant participants. The idea of the site of engagement takes from practice/activity theory (as well as from interactional sociolinguistics) the insistence on the real-time, irreversible, and unfinalizable nature of social action. A mediated action is not a class of actions but a unique moment in history. Its interpretation is located within the social practices which are linked in that unique moment. The cup of coffee/coffee conversation in San Diego is theoretically taken as unique and unfolding in that moment and bears only a loose, indirect, and highly problematical relationship with another cup of coffee at a Starbucks® in San Luis Obispo among the same participants a week later if for no other reason that the first is part of the history of the second.

Mediational means: A mediated action is carried out through material objects in the world (including the materiality of the social actors—their bodies, dress, movements) in dialectical interaction with structures of the habitus. We take these mediational means to always be multiple in any single action, to carry with them historical affordances and constraints, and to be inherently polyvocal, intertextual, and interdiscursive. Further, these multiple mediational means are organized in a variety of ways, either in hierarchical structures of activities or in relatively expectable relations of salience or importance.

While I have focused on the cup in this sketch, this cup of coffee has also equally entailed the physical spaces of the coffee shop, the coins and bills exchanged, the servers, the counters, the coffee machines, the tables and chairs, the other customers of the shop, the San Diego sunshine—a significant materiality of that particular action—and our own habitus, latte for me, chai latte for my friend. The polyvocality, intertextuality, and interdiscursivity of the cup has been noted above. To this we add the Southern California décor which sets this particular shop in its place on earth and departs so radically from the 'same' company's shops in Washington, DC, Beijing, and London.

Practice and social structure: For this mediated action to take place in this way there is a necessary intersection of social practices and mediational means which in themselves reproduce social groups, histories, and identities. A mediated discourse analysis takes it that a mediated action is only interpretable within practices. From this point of view 'having a cup of coffee' is viewed as a different action in a Starbucks®, in a cafeteria, and at home. The difference lies both in the practices (how the order is made, for example) and in the mediational means (including the range from the espresso machines to the décor of the spaces in which the action is taken). That is to say, a mediated discourse analysis does not neutralize these practices and social structures as 'context', but seeks to keep them alive in our interpretations of mediated actions.

Nexus of practice: Mediated discourse analysis takes a tight or narrow view of social practice as social practices—ordering, purchasing, handing and receiving—and so then sees these as practices (as count nouns, not as a mass noun). These practices are linked to other practices discursive and non-discursive over time to form nexus of practice. So we might loosely at least want to talk about an early 21st Century American 'designer coffee shop' nexus of practice which would provisionally include such things as pricing practices (high), ordering practices (the distinctions between caffe latte, café au lait, regular coffee with milk, cappuccino), drinking practices (alone with newspapers, in conversation with friends), discursive practices (being able to answer to 'whole or skim?', knowing that 'tall' means the smallest cup on sale or that 'for here' means in a porcelain cup rather than a paper one), physical spacing practices (that the queuing place and delivery place are different) and the rest.

The concept of the nexus of practice works more usefully than the concept of the community of practice which was the earlier framing (Scollon 1998) in that it is rather loosely structured and structured over time. That is, a nexus of practice, like practices themselves is formed one mediated action at a time and is always unfinalized (and unfinalizable). The concept of the nexus of practice is unbounded (unlike the more problematical community of practice) and takes into account that at least most practices (ordering, purchasing, handing and receiving) can be linked variably to different practices in different sites of engagement and among different participants. From this point of view, the practice of handing an object to another person may be linked to practices which constitute the action of purchasing in a coffee shop, it may be linked to practices which constitute the action of giving a gift to a friend on arriving at a birthday party, or even to handing a bit of change to a panhandler on the street. Mediated discourse analysis takes the position that it is the constellation of linked practices which make for the uniqueness of the site of engagement and the identities thus produced, not necessarily the specific practices and actions themselves.

This mediated action of having a cup of coffee and the concurrent and dialogically chained prior and subsequent mediated actions could be analyzed with a great deal more care than I have been able to do here. My purpose has been simply to make these five points:

❏ The mediated action (within a dialogical chain of such social actions) is the focus of mediated discourse analysis.
❏ The focus is on real-time, irreversible, one-time-only actions rather than objectivized, categorical analyses of types of action or discourses and texts.
❏ An action is understood as taking place within a site of engagement which is the real-time window opened through an intersection of social practices and mediational means.
❏ The mediational means are multiple in any case and inevitably carry histories and social structures with them.
❏ A mediated action produces and reproduces social identities and social structures within a nexus of practice.

Issues to consider
❏ Scollon says that the main task of mediated discourse analysis is finding out a way to understand the relationship between the actions that we take and larger 'capital D Discourses' 'without giving either undue weight to the action without reference

to the Discourse or to the Discourse without reference to the actions within which it is appropriated'. What are some of the challenges involved in this task? How is the way mediated discourse analysis goes about this task different from the way critical discourse analysis (see sections A4, B4, C4 and D4) does?

❑ According to Scollon, a 'nexus' of practice occurs when a number of practices are linked to other practices in predictable ways. The example he gives is 'early 21st Century American "designer coffee shop" nexus of practice'. How does this definition of nexus of practice compare to Gee's definitions of 'cultural models' and 'capital D Discourses' and with Swales's definition of 'discourse communities'?

❑ Scollon notes that when we take social actions we inevitably make claims about 'who we are', the communities to which we belong. He also notes that these same actions have the effect of producing 'others' who are constructed as not members of the relevant nexus of practice. How is the way mediated discourse analysis approaches issues of social identity similar to and different from the way interactional sociolinguistics and critical discourse analysis do?

Popcorn, movie stars and regulatory discourse

Rodney H. Jones

Rodney H. Jones (reprinted from Jones, R. (2014) Mediated discourse analysis. In S. Norris and C.D. Maier (eds.) *Interactions, Images and Texts: A Reader in Multimodality*. New York: Mouton de Gruyter, 39–52)

An example of how mediated discourse analysis can help us to unravel the complex chains of discourse and practice that combine to make a particular action possible can be seen in my own act of choosing a box of Newman's Own Oldstyle Picture Show Microwave Popcorn from a shelf in a supermarket in Hong Kong where I live. This purchase is inextricably tied up with my own particular set of practices around shopping, popcorn eating and movie watching. My partner and I have becoming accustomed to spending our Friday evenings watching a movie on our big screen television, and making a bowl of popcorn has become an expected part of that practice. The practice of eating popcorn while watching movies is of course not unique to us, but has a long history going back to the Great Depression when cinema owners, watching their profits from ticket sales decline, started to sell candy and other snacks in their theaters, and to World War II, when sugar rations resulted in popcorn replacing candy at theater concessions stands. The migration of this practice into people's homes, including my own, can be traced back to other chains of technological development including the invention of 'home theaters' and microwave ovens.

Why I choose this particular brand is slightly harder to unravel. Part of it has to do with the kind of inertia that often accompanies purchasing behavior – I buy this brand because, for as long as I can remember, I have bought it. Part of it has to do with my own 'historical body', the fact that I grew up watching Paul Newman movies, that I'm a Democrat and Paul Newman has always supported liberal causes, the fact that I prefer savory snacks to sweet ones, and a host of other practices and preferences that have become deeply sedimented in my 'historical body'. Also relevant here is the itinerary of discourse and action that led to Paul Newman himself to find his face on a box of microwave popcorn, an itinerary that began with his birth in Shaker Heights, Ohio in

1925, extends through a successful acting career to 1982 when he stared the Newman's Own line of food products, chiefly as a way of earning money for charities for seriously ill children. Finally, this box of popcorn would not be available for me to choose were it not for the itineraries that led up to it being placed on this particular shelf, itineraries that stretch back to cornfields in Iowa, company board rooms in Westport, Connecticut, and factories in China. Finally, this package of popcorn, its presence in this supermarket, and my act of reaching for it are all bound up with the itineraries of large-scale systems of economic exchange, of wealth and poverty, production and environmental degradation over which neither me nor Paul Newman seem to have much control, but which would not function if not for me and people like me taking the tiny action of reaching for a product in a supermarket (Scollon, 2005).

The point is that there are multiple itineraries of discourse and action on many levels from the cultural to the corporate to the personal that conspire to drive the action of me reaching for this package and dropping it into my shopping basket, itineraries that I am not fully conscious of but nevertheless are inseparable from that momentary action and how it gets done. Although most of the chains of action that converge at this moment are deeply submerged in my historical body and in the practices and architecture of the supermarket, the corporate structure of the company that manufacturers the product, and the culture of popcorn eating of movie watchers everywhere, if pressed, I and most other shoppers could unravel these chains, could, for example, explain why we are buying this particular brand or venture a guess as to why Paul Newman is selling it. The reason for this is that we are not separate 'historical bodies' choosing a box of popcorn, but rather members of broader 'communities of practice' (Lave and Wenger, 1991), communities that are bound together by thousands of banal practices like movie going and popcorn eating and supermarket shopping.

Most discourse analysts confronted with this package of popcorn would focus on the strategic use of language and other modes: They might for example point out the interdiscursivity on the front of the package which shows an old style movie marquee in which the name of the product appears like the name of a movie. They might point out the intimacy created by the headshot of Paul Newman gazing directly out at the viewer and smiling. They might point out the grammatical construction of phrases like 'No Trans Fats' and 'All Profits to Charity', especially how processes are elided. They might point out how the words on the package like 'oldstyle', 'natural' and 'charity' (as in 'All Profits to Charity') go together to reproduce a certain ideology that resonates with customers like me who grew up in the 60s in the US. They might also turn their attention to issues like font and color, pointing out that the word 'Natural' is printed in bold white font against a purple background, as opposed to the word 'flavoring' to the right of it, printed in a harder to see small, dark font, and how this might potentially mislead customers.

The problem with such an analysis is that it would totally ignore all of those itineraries mentioned above. Gone would be the movie theater concession stands, the microwave ovens, and the Iowa farmers without which this package would not have been possible. And, most important, gone would be all of the actions in my life that led up to me choosing this product, an itinerary of discourse and action in which the grammar and font of the words on the package are rather peripheral.

In fact, much of the communicative work of the *discourse* on this package play no role at all in the action of me plucking it from the supermarket shelf. The only really relevant thing about the colors, fonts, words and smiling face of Paul Newman for me at this moment is that they make it *recognizable* as the same product that I have bought before. In fact there are large parts of this text that I have never read. I've never read the ingredients or the nutritional information on the side of the box (maybe because somewhere deep down I trust Paul Newman), and I've never, until recently, read the additional promotional paragraph printed on the bottom of the box, which reads:

Top-of-The-Crop
Taste. No
Trans Fats. No
Hydrogenated Oils!

It's our great,
crispy, fresh tasting
popcorn without
the trans fats and
hydrogenated oils.
It's deliciously
all natural and
pops to perfection
in two to five minutes.

A diligent discourse analyst would no doubt have included this passage in her analysis, and there is plenty to analyze here, including more literary uses of language like rhyme and alliteration (Carter, 2004). But as a shopper, this text was completely invisible to me until the last time I went searching for the product and found it altered, portions of it redacted with black magic marker.

Top-of-The-Crop
Taste. ▉
▉▉▉ No
Hydrogenated Oils!

It's our great,
crispy, fresh tasting
popcorn ▉▉▉
▉▉▉ and
hydrogenated oils.
It's deliciously
all natural and
pops to perfection
in two to five minutes.

Of course, there is a lot about this new text that is problematic from the point of view of discourse, not least of which is the fact that now it 'means' something totally different than it did before. Before I was buying 'fresh tasting popcorn without … hydrogenated oils', and now I am buying 'fresh tasting popcorn … and hydrogenated oils'. This in itself, however, (since I have very little knowledge of hydrogenated oils) is not nearly as important as the *physical* presence of black marks on the package, the *physical* fact that the product package has been altered by somebody other than Paul Newman or his employees.

Suddenly a piece of discourse that I could safely keep in the background when purchasing this product has been pushed into the foreground, demanding that I take some kind of action with it. But, not understanding the hidden chain of actions that led to these words being hidden, I do not know what action to take. What is important here, what has suddenly disrupted my popcorn purchase, is not *discourse* per se, but *action*, the action of somebody somewhere taking a black magic marker and defacing this package. This 'frozen action' (Norris, 2004) embodied in these black marks on the package is enough to interrupt my purchase, to make me consider buying something else instead.

There is, in fact, nothing sinister going on here. The black marks on this package are the result of an itinerary of discourse and action that can be traced back to the passage of a new Food and Drug Composition and Labeling Regulation by the Hong Kong Legislative Council in May 2008, which imposes strict new rules about what can and cannot appear on food labels. Among these is the rule that in order to make the claim 'zero trans fat', a product must fulfill three conditions: 1) it must contain no more than .03 grams of trans fats per 100 grams; 2) the sum of trans fats and saturated fats must not exceed 1.5 grams per 100 grams; 3) the sum of trans fats and saturated fats must not contribute to more than 10% of the energy. The fact is, Newman's Own Microwave Popcorn, while actually containing 0 trans fats, contains 6.6 grams of saturated fat per 100 grams, and therefore is not legally permitted to bear the claim 'zero trans fats' (despite the fact that the amount of trans fats in the product equals zero).

The fact that this regulation is rather confusing, however, is not the main problem here. The problem comes in the actions that must be taken to comply with the regulation. Since Hong Kong is such a small market, few major food manufactures are willing to change their packages to comply with these unique rules. Therefore, shopkeepers and supermarket employees are forced to alter packages before they put them on the shelves to avoid falling foul of the law. Once the package finds its way onto the shelves ready for me to reach for it, all of those actions of legislation, regulation, and compliance have become invisible. All that is left are the black marks. The problem is not that I don't know what the words *mean*, but that I don't even know what the words are.

The goal of the government was to help me make healthy choices about my diet. However, the result is the opposite. Not knowing what is behind those black marks, I immediately become suspicious of Paul Newman and decide to choose another snack item, one with no unsightly black marks because the manufacturer of this particular item, chock full of trans fats, has chosen not to make any claims to the contrary. And so I trade in a healthy item for a less healthy one, perhaps beginning a new itinerary leading up to possible heart disease in my later years.

The point I'm trying to make here is that the real problem with this text is not so much that I can't figure out what it means as it is that I can't figure out what it *does*. What interrupts my practice of popcorn buying, steering it in a new and dangerous direction, is not discourse *per se*, but the convergence of multiple itineraries of discourse and action, many of which, like the blacked-out words, are invisible to me.

Not only would analyzing this discourse divorced from the actions it is used to take not help me much in understanding this text, but it is this focus on discourse (meaning) at the expense of considering how it is used to take action that is, in fact, the problem here. In its effort to protect me from the non-existent trans fats in this product, the Hong Kong government has focused only on the words and their 'technical' meanings without considering the complex chains of actions in which these words (and their disappearance) are implicated.

Issues to consider

❏ In this article Jones argues not just that the act of him buying popcorn in the supermarket is 'bound up with the itineraries of large-scale systems of economic exchange, of wealth and poverty, production and environmental degradation', but that these systems are made possible by this act. What does he mean by this? If this is the case, how can mediated discourse analysis help us to take more responsible, socially conscious or environmentally sound actions?

❏ Jones argues that sometimes measures we take to change discourse (such as food labelling laws) can actually have unintended consequences if we don't take into account the 'interaction orders' and 'historical bodies' with which this discourse might interact. Can you think of other examples in which texts have consequences that are different from the intentions of those that produced them?

D9   TWO PERSPECTIVES ON MULTIMODALITY

The excerpts reprinted in this section represent the two broad approaches to multimodality which were introduced in section A9. The first is from Gunther Kress and Theo van Leeuwen's classic, *Reading Images: The Grammar of Visual Design*. In this excerpt the authors make an argument that visual design, like language, constitutes an organised system of meaningful choices which can be analysed with reference to linguistic theories. At the same time, they warn against adopting the same concepts used to analyse language to analyse other modes, which necessarily involve different kinds of resources from making meaning. They then go on to explain the 'grammar' of visual design in terms of Halliday's tripartite model of meaning: ideational meaning, interpersonal meaning and textual meaning.

In the second excerpt, Sigrid Norris makes an argument for moving beyond a view of interaction that focuses primarily on spoken language, insisting that other modes such as gesture, gaze, posture and the layout of furniture are just as important, and sometimes more important, than speech. She then goes on to explain how principles from mediated discourse analysis (see section D8) can help to organise the multimodal analysis of interactions.

As you read through these excerpts, consider not just how the two approaches differ from each other, but also how they appropriate and build upon concepts from other approaches to discourse that have been discussed in this book.

A. Reading images

Gunther Kress and Theo van Leeuwen (reprinted from *Reading Images: The Grammar of Visual Design* 2nd edition. London: Routledge 2006, pp. 17–20, 41–43)

Gunther Kress and Theo van Leeuwen

A social semiotic theory of communication

In order to function as a full system of communication, the visual, like all semiotic modes, has to serve several representational and communicational requirements. We have adopted the theoretical notion of 'metafunction' from the work of Michael Halliday for this purpose. The three metafunctions which he posits are the ideational, the interpersonal and the textual. In the form in which we gloss them here they apply to all semiotic modes, and are not specific to speech or writing.

The ideational metafunction

Any semiotic mode has to be able to represent aspects of the world as it is experienced by humans. In other words, it has to be able to represent objects and their relations in a world outside the representational system. That world may of course be, and most frequently is, already semiotically represented. In doing so, semiotic modes offer an array of choices, of different ways in which objects, and their relations to other objects and to processes, can be represented. Two objects may be represented as involved in a process of interaction which could be visually realized by vectors:

But objects can also be related in other ways, for instance in terms of a classification. They would be connected, not by a vector but, for instance, by a 'tree' structure:

The interpersonal metafunction

Any semiotic mode has to be able to project the relations between the producer of a (complex) sign, and the receiver/reproducer of that sign. That is, any mode has to be able to represent a particular social relation between the producer, the viewer and the object represented.

As in the case of the ideational metafunction, modes offer an array of choices for representing different 'interpersonal' relations, some of which will be favoured in one form of visual representation (say, in the naturalistic image), others in another (say, in the diagram). A depicted person may be shown as addressing viewers directly, by looking at the camera. This conveys a sense of interaction between the depicted person and the viewer. But a depicted person may also be shown as turned away from the viewer, and this conveys the absence of a sense of interaction. It allows the viewer to scrutinize the represented characters as though they were specimens in a display case.

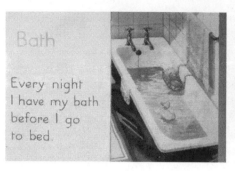

Figure D9.1 Bath I.   *Figure D9.2* Bath II.

The textual metafunction

Any semiotic mode has to have the capacity to form texts, complexes of signs which cohere both internally with each other and externally with the context in and for which they were produced. Here, too, visual grammar makes a range of resources available: different compositional arrangements to allow the realization of different textual meanings. In Figure D9.1, for example, the text is on the left and the picture on the right. Changing the layout (Figure D9.2) would completely alter the relation between written text and image and the meaning of the whole. The image, rather than the written text, would now serve as point of departure, as 'anchor' for the message.

Issues to consider

❑ In the beginning of this excerpt Kress and van Leeuwen give a historical account of the relationship between text and image beginning with the fifteenth century. How do you think the importance of images in communication has changed over time, especially in relation to media such as the Internet and mobile phones? Do you think images function differently in communication than they did before?

❑ Kress and van Leeuwen say 'both language and visual communication express meanings belonging to and structured by cultures in the one society'. Does this mean that the visual grammar of different cultures is likely to be as different as their languages? To what degree does visual communication transcend different cultures in ways that language cannot?

❑ Look at Figures D9.1 and Figure D9.2. Which arrangement of text and image seems more 'natural' to you? Can you 'translate' the differences between these two arrangements into language?

B.

Sigrid Norris

Sigrid Norris (reprinted from *Analyzing Multimodal Interaction: A methodological framework.* London: Routledge, 2004, pp. 1–3, 9–13)

Multimodal interaction analysis

All interactions are multimodal. Imagine, for example, a simple two-person interaction, a conversation with a friend. During this interaction, you are aware of your friend's spoken language, so that you hear the verbal choices, the content, the prosody, and the pitch. You are also aware of the way that your friend is standing or sitting, the way that your friend is nodding or leaning back or forward; you are aware of your friend's facial expression, and clothing, just as you are aware of the environment in which this interaction takes place. If there is music playing in the background, even though you are not focusing on the music, you are aware of it. All of these elements play a part in this conversation. You may react to the words that your friend is speaking as much as you may react to your friend's facial expression or the posture that your friend is taking up towards you. You may speak quickly or slowly, depending on the music playing in the background or the given environment that the interaction takes place in.

Intuitively we know that we draw on all of these communicative channels or modes when interacting with others. We also know that we are aware of many things that surround us while we interact with others. Let us keep thinking about a conversation. No matter where it may take place, you are certainly aware whether other people are present in close proximity. Thus, if your conversation takes place at a table in a cafeteria, you are aware of others talking, eating, or passing by your table. You may not take much notice of these other people, because you are focused on your conversation, but you are aware of them nevertheless.

Interactional meaning

Generally it is assumed that we can communicate best through our use of language. Language seems to have the most informative content, which can easily be employed without a need for other channels. We may speak on the phone, write emails, or go to chat-rooms. In each case, we use language, either spoken or written, to communicate.

But when thinking about TV or the Internet, it is clear that we also communicate through images. Often, viewing an image may carry more. We may even feel that the image has more "reality" to it than a written description of the same image would have. This realization questions the notion that the process of communicating is dependent upon language. Just as moving images or still photos can communicate meaning to the viewer, nonverbal channels such as gesture, posture, or the distance between people can—and do—carry meaning in any face-to-face interaction.

All movements, all noises, and all material objects carry interactional meaning as soon as they are perceived by a person. Previously, language has been viewed as constituting the central channel in interaction, and nonverbal channels have been viewed as being subordinated to it. While much valuable work on the interplay between the verbal and nonverbal has been established, I believe that the view which unquestionably positions language at the center limits our understanding of the complexity of interaction.

Therefore, I will step away from the notion that language always plays the central role in interaction, without denying that it often does. Language, as Kress et al. (2001) have noted, is only one mode among many, which may or may not take a central role at any given moment in an interaction. In this view, gesture, gaze, or head movement may be subordinated to the verbal exchanges going on as has been shown in much research.

However, gesture, gaze, and head movement also may take the superior position in a given interaction, while language may be subordinated or absent altogether.

Alternatively, sometimes many communicative channels play an integral part in a given interaction, without one channel being more important than another.

While we all intuitively know that people in interaction draw on a multiplicity of communicative modes, and that people in interaction are aware of much more than just what they are focused upon, an analysis of such multimodal interaction brings with it many challenges.

Structure and materiality

One challenge for the analysis of multimodal interaction is that the different communicative modes of language, gesture, gaze, and material objects are structured in significantly different ways. While spoken language is sequentially structured, gesture is globally synthetically structured, which means that we can not simply add one gesture on to another gesture to make a more complex one. In language, we can add a prefix to a word, making the word more complex; or we can add subordinate clauses to a main clause, making the sentence more complex. With gestures, this is not possible, since gestures that are linked to language inform about global content or intensity. Gaze, however, may be sequentially structured, and during conversation it often is. But, during other interactions, gaze can be quite random. For example, when you walk through the woods with a friend, your gaze may wander randomly, focusing on a tree, a rock, or nothing at all. Then there are other communicative modes, which are structured even more differently.

As we will see, furniture is a mode, and when thinking about it, we find a functional structure. Chairs are usually located around a table, or a reading lamp is located next to an easy chair. Thus, different modes of communication are structured in very different ways.

Another challenge for the analysis of multimodal interaction is the fact that different communicative modes possess different materiality. For example, spoken language is neither visible nor enduring, but it does have audible materiality. Gesture, however, has visible materiality but is also quite fleeting. The mode of print has more visible materiality and is also enduring; and the mode of layout, thinking about furniture, for example, has highly visible materiality and is extensively enduring.

*****

Heuristic units

The first step to a multimodal analysis of interaction is a basic understanding of an array of communicative modes. Modes such as proxemics, posture, head movement, gesture, gaze, spoken language, layout, print, music, to name several, are essentially systems of representation. A system of representation or mode of communication is a semiotic system with rules and regularities attached to it (Kress and Van Leeuwen, 2001). I like to call these systems of representation *communicative modes* when I emphasize their interactional communicative function.

A communicative mode is never a bounded or static unit, but always and only a *heuristic* unit. The term "heuristic" highlights the plainly explanatory function, and also accentuates the constant tension and contradiction between the system of representation and the real-time interaction among social actors. A system of representation—a writing system, for example—is usually thought of as a given system that exists in and by itself once it is developed.

While such a system changes over time, we can describe the system in the form of dictionaries and grammars, showing the rules and regularities that exist. Taking this thought further, we could describe systems of representation like gesture, gaze, layout, etc. in a similar way to a written language, by developing certain dictionaries and grammars of these communicative modes.

Communicative modes in interaction

When observing an interaction and trying to discern all of the communicative modes that the individuals are utilizing, we soon notice that this is a rather overwhelming task. People move their bodies, hands, arms, and heads, and while the observer may try to understand the content of what is being spoken, they have already missed many important messages which each speaker is sending—intentionally or not—and the other speaker is reacting to through other modes. Yet, a multimodal interactional analysis is not as impossible as one may think. First, the analyst needs to become skilled at distinguishing one communicative mode from others. Then the analyst is ready to investigate how modes play together in interaction.

When working with real-time interaction, we discover that there is constant tension and contradiction between the system of representation and the event. Individuals in interaction draw on systems of representation while at the same time constructing, adopting, and changing those systems through their actions. In turn, all actions that individuals perform are mediated by the systems of representation that they draw on.

Unit of analysis

As I mentioned in the introduction, the differing structures and materiality of modes were challenges that needed to be overcome, as an integrative multimodal approach required a single unit of analysis that allowed for the communicative modes to be structurally and materially different. In multimodal interactional analysis, the mediated action is the unit of analysis, and since every action is mediated, I will simply speak of the action as the unit of analysis. The action as unit of analysis, however, is still a complicated issue, because there are smaller (lower-level) and larger (higher-level) actions. Take, for example, a person uttering the words "good morning." This is an intonation unit, the unit that discourse analysts rely on. But this intonation unit can also be defined as an action, and more specifically, as a lower-level action. Now, take a meeting among three friends, which can be called a conversation, a moment in time, or a social encounter. This meeting can also be called an action, however, and more specifically, a higher-level action. This use of action as a unit of analysis may seem confusing at first sight. However, let us think about the specific example of a meeting among three friends—to illustrate the usefulness of this unit of analysis. The meeting is taken to be the higher-level action. This higher-level action is bracketed by an opening and a closing of the meeting and is made up of a multiplicity of chained lower-level actions. All intonation units that an individual strings together become a chain of lower-level actions. All gesture units that an individual performs become a chain of lower-level actions. All postural shifts that an individual completes become a chain of lower-level actions. All gaze shifts that an individual performs become a chain of lower-level actions, and so on. Consequently, all higher-level actions are made up of multiple chains of lower-level actions.

The chains of lower-level actions are easily understood when talking about embodied communicative modes like gaze, gesture, or spoken language. But disembodied modes can play just as important a role in interaction as do the embodied modes.

Modes like print—a magazine that participants are reading or that is just lying on a table for anyone to see; or layout—the furniture in a room, pictures hung on a wall, or a busy street with signs, buildings, and walkways, are disembodied modes. These modes can also be analyzed by using the unit of analysis, the (mediated) action. However, here the unit of analysis is the frozen action. Frozen actions are usually higher-level actions which were performed by an individual or a group of people at an earlier time than the real-time moment of the interaction that is being analyzed.

These actions are frozen in the material objects themselves and are therefore evident. When we see a magazine lying on a table, we know that somebody has purchased the magazine and placed it on the table. Thus, the chains of lower-level actions that somebody had to perform in order for the magazine to be present on the table are perceptible by the mere presence of the magazine itself. The same is true for furniture, pictures on walls, houses in cities, or a CD playing. Material objects or disembodied modes, which we are concerned with here because individuals draw upon them in interaction, necessarily entail higher-level actions (which are made up of chained lower-level actions).

We can think of lower-level actions as the actions that are fluidly performed by an individual in interaction. Each lower-level action is mediated by a system of representation (which includes body parts such as the lips, etc. for spoken language; or hands, arms, and fingers for manual gestures). Higher-level actions develop from a sum of fluidly performed chains of lower-level actions, so that the higher-level actions are also fluid and develop in real-time. Every higher-level action is bracketed by social openings and closings that are at least in part ritualized. When the three friends get together for their meeting, the higher-level action of that meeting is opened up by the physical coming together or the friends and by ritualized greetings. Similarly, this overarching higher-level action will be ended by ritualized greetings and a parting of the individuals. Embedded within such a higher-level action, we find other higher-level actions such as a conversation between two or three members, or another conversation among all three of them. Besides conversations, we may also find higher-level actions which develop from a sum of other lower-level actions in which there is little or no talk involved, like the higher-level action of consuming food and/or drink.

While lower-level and higher-level actions are fluidly constructed in interaction, frozen actions are higher-level actions, which are entailed in an object or a disembodied mode. To understand this concept, we can think about ice. Similarly to the freezing of water, actions are frozen in the material objects present in interaction.

Issues to consider

❑ Norris talks about how the materiality of a mode affects the way it structures meaning and action. What implications does this have when people wish to 'translate' meanings from one mode to another? Can you give some examples?

❑   'A communicative mode', says Norris, 'is never a bounded or static unit, but always and only a *heuristic* unit'. What does she mean by this? What are the advantages of keeping the concept of 'communicative mode' flexible and contingent?

CORPUS-ASSISTED DISCOURSE ANALYSIS   D10

The following excerpt illustrates how corpus techniques can be used to aid discourse analysis on the portrayal of Muslims in the media. In it, Paul Baker demonstrates how an analysis of collocates of word 'Muslim' can reveal the ideological bias in a corpus of British newspaper articles. At the same time, he also shows how this apparent bias needs to be critically evaluated through closer analysis of the texts.

Using corpus linguistics methods with critical discourse analysis

Paul Baker (reprinted from *Critical Discourse Studies* 9 (3), 2012, pp. 247–256)   Paul Baker

The main aim of analysing a corpus of newspaper articles which referred to Islam and/ or Muslims was to identify how these concepts were represented in the British press … While earlier studies had incorporated CDA and/or aspects of quantitative analysis, none of the previous research on the subject had incorporated corpus-driven methods (such as keyword analysis) on an extremely large sample of data consisting of over 100 million words. Our research team were interested in ascertaining whether such a corpus analysis would produce a similar pattern of negative bias or whether it would result in a more complex picture. Unlike more traditional CDA [Critical Discourse Analysis] research, we approached our corpus in a relatively naïve way. This meant that while we were aware that other research had found negative bias, we did not intend to specifically look for such bias ourselves. Instead, we hoped that the identification of frequent and salient linguistic patterns in the corpus would provide a 'way in' to the data – we would thus need to account for whatever the corpus analytical techniques highlighted, negative or positive.

For example, one early strand of our analysis involved focussing on the word Muslim and its plural form. This word seemed to be a good place to start because it was both highly frequent in the corpus and it appeared to be used as both an adjectival modifier of nouns (e.g. Muslim woman) and as a noun itself (e.g. a Muslim). Interestingly, its use as an adjective appeared to be more frequent (about 70% of the time), so we decided to focus on the most typical contexts in which Muslim occurred as a pre-modifying adjective. We found that one common pattern in this context concerned words relating to extreme belief, such as extremist(s), fundamentalist(s) and militant(s). Such words also were common when Muslim was a noun, and they also occurred frequently with two other high-frequency words Islam and Islamic.

In order to obtain a better picture of what sort of contexts these extreme-belief words occur in we used Sketch Engine's Word Sketch function (Kilgarriff, Rychly, Smrz, & Tugwell, 2004). Table D10.1 shows the 10 most statistically salient (using the logDice metric) adjective and verb collocates of the extreme belief words (when they occur as

Table D10.1 Word sketch of extreme belief words

Extreme belief word	Adjectives	Verbs (subject)	Verbs (object)
fanatic	*murderous, Islamic, Muslim, religious, home-grown, evil, suicidal, fundamentalist, ruthless, hate-filled*	brainwash, plot, behead, plan, abuse, hate, preach, target, hijack, rant	*brainwash, deport, appease, defeat, fear, curb, isolate, link, brand, prepare*
extremist	Islamic, Muslim, violent, suspected, right-wing, religious, home-grown, far-right, Algerian, animal	target, brainwash, infiltrate, plot, hijack, preach, exploit, murder, plan, pose	*isolate, deport, tackle, link, suspect, determine, prosecute, appease, defeat, confront*
militant	*Islamic, suspected, Palestinian, Hamas, Kashmiri, wanted, loyal, armed, alleged, Pakistani*	*fire, kidnap, storm, attack, threaten, seize, behead, target, bomb, ambush*	*suspect, link, hole, arrest, arm, assassinate, blame, mask, kill, disarm*
fundamentalist	*Islamic, Christian, Muslim, religious, reluctant, Protestant, crazed, fanatical, extreme, Algerian*	*infiltrate, object, wish, favour, preach, hate, target, threaten, wage, exploit*	*poise, appease, anger, offend, upset, fuel, oppose, link, criticise, suspect*
separatist	Basque, Kashmiri, Kurdish, Tamil, Flemish, Croat, Sikh, Albanian, suspected, Muslim	operate, seize, try, fight, threaten, seek, want, begin, claim, call	*blame, crush, defeat, suspect, encourage, support, fight, accuse, join, include*
radical	*Islamic, British-based, left-wing, non-violent, suspected, home-grown, Islamist, Muslim, anti-Western, so-called*	*brainwash, plot, preach, exploit, influence, recruit, hijack, kidnap, pose, want*	*deport, inflame, counter, determine, suspect, tackle, jail, confront, investigate, invite*
hardliner	*embattled, unelected incumbent, clerical, Iranian, Croat, Hamas, loyal, furious, outspoken*	*wield, control, oppose, exploit, dominate, ally, block, attempt, fear, replace*	*appease, embolden, anger, galvanise, infuriate, strengthen, isolate, alienate, enable, oppose*
firebrand	*left-wing, one-eyed, Unionist, populist, one-time, bearded, socialist, far-right, clerical, Protestant*	endanger, head, launch, support, lead, run, tell	*N/A*

nouns). Sketch Engine allows us to distinguish between verb collocates that position a noun as either a subject (e.g. A fanatic plotted …) or an object (e.g. A fanatic was deported). While there is not enough space here to carry out detailed analyses of these collocates, it is notable how many of these collocates refer to crime, violence, terrorism, conflict and ideological influence. In these articles then, the concept of extremisms is not strongly linked to more positive representations like piety.

Having determined that these extreme belief words tended to occur in negative contexts, we decided to examine their dispersion across the corpus.

The corpus consisted of approximately 143 million words (200,000 articles) taken from the British national press between 1998 and 2009. We used the online database Nexis UK to identify articles which contained relevant search terms like Muslim and Islam. The newspapers in our corpus were *The Star, The Mirror, The Sun, The Daily Mail, The Daily Express, The Daily Telegraph, The Times, The Independent* and *The Guardian* and all of the Sunday versions of these papers. Two other newspapers, *The Business* (which appeared weekly but stopped publication in 2008) and *The People* (a Sunday newspaper with no daily equivalent), were also included. It is possible to distinguish British national newspapers along numerous dimensions such as political leaning (whether the newspaper advocates broadly conservative or liberal economic and/or social values) or format/style (whether the newspaper takes the form of a more serious 'quality' broadsheet reporting or whether it tends towards a more populist tabloid format).

Figure D10.1 shows the overall frequencies of occurrences of the words fanatic(al), militant, extremist, fundamentalist, radical, separatist, hardline(r) and firebrand, and their plurals,occurring directly next to (either to the right or left) of the words Muslim(s), Islam or Islamic, for each newspaper in the corpus.

A number of conclusions of a descriptive nature can be drawn from Figure D10.1. First, the direct and close association of extreme belief words with Islamic appears to be more frequent than for Muslim(s) and Islam. Notably, the difference in frequencies

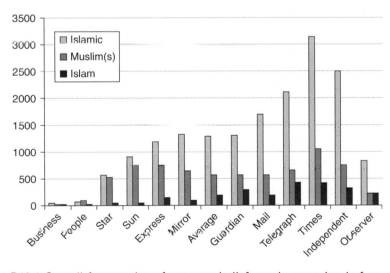

Figure D10.1 Overall frequencies of extreme belief words occurring before or after Muslim(s), Islamic and Islam for each newspaper.

appears to be largest between Islam and Islamic. Second, some newspapers seem to use these extreme belief terms to represent Muslims and Islam much more frequently (*The Times, The Independent*) than others (*The Business, The People*). However, Figure D10.1 is based only on frequency alone. It is indeed interesting that *The Times* has a high occurrence of terms like extremist Muslim, but this could be due to the fact that *The Times* is a daily broadsheet newspaper which contains more text than some of the other newspapers. A supplementary way of comparing newspapers would be to take into account the total number of times that each one uses the terms Muslim(s), Islamic and Islam, and then calculate the proportion of times that such words co-occur with an extreme belief word. This is shown in Figure D10.2.

In one way, the picture which emerges when proportional frequencies are taken into account is not so different to Figure D10.1. The word Islamic still appears to be a stronger 'attractor' of extreme belief terms. However, when we compare newspapers against each other, a very different picture emerges. Here, *The People* (a conservative tabloid) has the highest proportional frequency of writing about extremist Muslims, whereas *The Guardian* (a liberal broadsheet) has the lowest proportional frequency (at least for the words Muslim(s) and Islamic).

It is thus useful to take both raw and proportional information into account. Figure D10.1 indicates that some newspapers write a lot about extremist Muslims, possibly because they simply contain much more text than other newspapers, whereas Figure D10.2 tells us that some newspapers tend to write about Muslims as extremist because they have relatively more constructions of Muslims as extremists as opposed to Muslims as something else. Our quantitative analysis has thus uncovered evidence for a semantic prosody ... of Muslims and Islam as extreme, which is more prevalent in some newspapers than others.

This is not the end of the analysis, however ... Care must be taken, however, in assuming that words have the meanings and connotations that we assign to them. Take, for example, the term devout Muslim, (can be taken to indicate) 'strong but not

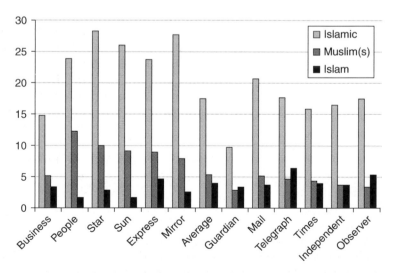

Figure D10.2 Proportion of times (per cent) that extreme belief words occur before or after Muslim(s), Islamic and Islam for each newspaper.

extreme belief'. A more detailed analysis of this term revealed that it often occurred near the word described. The example below shows one such case.

> Ragab el-Swerkie, 56, who owns a chain of clothes stores and is described by his employees as a devout Muslim, preyed mainly on beautiful young females, say prosecutors.
>
> (Sunday Telegraph, 24 June 2001)

Therefore, the phrase described ... as a devout Muslim appears to highlight cases where devout Muslims are actually more problematic. It could be argued then that readers are being primed to suspect that (some) devout Muslims are actually not devout at all, or, worse, that devout is merely a euphemism for extremist (or other 'extreme belief' words).

As noted previously, terms like extremist Muslim are used uncritically in the corpus, although the analysis of devout Muslim is useful in that it reveals that there are other ways in which extreme beliefs can be implied, without actually using a word like extremist. The example of devout Muslim is useful in warning us not to read frequencies at face value. However, if we simply focus on the figures, we can summarise the patterns regarding extent of belief with the following statements:

❑ References to extreme forms of Islam or Muslims are 21 times more common in the corpus than references to moderate Islam/Muslims.

❑ There is variation across the terms; almost 1 in 6 cases of Islamic are modified by an extreme belief word. This is 1 in 20 for Muslim(s) and 1 in 25 for Islam.

❑ There is variation across newspapers – in *The People*, 1 in 8 Muslims are described as extreme. In *The Guardian* this is 1 in 35.

Critically considering bias

So far, the analysis had been fairly descriptive, although a very basic form of interpretation was required to make sense of the patterns. [From these patterns I have concluded that] the British press are biased against Muslims because they tend to over-focus on Muslims who are extreme, or they often associate Islam with extremism ...

Yet, casting a critical eye back over my [conclusion] about the British press being biased, I wondered to what extent others would agree with me ... First, it could be argued that the majority pattern is that the words Muslim(s), Islam and Islamic are not normally referred to by extremist belief words. Take one of the 'most biased' newspapers, *The People,* which directly links the words Muslim(s) to an extremist word 12% of the time (or 1 in 8 cases). However, there are 7 out of 8 cases where *The People* does not directly link the words Muslim(s) to an extremist word. Someone could argue then that a negative representation is acceptable as long as it is not the majority representation ...

A second position could take a very different view – that Muslims should never (or only in particular circumstances, for example, if they self-identify) be described as extreme (particularly because when we looked at representations of 'extreme Muslims', they tended to be associated with very negative contexts such as terrorism and conflict). Even 1 in 100 cases would therefore be a problem. Therefore, all of the British press could be seen as unacceptably biased.

A third view might try to compare the newspapers against each other. It might accept that completely avoiding negative representation of all of the members of a large and diverse social group is impossible, and so instead we should judge the newspapers in relation to each other. For example, in Figure D10.2, The Guardian has the smallest proportion of cases where the words Muslim(s) and Islamic are linked to extremist belief. We might say that this newspaper could act as a benchmark, giving us an idea of a 'responsible' way of reporting on Islam and that others should be judged according to how far they deviate from *The Guardian*. Or we could look at the figures for the averages in Figures D10.1 and D10.2. That would at least allow us to identify which newspapers have extreme belief representations which are more frequent than the average.

Fourth, a different perspective might argue that the British press does not write about extremist Muslims enough. They could accuse the press (and particularly *The Guardian*) of downplaying the importance of such news stories, sacrificing news-values for 'political correctness'.

Finally, faced with such a wealth of (hypothetical) disagreement, we may decide to be cautious in making any definitive conclusions about the extent that bias exists and whether or not it is acceptable, and instead simply present the descriptive information in the form of the figures, allowing readers to draw their own conclusions.

All of the above strategies carry their own problems, at least from the perspective of someone who wishes to claim that a corpus approach enables an objective analysis. The first four betray the analyst's own biases, while the last one attempts to 'sit on the fence' and fails to fully engage with the remit of CDA which is to go beyond a mere descriptive account of linguistic patterns in texts. If we want to fully carry out CDA then, it appears that the political biases of the analyst must come into play. Traditional CDA practitioners might see no problem with this, although as someone who has argued that corpus approaches help to reduce researcher bias, it is ironic to find that bias has crept back in again at the end. Putting aside the question of whether a text producer is negatively biased or not, a further set of issues relates to how we decide whether the amount of bias is cause for concern. There appear to be a number of different factors that need to be taken into account when considering whether a particular representation of group can be labelled as problematic.

First, there is the overall frequency of the negative representation (see Figure D10.1). So, a group may be negatively represented only 5% of the time it gets referred to. But, it may get talked or written about so much, that that 5% will still amount to recipients of texts being exposed to a great deal of negative representation.

Second, there is the proportional frequency of the negative representation (Figure D10.2). So, if a social group tends to be represented negatively much more than it is represented positively, then this also could be seen as cause for concern. It is, of course, unlikely that analysts will be able to agree on the 'acceptable' or 'problematic' frequencies for these two factors.

A third factor relates to the social group under discussion. One way of deciding whether a particular representation is a cause for worry could be to compare it against another (similar) social group. For example, if we know how often Muslims are represented as extreme in the press, then how does this compare to Christians?

Similar to comparing frequencies of representations across different newspapers, this could be another way of reaching benchmarks about what is typical in certain discourse communities. However, it may not be a good idea to base standards of acceptable and unacceptable representation frequency by comparing groups who may be similar in one dimension (e.g. both Christians and Muslims are religious groups) but could also be different in many other ways. It could be argued that CDA practitioners should be especially concerned if vulnerable groups like Muslims, immigrants, gay people, disabled people, women, working class people, older people, children or ethnic minority groups are represented negatively. Traditionally, these groups are either numerically in a minority (in the UK at least); so even in a democracy they may not have 'power in numbers', or they may not be able to protect their own interests, or they may already suffer from societal and personal prejudice and discrimination. Also, what if the group under examination is one which is or has been relatively powerful, like bankers, who have been held responsible for the global recession of 2008? If a corpus analysis of the media representation of bankers found that they were negatively represented as greedy, irresponsible, etc. then should this be raised as a point of concern with recommendations for curbing such representations? It is also unlikely that a 'hierarchy of vulnerability', along with cut-off points as to who deserves their media representation to be closely monitored, can be agreed upon. On the other hand, some people may view any form of negative representation of any social group to be problematic, no matter what certain members of that social group may or may not have done in the past.

A fourth factor is the strength of negativity of the negative representation. So, in the illustrative example discussed in this paper, I only considered constructions of Muslims or Islam in relationship to extremist belief. I have argued that this is a negative representation and therefore a problem if it happens (too) often. However, this was not the only negative representation in the research on Islam that I discovered. Elsewhere in the corpus, Muslims were represented as terrorists, 'scroungers' or as easily offended and difficult. At other points, they were viewed as susceptible to radicalisation or as victims of prejudice. So, as with a hierarchy of vulnerability, we could also conceive of a hierarchy of negativity, with some representations being viewed as more problematic than others. Again, analysts would need to make decisions with regard to the point that the frequency of certain types of representation crosses a line. Potentially, each type of representation could collectively contribute towards an overall negative or positive stance.

Fifth is a factor relating to the context of the representation (particularly concerning issues of text production and reception). Is it more of a problem if representations of Muslims as extreme tend to be very frequent in political speeches made by government ministers, or if they occur in people's personal blogs? Negative representations of social groups are problematic whatever context they occur in, but certain contexts, such as those which are made by powerful or influential text producers or are received by powerful people and/or reach very large numbers of people, may result in more immediate and damaging consequences.

These issues do not relate merely to corpus approaches to CDA but all forms of CDA. However, once we are in a position to start quantifying bias, based on analysis of very large representative (or even totally inclusive) samples of data, these questions regarding interpretation and evaluation of linguistic patterns become much more pertinent.

Issues to consider

❏   What does Baker's analysis of the word 'devout', which is normally seen as a word with a positive connotation, in the quote from *The Sunday Telegraph* above tell us about the limitations of using corpus tools in assisting discourse analysis? How can other analytical tools you learned about in this book help to uncover the meaning of the word 'devout' in this quote?

❏   Baker raises an interesting point about 'bias' when he imagines that a corpus analysis of 'bankers' might find them to be negatively represented as 'greedy' or 'irresponsible'. Could such representations be considered 'biased' in the same way representations of Muslims as 'extreme' are? Is 'bias' always a bad thing?

FURTHER READING

Strand 1: What is discourse?

There are many good overviews of discourse analysis, including Brown and Yule (1983), Carter (1997), Paltridge (2006) and Widdowson (2007). Good edited collections are Schiffrin *et al.* (2004) and Hyland and Paltridge (2011). Bhatia *et al.* (2007) focus on more recent developments in the field. Jaworski and Coupland (2006) is a fine compilation of key readings. For an elaboration of the three approaches to discourse, see Schiffrin (1994). For more on 'capital D Discourses', see Gee (2010).

Strand 2: Texts and texture

For a thorough treatment of cohesion and other aspects of texture, see Martin (1992). Stoddard (1991) is also a good introduction. Eggins (1994) provides a more general overview of systemic functional linguistics. A classic compilation of papers on coherence in discourse is Tannen (1984). Other important works on the structure and comprehension of narrative are Labov and Waletzky (1967) and Kintsch (1977). Carrell (1984) discusses the effects of schema on second language readers. Van Dijk and Kintsch (1983) provide another perspective on discourse coherence. Liu and O'Halloran (2009) discuss cohesion from a multimodal perspective.

Strand 3: Texts and their social functions

Apart from Bhatia (1993) and Swales (1990), Berkenkotter and Huckin (1995) is a good introduction to genre analysis. Johns (1997) and Swales (2004) focus more on academic genres. Bhatia (2004) gives a more detailed treatment of the field of genre analysis. See Christie and Martin (1997) for a systemic functional view of genre. Bateman (2008) takes a multimodal approach to genre analysis. A more detailed analysis of 'It Gets Better' videos can be found in Jones (2015). Vasquez (2014) gives a thorough analysis of online reviews. For a perspective on YouTube genres, see Simonsen (2011), and for a genre analysis of Internet memes, see Wiggins and Bowers (2015).

Strand 4: Discourse and ideology

The Routledge English Language Introduction that focuses most on discourse and ideology is Simpson and Mayr (2009) *Language and Power: A Resource Book for Students.*

A Routledge English Language Introduction that offers more information on aspects of grammar covered in this strand is Jackson (2002) *Grammar and Vocabulary: A Resource Book for Students*. Hodge and Kress (1988) and Fairclough (1992) are classic works in the critical analysis of discourse. Good collections of papers on critical discourse analysis are Fairclough (1995) and Wodak and Meyer (2001). Fairclough (2003) gives an excellent practical introduction to the critical analysis of texts, and van Leeuwen (2008) provides a more practice-based approach to critical discourse analysis. Silverstein (2003) presents a rather dense treatment of indexical orders. A more readable explanation can be found in Johnstone *et al.* (2006). Jones (2017) presents a more detailed analysis of surveillance signs.

Strand 5: Spoken discourse

A good overview of different approaches to spoken discourse is Jones (2016). The Routledge English language introduction that focuses most on spoken discourse is Cutting (2007) *Pragmatics and Discourse: A Resource Book for Students*. Coulthard (1992) is a classic edited collection on the analysis of spoken language. Austin's speech act theory was further developed by Searle (1966). Good introductions to pragmatics include Mey (2001) and Verschueren (1999), and good introductions to conversation analysis include Hutchby and Wooffitt (2008), Schegloff (2007) and ten Have (2007). The lectures of Harvey Sacks are collected in Sacks (1992). Drew and Heritage (1993) deals with talk in institutional settings.

Strand 6: Strategic interaction

The classic work on face strategies is Brown and Levinson (1987). A more recent book on face and politeness is Watts (2003). For more information on framing in interaction, see Tannen (1993). Tannen (2005) is a good overview of conversational strategies. An excellent collection on discourse and identity from an interactional sociolinguistic perspective is De Fina *et al.* (2006). A collection dealing with speech styles and social languages is Auer (2007). For another approach to conversational strategies, see the work of Harré and van Langenhove (1999) on positioning theory. For studies on conversational strategies in computer-mediated communication, see Morand and Ocker (2003), Losh (2008) and Talamo and Ligorio (2001).

Strand 7: Context, culture and communication

Duranti and Goodwin's (1992) edited collection provides multiple perspectives on the problem of context. van Dijk (2008) examines context from a socio-cognitive perspective. A very accessible introduction to culture and conversation is Agar (1994). Bauman and Sherzer (1989) presents an overview of the principles and practices associated with the ethnography of communication, and Philipsen (1975) is a good example of an application of this method. For more information on ethnographic research methods, see Agar (1996) and Hammersley and Atkinson (1995).

Strand 8: Mediated discourse analysis

Wertsch (1993) provides a good introduction to the socio-cultural theory on which mediated discourse analysis is based. The seminal texts on mediated discourse analysis and nexus analysis are Scollon (2001) and Scollon and Scollon (2004). Norris and Jones (2005) is a collection that shows the wide range of contexts to which mediated discourse analysis can be applied. It also contains a clear explanation of the principles and terminology used in MDA. An alternative approach to the analysis of computer-mediated discourse can be found in Herring (2001).

Strand 9: Multimodal discourse analysis

Kress and van Leeuwen (2001) is a good theoretical introduction to multimodal discourse analysis. O'Halloran (2004) and Royce and Bowcher (2006) are good collections of studies from a systemic functional perspective. The papers in Jewitt (2014) present a more varied range of perspectives. Machin (2007) takes a critical approach to multimodality, and Forceville and Urios-Aparisi (2009) present an approach informed by cognitive linguistics. Kendon (1990) is a classic work on analysing gesture. For more information on the transcription of multimodal data, see Baldry and Thibault (2005) and Norris (2004). A clear and up to date overview of different approaches to multimodality can be found in Jewitt, Bezemer and O'Halloran (2016).

Strand 10: Corpus-assisted discourse analysis

The Routledge resource book that focuses on corpus-based analysis is McEnery and Xiao (2006) *Corpus-based Language Studies: An Advanced Resource Book*. Stubbs (1996) is a well-known introductory text for corpus-based linguistics. Other good introductions are Biber *et al.* (1998) and Hunston (2002). Baker (2006) provides a clear overview of using corpora in discourse analysis. A classic application of corpus-based methods to critical discourse analysis is Orpin (2005).

REFERENCES

Agar, M.H. (1994). *Language shock: Understanding the culture of conversation*. New York: William Morrow. (Further reading)

Agar, M. (1996). *The professional stranger: An informal introduction to ethnography*, 2nd edition. New York: Academic Press. (Further reading)

Agha, A. (2003). The social life of cultural value. *Language and Communication 23*, 231–273. (D4)

Albawardi, A. (2018). Digital literacy practices of Saudi female university students. Unpublished PhD Thesis. University of Reading, UK. (C9)

Androutsopoulos, J. (2008). Potentials and limitations of discourse-centred online ethnography. *Language@Internet 5*, article 9. (D7)

Auer, P. (ed.) (2007). *Style and social identities: Alternative approaches to linguistic heterogeneity*. Berlin: Mouton de Gruyter. (Further reading)

Austin, J.L. (1976, 1990). *How to do things with words*, 2nd edition. (J.O. Urmson and M. Sbisa, eds) Oxford: Oxford University Press. (B1, B5, D5)

Baker, P. (2005). *Public discourses of gay men*. London: Routledge. (A10)

Baker, P. (2006). *Using corpora in discourse analysis*. London: Continuum. (A10, B10 Further reading)

Baker, P. (2012). Acceptable bias? Using corpus linguistics methods with critical discourse analysis. *Critical Discourse Studies*, *9*(3), 247–256. (D10)

Baker, P. and McEnery, T. (2005). A corpus-based approach to discourses of refugees and asylum seekers in UN and newspaper texts. *Journal of Language and Politics*, *4*(2), 197–226. (B10)

Bakhtin, M. (1981). *The dialogic imagination*. (C. Emerson and M. Holquist, (eds.), and V.W. McGee, Trans.) Austin, TX: University of Texas Press. (A4, D4)

Bakhtin, M. (1986). *Speech genres and other late essays*. (C. Emerson and M. Holquist, eds, and V.W. McGee, Trans.) Austin, TX: University of Texas Press. (D4)

Baldry, A. and Thibault, P. (2005). *Multimodal transcription and text analysis*. Oakville, CT: Equinox. (Further reading)

Basso, K. (1970). To give up on words: Silence in Western Apache culture. *Southwestern Journal of Anthropology*, *26*(3), 213–230. (B7)

Bateman, J. (2008). *Multimodality and genre: A foundation for the systematic analysis of multimodal documents*. Basingstoke, UK: Palgrave Macmillan. (Further reading)

Bateson, G. (1972). *Steps to an ecology of mind: Collected essays in anthropology, psychiatry, evolution, and epistemology*. Chicago, IL: University of Chicago Press. (D8)

Bauman, R. and Sherzer, J. (1989). *Explorations in the ethnography of speaking*, 2nd edition. Cambridge: Cambridge University Press. (Further reading)

Baynes, C. (2017, August 16). Baby dolphin dies after being passed around for selfies with tourists on beach. Retrieved 19 February 2018, from http://www.independent. co.uk/news/world/europe/baby-dolphin-dies-passed-tourists-photographed-almeira-spain-moj-car-a7896376.html (C2)

Berkenkotter, C. and Huckin, T.N. (1995). *Genre knowledge in disciplinary communication—cognition/culture/power*. New Jersey: Lawrence Erlbaum Associates. (D3)

Bhatia, V.K. (1993). *Analysing genre: Language use in professional settings*. London: Longman. (A3)

Bhatia, V.K. (1995). Genre-mixing and in professional communication: The case of 'private intentions' v. 'socially recognized purposes.' In P. Bruthiaux, T. Boswood and B. du Babcock (eds.) *Explorations in English for professional communication*. Hong Kong: Department of English, City University of Hong Kong. (D3)

Bhatia, V.K. (1997). The power and politics of genre. *World Englishes, 16*(3), 359–371. (B3, D3)

Bhatia, V.K. (2004). *Worlds of written discourse: A genre based view*. London: Continuum. (Further reading)

Bhatia, V.K. (2016). *Critical Genre Analysis: Investigating interdiscursive performance in professional practice*, 1st edition. New York, NY: Routledge (D3).

Bhatia, V.K., Flowerdew, J. and Jones, R. (eds.) (2007). *Advances in discourse studies*. London: Routledge. (Further reading)

Biber, D., Conrad, S. and Reppen, R. (1998). *Corpus linguistics: Investigating language structure and use*. Cambridge: Cambridge University Press. (Further reading)

Birch, D. (1989). *Language, literature and critical practice: Ways of analyzing texts*. London: Routledge. (D4)

Bizzell, P. (1987). Some uses of the concept of 'discourse community'. Paper presented at the Penn State Conference on Composition, July. (D3)

Blommaert, J. (2007). On scope and depth in linguistic ethnography. *Journal of Sociolinguistics, 11*(5), 682–688. (D7)

Blommaert, J. (2010). *The sociolinguistics of globalization*. Cambridge: Cambridge University Press. (D4)

Blommaert, J. and Dong, J. (2009). *Ethnographic fieldwork. A beginner's guide*. Bristol: Multilingual Matters. (D7)

Brown, P. and Levinson, S. (1987). *Politeness: Some universals in language usage*. Cambridge: Cambridge University Press. (A6, Further reading)

Brown, G. and Yule, G. (1983). *Discourse analysis*. Cambridge: Cambridge University Press. (Further reading)

Butler, J. (1990/2006). *Gender trouble: Feminism and the subversion of identity*. London: Routledge. (D5)

Caldas-Coulthard, C.R. (1993). From discourse analysis to critical discourse analysis: The differential re-presentation of women and men speaking in written news. In J.M. Sinclair, M. Hoey and G. Fox (eds.) *Techniques of description: Spoken and written discourse* (pp. 196–208). London: Routledge. (D2)

Carrell, P.L. (1984). The effects of rhetorical organization on ESL readers. *TESOL Quarterly, 18*(3), 441–469. (Further reading)

Carter, R. (1997) *Investigating English discourse*. London: Routledge. (Further reading)

Chouliaraki, L. and Fairclough, N. (1999). *Discourse in late modernity: Rethinking critical discourse analysis*. Edinburgh: Edinburgh University Press. (D8)

Christie, F. and Martin, J.R. (1997). *Genre and institutions: Social processes in the workplace and school*. London: Cassell. (Further reading)

Coleman, G.E. (2010). Ethnographic approaches to digital media. *Annual Review of Anthropology 39*, 487–505. (D7)

Coulthard, M. (ed.) (1992). *Advances in spoken discourse analysis*. London: Routledge. (Further reading)

Cutting, J. (2007). *Pragmatics and discourse: A resource book for students*, 2nd edition. London: Routledge. (Further reading)

Danet, B., Ruedenberg, L. and Rosenbaum-Tamari, Y. (1997). "Hmmm … Where's that smoke coming from?" Writing, play and performance on Internet Relay Chat. In S. Rafaeli, F. Sudweeks and M. McLaughlin (eds.) *Network and netplay: Virtual groups on the Internet* (pp. 119–157). Cambridge, MA: AAAI/MIT Press. (C6)

De Fina, A., Schiffrin, D. and Bamberg, M. (eds.) (2006). *Discourse and identity*. Cambridge: Cambridge University Press. (Further reading)

Djonov, E. (2007). Website hierarchy and the interaction between content organization, webpage and navigation design: A systemic functional hypermedia discourse analysis perspective. *Information Design Journal 15*(2), 144–162. (A9)

Drew, P. and Heritage, J. (1993). *Talk at work: Interaction in institutional settings*. Cambridge: Cambridge University Press. (Further reading)

Duranti, A. and Goodwin, C. (eds.) (1992). *Rethinking context: Language as an interactive phenomenon*. Cambridge: Cambridge University Press. (Further reading)

Eggins, S. (1994). *An introduction to systemic functional linguistics*. London: Pinter Pub. (B2, Further reading)

Fairclough, N. (1992). *Discourse and social change*. London: Polity. (D2, D4, Further reading)

Fairclough, N. (ed.) (1995). *Critical discourse analysis: The critical study of language*. London; New York: Longman. (B1, D2, Further reading)

Fairclough, N. (2001). *Language and power*, 2nd edition. Essex: Longman. (B4)

Fairclough, N. (2003). *Analysing discourse: Textual analysis for social research*. London: Routledge. (Further reading)

Ferguson, C.A. (1985). Editor's introduction. Special language registers, Special issue of *Discourse Processes 8*, 391–394. (D6)

Fillmore, C. (1975). An alternative to checklist theories of meaning. In C. Cogen, H. Thompson, K. Wistler and J. Wright (eds.) *Proceedings of the first annual meeting of the Berkeley Linguistics Society* (pp. 123–131). Berkeley, CA: University of California Press. (D4)

Firth, J.R. (1957). *Papers in linguistics 1934–1951*. London: Oxford University Press. (A7, B10)

Forceville, C.J. and Urios-Aparisi, E. (eds.) (2009). *Multimodal metaphor*. Berlin and New York: Mouton de Gruyter. (Further reading)

Foucault, M. (1972). *The archaeology of knowledge*. New York: Pantheon. (A4, B1)

Foucault, M. (1984). The order of discourse. In Shapiro, M. (ed.) *Language and politics* (pp. 108–138). London: Basil Blackwell. (D4)

Fullick, N. (2013). 'Gendering' the self in online dating discourse. *Canadian Journal of Communication*, 38, 545–562. (C4)

Gee, J.P. (1996). *Social linguistics and literacies: Ideology in discourses*. London; Bristol, PA: Taylor and Francis. (A4, B1, D4)

Gee, J.P. (2010). *Introduction to discourse analysis: Theory and method*, 3rd edition. London: Routledge. (D1, B2, B4 Further reading)

Geertz, C. (1973). *The interpretation of cultures*. New York: Basic Books. (D7)

Gershon, I. (2010). *The breakup 2.0: Disconnecting over new media*. Ithaca, NY: Cornell University Press. (C8)

Goffman, E. (1959). *The presentation of self in everyday life*. New York: Anchor Books. (A6)

Goffman, E. (1967). *Interaction ritual: Essays on face-to-face behavior*. Chicago, IL: Aldine. (A6, D6)

Goffman, E. (1974). *Frame analysis*. New York: Harper and Row. (A6, B6, D6)

Goffman, E. (1981). *Forms of talk*. Philadelphia, PA: University of Pennsylvania Press. (D6)

Grice, H.P. (1975). Logic and conversation. In Cole, P. and Morgan, J. (eds.) *Syntax and semantics*, Vol 3. New York: Academic Press. (B5)

Grice, H.P. (1991). *Studies in the way of words*. Cambridge, MA; London: Harvard University Press. (B1)

Gumperz, J.J. (1982). *Discourse strategies*. Cambridge: Cambridge University Press. (B6)

Halliday, M.A.K. (1968). Notes on transitivity and theme in English. *Journal of Linguistics* 4(1), 179–215. (B2)

Halliday, M.A.K. (1976). The teacher taught the student English: An essay in Applied Linguistics. In P.A. Reich (ed.) *The second LACUS forum* (pp. 344–349). Columbia: Hornbeam Press. (D4)

Halliday, M.A.K. (1978). *Language as social semiotic: The social interpretation of language and meaning*. London: Edward Arnold. (A2, A7)

Halliday, M.A.K. (1985, 1994). *An introduction to functional grammar*. London: Edward Arnold. (A2, A4, B1, D2)

Halliday, M.A.K. and Hasan, R. (1976). *Cohesion in English*. London: Longman. (B2, D1, D2)

Hammersley, M. and Atkinson, P. (1995). *Ethnography: Principles in practice*, 2nd edition. London: Routledge. (Further reading)

Harré, R. and van Langenhove, L. (eds.) (1999). *Positioning theory*. Oxford: Blackwell. (Further reading)

Harris, Z. (1952). Discourse analysis. *Language, 28*(1), 1–30. (D1)

Herring, S. (2001). Computer-mediated discourse. In D. Tannen, D. Schiffrin and H.E. Hamilton (eds.) *Handbook of discourse analysis* (pp. 612–634). Oxford: Blackwell. (C6, Further reading)

Herring, Susan C. (2004). Computer-mediated discourse analysis: An approach to researching online behavior. In Barab, S. R. Kling and J. H. Gray (eds.) *Designing for virtual communities in the service of learning.* New York: Cambridge University Press, 338–376. (D7)

Herring, S.C., Scheidt, L.A., Bonus, S. and Wright, E. (2004). Bridging the gap: A genre analysis of weblogs. *Proceedings of HICSS-37.* Los Alamitos: IEEE Press. (Further reading)

Hine, Christine (2000). Virtual ethnography. London: Sage. (D7)

Hodge, R. and Kress, G. (1988). *Social semiotics.* Cambridge: Polity Press. (B4, Further reading)

Hoey, M. (1983). *On the surface of discourse.* London: Allen and Unwin. (B2)

Hofstadter, D. and the Fluid Analogies Research Group (1995). *Fluid concepts and creative analogies: Computer models for the fundamental mechanisms of thought.* New York: Basic Books. (D4)

Holyoak, K.J. and Thagard, P. (1995). *Mental leaps: Analogy in creative thought.* Cambridge, MA: MIT Press. (D4)

Hunston, S. (2002). *Corpora in applied linguistics.* Cambridge: Cambridge University Press. (D10, Further reading)

Hutchby, I. and Wooffitt, R. (2008). *Conversation analysis.* Malden, MA: Polity Press. (Further reading)

Hyland, K. and Paltridge, B. (eds.) (2011). *Continuum companion to discourse analysis.* London: Continuum. (Further reading)

Hymes, D. (1974). *Foundations in sociolinguistics: An ethnographic approach.* Philadelphia: University of Pennsylvania Press. (A7, D7)

Hymes, D. (1986). Models of the interaction of language and social life. In J.J. Gumperz and D. Hymes (eds.) *Directions in sociolinguistics* (pp. 296–336). Oxford: Basil Blackwell. (D7)

Hymes, D. (1987). Communicative competence. In U. Ammon, N. Dittmar and K.J. Mattheier (eds.) *Sociolinguistics: An international handbook of the science of language and society* (pp. 219–229). Berlin: Walter de Gruyter. (D7)

Hymes, D. (1993). Anthropological linguistics: A retrospective. *Anthropological Linguistics 35*, 9–14. (D7)

Iedema, R. (2001). Resemiotization. *Semiotica, 137*(1/4), 23–39. (A9)

Jackson, H. (2002). *Grammar and vocabulary: A resource book for students.* London: Routledge. (Further reading)

Jakobson, R. (1990). *Roman Jakobson on language.* (L.R. Waugh and M. Halle, eds.). Cambridge, MA: Harvard University Press. (B7)

Jaworski, A. and Coupland, N. (eds.) (2006). *The discourse reader*, 2nd edition. London: Routledge. (Further reading)

Jewitt, C. (ed.) (2014). *The Routledge handbook of multimodal analysis*, 2nd edition. London: Routledge. (Further reading)

Jewitt, C., Bezemer, J. and O'Halloran, K. (2016). *Introducing multimodality*. London: Routledge. (Further reading)

Johns, A.M. (1997) *Text, role and context: Developing academic literacies*. Cambridge: Cambridge University Press. (Further reading)

Johnstone, B., Andrus, J. and Danielson, A.E. (2006). Mobility, indexicality, and the enregisterment of "Pittsburghese". *Journal of English Linguistics, 34*(2), 77–104. (Further Reading)

Jones, R. (2005). 'You show me yours, I'll show you mine': The negotiation of shifts from textual to visual modes in computer mediated interaction among gay men. *Visual Communication, 4*(1), 69–92. (A9)

Jones, R. (2008). Rewriting the city: Discourses of Hong Kong skateboarders. *A paper presented at Sociolinguistics Symposium 17*, April 3–5, Amsterdam. (C7)

Jones, R. (2011). Sport and re/creation: What skateboarders can teach us about learning. *Sport, Education and Society 16*(5), 593–611. (C7)

Jones, R. (2014) Mediated discourse analysis. In S. Norris and C.D. Maier (eds.) *Interactions, images and texts: A reader in multimodality* (pp. 39–52). New York: Mouton de Gruyter. (D8)

Jones, R. (2015) Generic intertextuality in online social activism: The case of the *It Gets Better* project. *Language in Society 44*(3): 317–339. (B3)

Jones, R. (2016) *Spoken discourse*. London: Bloomsbury. (Further Reading)

Jones, R. (2017). Surveillant landscapes. *Linguistic Landscapes 3*(2), 150–187. (Further reading)

Kamberelis, G. and Scott, D.S. (1992). Other people's voices: The coarticulation of texts and subjectivities. *Linguistics and Education, 4*, 359–403. (D2)

Kendon, A. (1990). *Conducting interaction*. Cambridge: Cambridge University Press. (Further reading)

Kiesler, S. (1986). Thinking ahead: The hidden messages in computer networks. *Harvard Business Review, 64*, 46–60. (C6)

Kintsch, W. (1977). On comprehending stories. In M. Just and P. Carpenter (eds.) *Cognitive processes in comprehension*. Hillsdale, NJ: Lawrence Erlbaum Associates.

Kitzinger, C. and Frith, H. (1999). Just say no? The use of conversation analysis in developing a feminist perspective on sexual refusal. *Discourse & Society, 10*(3), 293–316. (C6)

Kress, G. (1997). *Before writing: Rethinking the paths to literacy*. London: Routledge. (B9)

Kress, G. and van Leeuwen, T. (2001). *Multimodal discourse: The modes and media of contemporary communication*. London: Edward Arnold. (Further reading)

Kress, G. and van Leeuwen, T. (1996, 2006). *Reading images: The grammar of visual design*, 2nd edition, London and New York: Routledge. (A9, D9)

Labov, W. (1972a). *Sociolinguistic patterns*. Philadelphia, PA: University of Pennsylvania Press. (D1)

Labov, W. (1972b). *Language in the inner city: Studies in Black English Vernacular*. Philadelphia: University of Pennsylvania Press. (B2, B3, D2).

Labov, W. and Waletzky, J. (1967). Narrative analysis. In J. Helm (ed.) *Essays on the verbal and visual arts* (pp. 12–44). Seattle: University of Washington Press. (Further reading)

Ladegaard, H.J. (2011). 'Doing power' at work: Responding to male and female management styles in a global business corporation. *Journal of Pragmatics 43*, 4–19. (B6)

Lakoff, G. and Johnson, M. (1980). *Metaphors we live by*. Chicago: University of Chicago Press. (B9, D4)

Landow, G.P. (1992). *Hypertext: The convergence of contemporary critical theory and technology*. Baltimore, MD: Johns Hopkins University Press. (C6)

Lave, J. and Wenger, E. (1991). *Situated learning: Legitimate peripheral participation*. Cambridge: Cambridge University Press.

Lin, A.M.Y. (1996). Bilingualism or linguistic segregation: Symbolic domination, resistance and code-switching in Hong Kong schools. *Linguistics and Education 8*(1), 49–84. (B6)

Liu, Y. and O'Halloran, K.L. (2009). Intersemiotic texture: Analyzing cohesive devices between language and images, *Social Semiotics, 19*(4), 367–387. (Further reading)

Losh, E. (2008). In polite company: Rules of play in five Facebook games. *ACE '08 Proceedings of the 2008 International Conference on Advances in Computer Entertainment Technology*. Available online at https://eee.uci.edu/faculty/losh/LoshPoliteCompany.pdf (Further reading)

McEnery, A. and Xiao, R. (2006). *Corpus-based language studies: An advanced resource book*. London: Routledge.(Further reading)

Machin, D. (2007). *Introduction to multimodal analysis*. London and New York: Hodder Arnold. (Further reading)

McLuhan, M. (1964/2001). *Understanding media: The extensions of man*. Cambridge, MA: MIT Press. (B8)

Malinowski, B. (1923). The problem of meaning in primitive languages. In C.K. Ogden and I.A. Richards (eds.) *The meaning of meaning: A study of influence of language upon thought and of the science of symbolism* (pp. 296–336). New York: Harcourt, Brace and World. (A7)

Martin, J.R. (1985). Process and text: Two aspects of human semiosis. In J.D. Benson and W.S. Greaves (eds.) *Systemic perspectives on discourse*, Vol 1. Norwood, NJ: Ablex. (A3, D3)

Martin, J.R. (1992). *English text: System and structure*. Amsterdam: John Benjamins. (Further reading)

Mey, J.L. (2001). *Pragmatics: An introduction*, 2nd edition. Oxford: Wiley-Blackwell. (Further reading)

Morand, D.A. and Ocker, R.J. (2003). Politeness theory and computer-mediated communication: A sociolinguistic approach to analyzing relational messages, *Proceedings of the 36th Annual Hawaii International Conference on System Sciences (HICSS'03)*—Track1 (p.17.2), January 06–09. (Further reading)

Murphey, T. (1992). The discourse of pop songs. *TESOL Quarterly, 26*(4), 770–774. (C10)

Norris, S. (2004). *Analyzing multimodal interaction: A methodological framework*. London: Routledge. (A9, D9, Further reading)

Norris, S. and Jones, R.H. (eds.) (2005). *Discourse in action: Introducing mediated discourse analysis*. London: Routledge. (Further reading)

O'Halloran, K. (ed.) (2004). *Multimodal discourse analysis: Systemic functional perspectives*. New York and London: Continuum. (Further reading)

O'Halloran, K. (2005). *Mathematical discourse: Language, symbolism and visual images*. London: Continuum. (A9)

Oldenberg, A. (2010). Lady Gaga explains her VMA raw meat dress. *USA Today*, 13 September 2010. Retrieved 12 March 2011 from: http://content.usatoday.com/communities/entertainment/post/2010/09/lady-gaga-explains-her-vma-raw-meat-dress/1?csp=hfn (B2)

Orpin, D. (2005). Corpus linguistics and critical discourse analysis: Examining the ideology of sleaze. *International Journal of Corpus Linguistics*, 10, 37–61. (Further reading)

Ortega y Gasset, J. (1959). The difficulty of reading. *Diogenes* 28, 1–17. (D6)

O'Toole, M. (1994). *The language of displayed art*. London: Leicester University. (A9)

Paltridge, B. (2006). *Discourse analysis: An introduction*. London, New York: Continuum. (Further reading)

Philipsen, G. (1975). Speaking 'like a man' in Teamsterville: Culture patterns of role enactment in an urban neighborhood, *Quarterly Journal of Speech*, 61, 13–22. (Further reading)

Pöttker, H. (2003). News and its communicative quality: the inverted pyramid—when and why did it appear? *Journalism Studies*, 4(4), 501–511. (C2)

Propp, V. (1986). *Morphology of the folktale*. (L. Scott, trans.) Austin, TX: University of Texas Press.(B1)

Quinn, N. and Holland, D. (1987). Culture and cognition. In D. Holland and N. Quinn (eds.) *Cultural models in language and thought* (pp. 3–40). Cambridge: Cambridge University Press. (D4)

Rampton, B. (2003). Hegemony, social class, and stylisation. *Pragmatics*, 13(1), 49–83. (D4)

Reddy, M. (1979). The conduit metaphor—a case of conflict in our language about language. In A. Ortony (ed.) *Metaphor and thought* (pp. 384–324). Cambridge: Cambridge University Press. (D4)

Rey, J.M. (2001). Changing gender roles in popular culture: Dialogue in *Star Trek* episodes from 1966 to 1993. In D. Biber and S. Conrad (eds.) *Variation in English: Multi-dimensional studies* (pp. 138–156). London: Longman. (A10)

Royce, T.D. and Bowcher, W. (eds.) (2006). *New directions in the analysis of multimodal discourse*. London: Routledge. (Further reading)

Ruesch, J. and Bateson, G. (1968 [1951]). *Communication: The social matrix of psychiatry*. New York: W.W. Norton and Company. (C7)

Sacks, H. (1992). *Lectures on conversation* (G. Jefferson and E.A. Schegloff, eds). Oxford and Cambridge, MA: Basil Blackwell. (Further reading)

Schegloff, E.A. (1968). Sequencing in conversational openings. *American Anthropologist 70*, 1075–1095. (B5)

Schegloff, E. (2007). *Sequence organization in interaction: A primer in conversation analysis*. Cambridge: Cambridge University Press. (Further reading)

Schegloff, E.A. and Sacks, H. (1973). Opening up closings. *Semiotica 7*, 289–327. (B5, D5)

Schiffrin, D. (1994). *Approaches to discourse*. Oxford: Basil Blackwell. (Further reading)

Schiffrin, D., Tannen, D. and Hamilton, H.E. (eds.) (2004). *The handbook of discourse analysis*. Oxford: Wiley-Blackwell. (Further reading)

Scollon, R. (1998). *Mediated discourse as social interaction: A study of news discourse*. New York: Longman. (D8, Further reading)

Scollon, R. (1999). Mediated discourse and social interaction. *Research on Language and Social Interaction, 32*(1 and 2), 149–154. (D8)

Scollon, R. (2001). *Mediated discourse: The nexus of practice*. London: Routledge. (D8, Further reading)

Scollon, R. (2005). The discourses of food in the world system: Toward a nexus analysis of a world problem. *Journal of Language and Politics, 4*(3), 465–488. (D8)

Scollon, R. (2008). Discourse itineraries: Nine processes of resemiotization. In V.K. Bhatia, J. Flowerdew and R.H. Jones (eds.) (pp. 233–244). London: Routledge. (B8, D8)

Scollon, R. and Scollon, S.W. (2004). *Nexus analysis: Discourse and the emerging Internet*. New York: Routledge. (B8, Further reading)

Scollon, R., Tsang, W.K., Li, D., Yung, V. and Jones, R. (1998) Voice appropriation and discourse representation in a student writing task. *Linguistics and Education, 9*(3), 227–250. (D4).

Scollon, R., Scollon, S.W. and Jones, R.H. (2012). *Intercultural communication: A discourse approach*, 3rd edition. Oxford: Blackwell. (A6, B7)

Searle, J. (1966). *Speech acts*. Cambridge: Cambridge University Press. (Further reading)

Silverstein, M. (2003). Indexical order and the dialectics of sociolinguistic life. *Language & Communication, 23*(3–4). (B4, Further Reading)

Simonsen, T. M. (2011). Categorising YouTube. *MedieKultur: Journal of Media and Communication Research, 27*(51), 23. (Further Reading)

Simpson, P. and Mayr, A. (2009). *Language and power: A resource book for students*. London: Routledge.(Further reading)

Sinclair, J. (1991). *Corpus, concordance and collocation*. Oxford: Oxford University Press. (B10)

Stoddard, S. (1991). *Text and texture: Patterns of cohesion*. Norwood, NJ: Ablex. (Further reading)

Stubbs, M. (1996). *Text and Corpus Analysis*. Oxford: Blackwell.

Swales, J.M. (1990). *Genre analysis: English in academic and research settings*. Cambridge: Cambridge University Press. (A3, B3, D3)

Swales, J.M. (2004). Research genres: Explorations and applications. Cambridge: Cambridge University Press. (Further reading)

Talamo, A. and Ligorio, B. (2001). Strategic identities in cyberspace. *Cyberpsychology and Behavior, 4*(1), 109–122. (Further reading)

Tannen, D. (ed.) (1984). *Coherence in spoken and written discourse*. Norwood, NJ: Ablex Publishing Corporation. (Further reading)

Tannen, D. (1993). *Framing in discourse*. New York: Oxford University Press. (Further reading)

Tannen, D. (2004). Talking the dog: Framing pets as interactional resources in family discourse. *Research in Language and Social Interaction, 37*(4), 399–420.

Tannen, D. (2005). *Conversational style: Analyzing talk among friends*, 2nd edition. Norwood, NJ: Ablex Publishing.

Tannen, D. and Wallat, C. (1987). Interactive frames and knowledge schemas in interaction: Examples from a medical examination/interview. *Social Psychology Quarterly*, 50(2), 205–216. (D6)

ten Have, P. (2007). *Doing conversational analysis*, 2nd edition. London: Sage. (Further reading)

van Dijk, T.A. (2008). *Discourse and context: A sociocognitive approach*. Cambridge: Cambridge University Press. (A7)

van Dijk, T. and Kintsch, W. (1983). *Strategies of discourse comprehension*. New York: Academic Press. (Further reading)

van Leeuwen, T. (1999). *Speech, music, sound*. Basingstoke, UK: Macmillan. (A9)

van Leeuwen, T. (2008). *Discourse and practice: New tools for critical discourse analysis*. Oxford: Oxford University Press. (Further reading)

van Leeuwen, T. (2011). *The language of color: An introduction*. London: Routledge. (A9)

Vasquez, C. (2014). *The discourse of online consumer reviews*. London: Bloomsbury. (Further Reading)

Velghe, F. (2011). Lessons in textspeak from Sexy Chick: Supervernacular literacy in South African instant and text messaging. *Tilburg Papers in Culture Studies*, Paper 1. (D7)

Verschueren, J. (1999). *Understanding pragmatics*. London: Arnold. (Further reading)

Vygotsky, L.S. (1981). The instrumental method in psychology. In J.V. Wertsch (ed.) *The concept of activity in Soviet psychology* (pp. 134–143). Armonk, NY: M.E. Sharpe. (B8)

Walther, J.B. (1996). Computer-mediated communication: Impersonal, interpersonal and hyperpersonal interaction. *Communication Research*, 23(1), 3–43. (C6)

Watts, R. (2003). *Politeness*. Cambridge: Cambridge University Press.(Further reading)

Wertsch, J.V. (1993). *Voices of the mind: A sociocultural approach to mediated action*. Cambridge, MA: Harvard University Press. (Further reading)

Wertsch, J.V. (1998). *Mind as action*. Oxford: Oxford University Press. (D8, Further reading)

Widdowson, H.G. (1973). *An applied linguistic approach to discourse analysis*. (Unpublished doctoral dissertation). Department of Linguistics, University of Edinburgh. (D1)

Widdowson, H.G. (2007). *Discourse analysis*. New York: Oxford University Press. (B1, Further reading)

Wiggins, B.E. and Bowers, G.B. (2015). Memes as genre: A structurational analysis of the memescape. *New Media & Society*, 17(11), 1886–1906.

Wodak, R. and Meyer, M. (eds.) (2001). *Methods of critical discourse analysis*. London: Sage. (Further reading)

AUTHOR INDEX

Austin, J. 20, 39, 63, 65–66, 171, 180, 188

Baker, P. 36, 87–88, 90, 207–214
Bakhtin, M. 48, 163
Basso, K. 74
Bateson, G. 24, 118, 122, 179
Bhatia, V.K. 8, 76, 106, 156, 159–162
Blommaert, J. 6, 59, 163, 168–171
Brown, P. 23, 178–179
Butler, J. 174

Fairclough, N. 48, 56, 153–155, 159, 192, 216
Firth, J. 25–27, 90
Foucault, M. 17, 40, 170

Gee, J.P. 12, 15, 17, 31, 40, 47, 57, 60,
    81, 107, 140, 145–146, 156, 162–168,
    171, 192
Gershon, I. 123–124
Goffman, E. 21–22, 24, 72, 178, 180,
    183, 186
Grice, H.P. 20, 39, 62
Gumperz, J. 21, 24, 72, 186

Halliday, M.A.K. 5–7, 12–15, 26–27, 32, 39,
    42, 44–45, 81, 84, 125, 143, 146–150, 153,
    164–165, 200–201
Harris, Z. 38–39, 140–145, 146, 150, 152
Hasan 42, 44–45, 146–150
Hoey, M. 46
Hymes, D. 26–28, 74–76, 121, 186–188, 190

Iedema, R. 34

Jakobson, R. 74
Jefferson, G. 20
Jones, R. 33, 80, 119, 125, 153–156,
    191, 196–200

Kitzinger, C. 113
Kress, G. 32, 56, 81, 84–85, 87, 200–204

Labov, W. 39–40, 47, 50–51, 100, 140, 144,
    145–146, 150–153
Levinson, S. 23, 178–179
Lin, A. 71

Malinowski, B. 25–26
McEnery, T. 36, 90
McLuhan, M. 76

Norris, S. 86, 129, 199, 202–207

Propp, V. 39

Ruesch, J. 118, 122

Sacks, H. 20, 65, 174–177
Savage, D. 50
Schegloff, E. 20, 65–66, 171, 174–177
Scollon, R. 22, 28, 74, 78–80, 125, 146,
    153–156, 191–196, 197
Scollon, S.W. 74, 78–79
Searle, J. 20
Silverstein, M. 60, 169, 170
Swales, J. 10, 49–50, 54, 76, 156–159, 196

Tannen, D. 24, 71–73, 178–186

Van Leeuwen, T. 32, 81, 84–85,
    200–202, 204
Varis, P. 189–191
Vygotsky, L. 76–77

Wallat, C. 24, 71–73, 179–186
Wertsch, J.V. 192–193
White, T. 50
Widdowson, H.G. 140, 143–146, 150, 152

GLOSSARIAL INDEX

abstract 56
act sequence 75
actions: frozen actions 86; higher-level actions 86; lower-level actions 86
adjacency pair 65
affordances 77
agency 13
agent 13
ambiguity 2
analytical images 81
antecedent 99

circumstantial adjuncts 55
classificatory images 81
closings 67
coherence 7
cohesion 7; grammatical 42; lexical 42
collocation 90; span 90
common knowledge 7
communicative competence 26
communicative events 8
communicative mode 32
communicative purpose 9
concordance 89
concrete 56
conditional relevance 65
conjunction 42
connectives: additive 42; causative 42; contrastive 42; sequential 42
consent 110
constituency 147
constraints: of cultural tools 77; of genres 8
content words 89
context 25, 59

contextualisation cues 70
conversation analysis 20
conversational strategies 21; face strategies 21; see also face; framing: strategies
cooperative principle 62
corpus 34; British National Corpus 88; cleaning 87; reference 88; tagging 87; see also reference corpus
corpus-assisted discourse analysis 34
critical discourse analysis 107
cultural models 17
cultural tool 30

deictic expressions 18, 59
directives 111
discourse 2
discourse analysis 2
discourse community 10
discourse marker 71
discourse prosody 90
discourse representation 15
discourses 17
discourses in place 78
dispersion plots (concordance plots) 91
dispreferred response 66
distributional analysis 39

ellipses 42
ends 75
ethnography 27
ethnography of speaking (communication) 26
ethnomethodology 20

face 22; negative 23; positive 23
face strategies 21; independence 23;
    involvement 22
face systems 68; deference 68;
    hierarchical 69; solidarity 69
felicity conditions 64
field 26
force 64; illocutionary 64; locutionary
    64; perlocutionary 64
forensic linguistics 35
formal approach 38
frames 22
frameworks: generic 47; interpretive 41;
    primary 24
framing: strategies 21
function words 89
functional approach 38

gaze 31
genre 8; chains 104; constraints 9;
    conventions 9; ecologies 104; move
    structure 9; networks 104
genre analysis 8
gestures 31; beat gestures 129; deictic
    gestures 130; iconic gestures 130
grammar 2

heteroglossia 57
historical body 78

ideational 12
ideology 11
implicature 62
index 11, 59
indexical orders 60
indexicality, orders of 61
instrumentalities 75
interaction order 78
interactional sociolinguistics 21
interactive frames 24
interdiscursivity 17, 48
interlocutor 19
intermodal relationships 129
interpersonal 12
intertextuality 7

key 75
keyness 91; negative 91
keyword analysis 90

lexical chains 44

markedness 74
maxims (Gricean) 62; manner 62;
    quality 62; quantity 62; relevance 62
meaning 5
mediated action 30
mediated communication 19
mediated discourse analysis 29
mediation 29
modality 14
mode, of communication 4
mode, related to context 26
moves 49
move structure 9
multimodal discourse analysis 31
multimodal interaction analysis 32

narrative images 81
nominalisation 56
norms 75; of interaction 75;
    of interpretation 75

object handling 131
official absence 66
openings 67
orders 110
orders of discourse 17
orders of indexicality 61

paralinguistic cues 24
paraphrase 15
participants (in grammar) 12
participants (in speech events) 75
performatives 63
phonology 2
pragmatics 20
preferred response 66
presuppositions 48
processes 12; action 13; mental 13;
    relational 13; verbal 13

quotation 16

reading position 56
reference 42; anaphoric 43; antecedent 43; cataphoric 43; definite article 43; exophoric 43
reference corpus 88
refusal 110
register 15
'reporting' words 16
requests 110
resemiotization 33

schema 100
semantic field 6
semantic prosody 90
semiotic mode 32
sequentiality 32
setting 74
simultaneity 33
sites of engagement 78
situated language 3
slot 67
social approach 38

social identity 29
social language 15
social practice 29
SPEAKING model 27
speech acts 64
speech events 27
speech situations 73
speech vs. writing 18
substitution 42
synthetic personalization 56
systemic functional grammar 32

tenor 26
textual 12
texture 6
transduction 87
transitivity 13
type token ratio 89

vectors 81

'whos doing whats' 12
word frequency lists 89

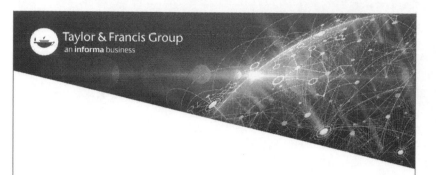

Made in the USA
Middletown, DE
20 January 2023

22669550R00139